TRANSITIONS: MILITARY PATHWAYS TO CIVILIAN CAREERS

TRANSITIONS:
MILITARY PATHWAYS
TO CIVILIAN CAREERS

by

Robert W. Macdonald,
Lt. Colonel, AUS (Ret.)

THE ROSEN PUBLISHING GROUP

New York

Published in 1988 by The Rosen Publishing Group, Inc.
29 East 21st Street, New York, NY 10010

First Edition

LIBRARY OF CONGRESS
Library of Congress Cataloging-in-Publication Data

Macdonald, Robert W.
  Transition: military pathways to a civilian career/
by Robert W. Macdonald.
     p.   cm.—(Military opportunity series)
  Bibliography: p.
  Includes index.
  Summary: Discusses the training and positions
available in military service which can prepare the
individual for civilian careers after leaving the service.
  ISBN 0-8239-0777-5: $14.95
  1. United States—Armed Forces—Vocational
guidance.   2. Occupations—United States.
[1. United States—Armed Forces—Vocational
guidance.   2. Vocational guidance.   3. Occupations.]
I. Title.   II. Series.
UB147.M325   1988
355'.0023'73—dc19   88-4693
                                                          CIP
                                                          AC

Acknowledgments

I am indebted to a large number of men and women, all former or retired members of the military services, for the development of the rationale and framework of this book—not to mention their encouragement.

Ed Kelly and Bill Fitzpatrick took time out from supervising a Non-Commissioned Officers Association Job Fair to talk to me about the problems they had observed in the transition from military service to a civilian career. Doug Carter, the energetic director of the very successful Officers' Placement Program operated by the Retired Officers Association, welcomed me to a preseparation briefing and provided other useful services.

Jerry Walker and Neil Thomas, two highly dedicated Veterans Employment Representatives with the Colorado State Job Service, were exceptionally generous in giving me extensive backgrounding from their personal experiences. Jerry Walker encouraged me to attend one of his weekly job-search seminars for former military men and women. From the Veterans Employment and Training Service (VETS) of the U.S. Department of Labor, Mike McGinty, in Denver, and Steve Guess, at Fort Bragg, gave much of themselves in responding to my questions.

Bob Daniels, founder of an employment service called Mil-Vets, Sam Wein, co-author of the innovative correspondence course Career Search, and Stan Hyman of Identity Research Institute freely discussed their personal initiatives to assist former and retired military men and women to find both themselves and civilian careers.

Others too numerous to mention here have contributed in many, often unexpected, ways to my work. To each of them I pay a silent but sincere tribute.

Needless to say, the approach and the opinions and conclusions expressed in the book are my own. Some risks are involved whenever anyone plows new ground, but I do not feel that anything expressed or implied in the chapters that follow lacks adequate documentation or echoes poor judgment.

Though much of the illustrative factual material that I have used is in the public domain, I wish specifically to credit the U.S. Department of Labor for the charts and graphs used throughout the text. Violet Moreton Cooper has been kind enough to allow me to make use of some of the survey data incorporated in her own excellent book, *How to Find Those Hidden Jobs*.

About the Author

Robert W. Macdonald retired as a Lieutenant Colonel after more than thirty years of Regular Army and Army Reserve service that he began as an infantry rifleman and ended as a Visiting Professor at the Army War College. When he retired, in 1975, Colonel Macdonald was awarded the Meritorious Service Medal for "outstandingly meritorious service as a Citizen Soldier."

During much of his military service Colonel Macdonald was an Operations and Training specialist. An early Army assignment as a service school instructor of tactics involved him with training military instructors—in part, at least, because of his previous graduate studies in education and career counseling. Later assignments afforded many opportunities to utilize this experience at higher levels.

In his civilian role Colonel Macdonald has been an educator, a social science researcher, a business executive, and a diplomat. He has taught in both public and private secondary schools as well as at the college and university level. His research activities emphasized public opinion and attitude studies and media analysis. Several successful business and consulting ventures, with a great deal of experience in industrial and small business development, have given him a thorough knowledge of the civilian world of work. His experience as a diplomat and subsequent service as a government contractor have afforded him exceptional exposure to the role of government at all levels—from the White House, Congress, and the federal court system to grass-roots village government across the United States.

Besides broad military schooling, ranging from basic training to Army Command and General Staff College, Colonel Macdonald holds degrees in Science, American Studies, and International Relations and has been a teacher, lecturer, and writer in all those fields. He resides in Colorado Springs, Colorado. When not actively engaged in research, writing, or teaching, he is likely to be found on a nearby ski slope or sailing the waters of the Atlantic Ocean and its bays, sounds, and tributaries.

Contents

Preface

The book that you hold in your hands is a story without an ending. It is one of the many "how-to-do-it" books that have recently flooded the market. Like all the others, it will lead you through some procedures and techniques: in this case, procedures and techniques for utilizing the available resources during your time in one of the military services to shape a civilian career that you can follow after you hang up your uniform. Like the other books, how you use those procedures and techniques is up to you. You have to write the final chapter.

This book has developed from an earlier one that I wrote, *Exploring Careers in the Military Services*. In that book I pursued a fact that everyone knows but relatively few people acknowledge: Every young man and woman who enters any of the uniformed services must eventually leave it. That means, in the simplest of terms, that everyone enters military service from the civilian world, and everyone returns to a civilian world. The only way to avoid that situation is to "die with your boots on," and the statistical chances of that happening, short of all-out war, are so slight that life insurance companies now often charge military members lower premiums than civilians.

In that earlier book I tried to show the ways in which military service can influence the people who serve in it. It doesn't much matter whether you serve a single tour of duty, plan a career in uniform, or are still trying to decide whether to "join up," military service does influence you in many ways.

Military service can help you develop a keen mind in a strong body. It can help you "grow up" to become a useful, effective adult by emphasizing the development of such personal qualities as self-esteem, self-discipline, initiative, and leadership. It can train you in a technical skill or a profession. And it can help you prepare yourself for that inevitable day when, older, wiser, and more experienced, you will take off the uniform for the last time and resume your role as a functioning member of civilian society.

So far, so good. But there is always a catch, and the catch is what this book is all about. The catch is that the civilian society you will eventually reenter is not likely to be the same as it was when you left it. While you have been changing, so has the rest of the world. The longer you remain in uniform, the more the civilian environment changes. When you extend that idea over time, the situation can become quite dramatic. As a minimum, leaving military service requires important adjustments in attitude and life-style.

So a corollary rule seems to be: The longer you remain in uniform, the longer you *want* to remain in uniform. What this really means is that you cannot quite face the prospect of rerentering the society into which you were born and in which you went to school and grew up. At some stage, usually in the case of those who stay in service ten years or more or qualify for retirement, leaving military service becomes very difficult—psychologically as well as materially. Yet the fact is that even those who stay for twenty years are young enough that they have about twenty-five years of productive work life ahead of them—or, to put it realistically, twenty-five years in which they have to earn a living, buy a home, put the kids through school, and stash away some savings that will help see them through their real retirement years. No one can live a dignified, useful life on "half pay." Obviously, those who leave service earlier have even longer periods of time ahead of them and no retirement pay or other benefits to ease the burden.

The military services as an institution recognize this situation, but they cannot do much about it. Too many personal variables are involved, in the first place. And, in the second place, the military services are not social service agencies. They have only limited jurisdiction over their retirees and almost none over those who have separated before retirement. They have no choice, therefore, but to give you a helping hand as far as the gate of the military installation and then wish you "Good luck!"

That is not to say that the military services do not care what happens to you on the other side of that gate. They do care, very much, for a variety of reasons. And they do recognize the fact that many people face difficult problems as they return to civilian society. They have even adopted a word to describe the process: *transition*, which means moving from one stage or condition to another.

Over the years since the era of the all-volunteer services began, the Department of Defense has launched several initiatives intended to help separating military members to walk out the gate with pride in themselves and confidence in the future. The *programs* have all failed, though the basic *structure* remains, available to anyone who wants to use it.

In part, the programs failed because of the persistent fact that the military services are not social service agencies. Each military service has a mission to perform. Full-scale transition programs can and do interfere with that mission. But the services keep trying. Perhaps they will succeed some day.

In part, the programs failed because the necessary civilian infrastructure on the other side of the gate did not exist. That situation has now improved considerably, as we shall see.

But the programs have failed for another reason, as well: You. The military services as a whole have scrapped programs but maintained the excellent institutions and career services that can ease the transition back to civilian life. The technical training and advanced education available to all men and women in uniform not only enhance their military performance but can prepare them for lifelong careers. Career services already include supervision of apprenticeship programs, counseling, testing, assistance with college and graduate school placement, professional certification, and much more.

The recruiting slogans speak for the services' interest in you. The Army says "Be All You Can Be." The Air Force urges you to "Aim High." And they mean what they say. The military services provide many of the resources needed to assist you over the bumps in the road back to civilian life. If you do not take advantage of the opportunities available to you and actively seek others, the military service has not failed. You have.

Time, not resources, is the factor most often overlooked by both the military services and the men and women in uniform who face or will face transition to civilian life. A combination of the demands of the military mission and the security of the military life-style can induce a certain lethargy—as well as an ambivalence toward the civilian environment—that leads to underestimating the time required to prepare oneself for the inevitable process or to delaying the process indefinitely. "Short-timers" look forward to the day they will be discharged like school kids looking forward to summer vacation.

Observers of the transition process urge that the planning begin at least one year before the anticipated separation from military service. I can go further and suggest that transition planning should start while a person is still considering military service as a career option. A wise choice of enlistment options can influence the entire service experience and color the transition process. Steps that must be taken *before* enlisting must be known and acted upon. Acting on a knowledge of the military opportunities for professional training (health services and law, for example) can change a college student's entire life. (Some of these are described in Appendix C.)

The standard "transition briefing" dictated by Department of Defense policy lasts about four hours and is given within ninety days of separation. The Army has developed and has tested at Fort Bragg a much more comprehensive transition program that begins 270 days prior to separation. The Air Force has requested proposals from civilian contractors for a similar program. The other services are becoming more interested in the whole subject, but their programs are still far in the future. Meanwhile your own future is out there just a few months or a few years away.

If you are a young first-term enlistee or are serving your obligated tour as an ROTC officer, you may feel that you have plenty of time to think about your future career after you leave military service. And you do. You have your entire adult life to think about it. Some people, in fact, never get beyond *thinking* about it.

During the research for this book I have met men and women who have been out of uniform for years and are still unemployed. They hang around the casual labor office hoping for a job for a day, a few days, or a few weeks. I have met others who have had a dozen or so jobs in the few years since they left military service because they cannot hold the jobs they have gotten. Some of these people feel that the military services have let them down. Others are bitter about the "system." Few of them have any idea what the system is.

What I have attempted to do in this book is to put the spurs into those people who are in uniform or who may be considering military service. The casual approach does not work. Everyone must do everything possible *while serving in uniform* to prepare for the transition from military service to a civilian career. Not to just any old *job*, but to a *career*. You owe this to yourself, to your military service, and, as the case may be, to your family. In the larger sense, you owe it to the society you will be living in.

What you do or how much you can do will depend on your circumstances. But no one can afford to wait until someone comes along with a program that fits his or her case and shouts "Fall in!" The problems are real, and they will affect *your* life. The transition career strategies and procedures suggested in this book can work for anyone who can read, write, and think. From where I view the state of the military services today, that means everyone now in uniform and all those who follow them.

"Knowledge is power," wrote Francis Bacon, the sixteenth-century English philosopher. He also wrote that "if a man begin with certainties, he shall end in doubts; but if he be content to begin with doubts he shall end in certainties." What a refreshing thought for most of us who are doubting and confused. The doubting man or woman is the one who asks the questions that lead to the truth. Can anyone afford not to open up his or her mind to the truth?

Military service can and does provide many resources and opportunities that can assist its members down the pathway to a happy, successful civilian career. The objective of this book is to put those career planning and development assets into focus and to show you how to use them to your own best advantage in a future out of uniform: *the rest of your life*. But when all is said and done the last chapter still has to be written. And *you* are the author.

Part I

Getting in Touch With the Real World

Chapter 1

An Introduction to the Real World

The Department of Defense and its separate military services and agencies, together with the United States Coast Guard, form one of the largest, possibly the most complex, and probably the least known workforce in the country.

The jobs performed by the two million full-time uniformed members who make up the core of the five military services range through the occupational alphabet from accountant to X-ray technician. On the face of things, then, the military workforce is engaged in many other pursuits than those combat roles that come most readily to mind: artilleryman, infantry soldier, jet pilot, seaman, and tank driver, for example. Indeed, most of the dozens of career fields and the thousands of jobs now available to this military workforce seem to have little to do with combat, though they support combat operations in one way or another.

Uniformed members of the armed forces work as air traffic controllers, broadcast technicians, carpenters, computer operators, detectives, electronic technicians, engineers, environmental health specialists, food service specialists, graphic artists, journalists, lawyers and paralegal assistants, mechanics of all kinds, medical technicians and doctors, musicians, nurses, office machine repairmen, photographers, plumbers and pipefitters, power plant mechanics, radio/TV repairers, recreation experts, riggers, secretaries and stenographers, teachers and educational administrators, weather forecasters, and welders, to name only a few military specialties. By and large, the men and women—and there are about two hundred thousand women in military service—are well-trained, competent people who are dedicated to their work. Futhermore, all the jobs and occupations in this list are common to the civilian workplace.

Nothing much new here, you might be saying if you are still in uniform or have only recently left military service. Nothing new for you, perhaps, but *news* for a lot of other people. People who, incidentally, will be among the employers that you may sooner or later be asking for a job. People who don't know much about the complexities of a military career and are not much interested in learning more.

3

People who, quite frankly, do not consider the military services to be part of the mainstream of life in the United States.

Before leaving military service to seek what will probably be your first real civilian job, you had better know that hardly anyone other than your family is waiting for you with open arms.

History Plus Tradition Equals Alienation

Traditionally, of course, all duties performed by the members of the armed forces contribute to the overall Department of Defense mission to protect and defend the United States, its territories, and its interests at home and abroad. However, circumstances that have deep historical roots tend to isolate, geographically and otherwise, what is now often called "the military establishment" from the economic, political, and social forces that drive the very country they serve.

To some extent, this situation is the result of deliberate national policy. The Founding Fathers opposed the establishment of permanent, professional armed forces in peacetime for fear that they might seize control of the political machinery of the new republic. Shortly after the Revolutionary War, in fact, Congress went so far as to disband the Continental Army and the Navy, a move that left the country with no organized national defense forces for about twenty years.

Even after Congress acted to authorize such "regular" forces, in the early eighteen hundreds, it deliberately kept them small and ineffectual, and they remained that way until after World War II. The military academy at West Point trained Army officers to be civil engineers, on the assumption that they could do something useful to the development of the nation since there were no enemy forces lurking about. The main chapters of the military history of the United States have, in fact, been written by the "citizen soldiers" of their day: the colonial militia of the Revolutionary War, the state militias of the Civil War, and the National Guard and Reservists of the two world wars in our own century.

Under the circumstances, the tasks performed by the early "regular" military services emphasized the traditional combat arms and combat support roles. Regular Army units, for example, could be "lean and mean" because civilians and contractors provided most technical and logistical services. The "regulars" of any service were commonly regarded as the castoffs and misfits of society.

In 1892, in his popular book *Barracks Room Ballads*, Rudyard Kipling wrote the famous lines about British soldiers that seemed at the time to apply to professional soldiers everywhere:

It's Tommy this, an' Tommy that,
an' "Chuck 'im out, the brute!"
But it's "Saviour of 'is country,"
when the guns begin to shoot.

Even officers, who were more likely to come from the upper levels of American society, were only somewhat more socially acceptable— at least until the chips were down. That situation prevailed until the onset of World War II, exacerbated by the Great Depression. Convicted criminals were sometimes offered the choice of going to jail or enlisting in the Army!

The small size and specialized functions of the professional military forces thus not only kept its members out of politics but also kept them out of sight most of the time. The public was grateful on both counts. In that continuing tradition, incidentally, military personnel have been encouraged to vote in political elections only since the end of World War II. As recently as March 1987 a senior member of Congress declared that a professional military force was "un-American."

Tradition dies hard. A 1986 Gallup poll showed that a majority of the American public has more confidence in the *leadership* of the armed forces than in many other national institutions—including Congress, the court system, and the media. Yet all too often the public image of *individual* service members seems to be a composite of worn-out stereotypes: harried recruits, brutal Marine "grunts," bumbling (or sadistic) sergeants, and incompetent (or neurotic) officers, for example. These and other stereotypes are in part fostered by the media, whether in its frantic search for "news" or in the name of entertainment or historical perspective. During interviews with military veterans who had entered the civilian job force, I was struck by the number who had somehow been made to feel that they had served in uniform only because they were unfit to do anything else—and, it follows, never would be.

In short, a large portion of the civilian population does not see the modern military services as part of the mainstream of American life today any more than it did two hundred years ago. This at a time when the services are emphasizing quality of personnel over quantity, providing unrivaled opportunities for job training and educational advancement, catering to the personal needs of service people and their families as never before, and preparing several hundred thousand young men and women to *leave* military service each year as responsible, mature adults ready to take their place in the larger society.

The fact that the active military forces are now composed entirely of volunteers contributes to continued public distaste for things military. And this fact by itself tends to confirm the historical isolation of the military establishment from a civilian population that has other things to worry about.

From another point of view, the public simply cannot identify with a military establishment that no longer "drafts" the boy next door or down the street for a couple of years of military training and then sends him back to his job or family. The volunteers who are the "professional" members of today's armed forces are less likely to be seen as doing their patriotic duty, even though this is frequently not the case at all. These and other circumstances point to increasing alienation of the civilian population from the military establishment despite the sophisticated public relations efforts now being employed by the Department of Defense.

Alienation in the Workplace

Anyone who knows anything at all about what is happening in the armed forces realizes that hardly anyone who enters military service can expect to serve in uniform during his or her entire adult working life. Most of the several hundred thousand men and women who leave the services each year are, indeed, not military professionals at all. They are first-term enlistees and Reserve junior officers who have completed their obligatory tours of duty and are looking forward to civilian careers. Moreover, the tough "up-or-out" retention policies adopted by the armed forces can frustrate the aspirations of even highly qualified members who do seek military careers. When these men and women are released from active duty, they leave with no benefits of any kind unless they qualify for separation pay. Those who are retained until they qualify for retirement, sometimes still only in their late thirties or early forties, have twenty or more years of productive life ahead of them. But they are seldom economically self-sufficient when they retire. In almost all cases, then, anyone who leaves military service must find civilian employment. Even if you accept this conclusion as more or less self-evident, finding a job after military service is not all that easy.

One result of the collapse of the Selective Service system in the aftermath of the Vietnam experience, for example, is that at least one generation of students has grown up and entered the civilian workforce without having had to think much about the possibility of being "drafted" into military service. These men and women have had little if any personal exposure to military life and the military establishment, which increasingly seems to be typecast by the media as a necessary evil existing outside the mainstream of society.

The public's historic distrust of professional military forces seems likely to be transferred to the civilian labor force as other generations of students join the first. Former military people are sometimes viewed as freeloaders who have unfair competitive advantages because of their veterans benefits. Retirees are often resented because they seem to have been awarded life incomes in return for very little. Employers sometimes attempt to hire retirees at lower salaries than their civilian peers.

Another consequence of the shelving of the military draft, sociological studies point out, is that the recruits—and many of the officers —required to sustain today's all-volunteer services come largely from the lower socioeconomic strata of the population. Most of these young people seek opportunity and upward mobility in the honorable American tradition, of course. The irony is that they are apt to be regarded by many in the society at large as having entered military service because they couldn't handle anything else. When they leave military service as better educated, occupationally qualified adults who are ready to take their place in that society, the reception they receive may be cold.

Military members who serve a hitch or two but leave the service before they qualify for retirement are especially vulnerable. A recent Department of Defense study showed that most men and women who drop out early do so for family or personal reasons. The two personal reasons cited most often are revealing: (1) lack of opportunity for upward mobility in the services, and (2) the desire to seek civilian careers. Most of these early leavers are not only personally ambitious; they have already acquired during their military service the skills and work habits needed in the civilian job market. But the public is fickle. The widespread perception that anyone who enters military service must be fundamentally incompetent may actually be reinforced by the suspicion that these young men and women are so lacking in positive attributes that they couldn't even cope with life in uniform.

Almost regardless of their reasons for leaving military service, many men and women will be disappointed. Most will find that they have been overtaken by events. The dynamic civilian society they left several—or many—years ago has passed them by while they were in uniform. Many will feel that the military services let them down somehow. Some will lose their self-esteem. Others will experience fear, disorientation, and other psychological trauma as they prepare to leave the familiar, highly structured military environment to re-enter a civilian world that is largely unknown, apparently unfriendly, and deliberately unstructured.

In some cases the results are dramatic. Personal stresses can lead to broken families. Nervous breakdowns are not uncommon. A few people commit suicide in their despair. What in sociological terms can be described as alienation of the general population from the military establishment can also mean that members of the military services may also be alienated from the civilian population. In practical terms, separating and retiring military personnel are already finding that the transition to civilian careers can be difficult. Indications are that it will become more difficult in the future.

Many men now in key management positions in civilian businesses have had less than happy personal experiences in the military services, especially those who served only briefly as "draftees." Their experiences are often resented as personally degrading; their military duties and assignments were often little short of meaningless. In some cases, these men act out their own frustrations by arbitrarily discarding job applications and résumés received from former members of the uniformed services. Evidence is emerging to suggest that some non-career enlisted men and officers who served honorably in Vietnam had been—and may still be—denied civilian employment simply because they mentioned that fact in their résumé.

Moreover, former Vietnam-era "flower children" and "peaceniks" have begun to exercise hire-and-fire authority as managers in civilian enterprises. Some of them still seem to identify former members of the military services with brutality, crime, drugs, or just sheer incompetence.

None of this is intended to suggest that anything like an anti-military conspiracy is abroad in the land. On the contrary, many civilian employers seek out former military personnel for employment, as much because of the positive character traits they acquired during service as for their training and experience. Legal remedies are available in other situations where employers actively discriminate against former military personnel. Still, as the old saying goes: "Forewarned is forearmed."

Coping with the Real World

The military services themselves recognize the problems that face exiting members and are beginning to take action to smooth the transition to the civilian economy. In fact, as those who wear the Army Green know, what used to be called Separation Processing is now known as Transition Processing. To varying degrees, the other services have adopted a similar approach as they implement policy directives of the Department of Defense. Unfortunately, what transition processing exists is not yet available to all members of all services.

In even the best programs, such processing now begins only about ninety days before separation or retirement, too late in most cases. Most authorities on the matter recommend that transition planning start at least one year and preferably two years before separation from military service.

All the services now also provide outreach programs to help retirees make successful transitions, and the Veterans Administration and the Department of Labor offer several transition programs to all former military personnel, including retirees. But, even counting the assistance that is available from all the sources that we will explore in this book, that transition from military to civilian status can be pretty rugged unless you have done some advance planning. To paraphrase a saying that is popular these days among career counselors, finding a civilian job may be the toughest job you will ever have had!

Systematic information gathering and realistic planning are essential to a successful career transition. Paradoxically, most career counselors who work with former military personnel report that their clients seldom have taken the opportunity to plan for a civilian career while still in uniform. The paradox is that most military personnel are engaged in planning their *military* career, continually studying to improve their personal and military skills; they seem unaware of or ignore the need to plan for their postmilitary career.

Ideally, of course, the process of career transition should begin on the day you raise your right hand and are sworn into service and never stop. That is not to suggest that you should slight your military obligations. It is simply a logical conclusion from the fact that hardly anyone can expect to spend his or her entire working life in military service. Why not use that time to prepare yourself for the rest of your life? Indeed, I believe strongly that some tentative planning for your eventual civilian career should already have been done at the time you decide to visit a recruiting station or enter a precommissioning program.

You could be in for a bad time if you wait until you have your discharge papers in your hand before you think seriously about what you are going to do after you have hung up the uniform for the last time. With no advance planning and few recognizable landmarks on the civilian landscape, you may flounder around like a fish out of water for months or even years. You may very soon wish that you were back in the service where you were more or less comfortable with the system and secure in the knowledge of who you are—or who you *were*. More and more people who have made their own painful transition from military service to the civilian job market are, in fact, urging that *you stay in uniform as long as you can while you complete your transition planning*.

The transition strategies and job-seeking techniques described in this book are designed to help you take advantage of the time that you have spent in military service, however long that may be, and to use the resources for training, work experience, and advanced education that are available to you while you are in uniform. Along the way, we will examine some characteristics of the civilian workplace that differ from those of the military services. We will also look at some trends that may influence your planning for a civilian career, particularly if you have a family.

In the last part of the book, you will find more detailed discussion of some of the transition options you may want to consider. Should you try to utilize the skills that you have acquired in military service as a basis for a civilian career? Or are you interested in shifting gears and carving out a career in an entirely different field? Perhaps you have always wanted to have a business of your own: What does it take? How do you get started?

A final word of caution: Reading the book should help you get started, but it won't get you the job you want or think you want. Only you can do that. Those counselors I mentioned have the right idea: Getting a civilian job could well be the hardest job you will ever have. There is no easy way for most of us, but getting to work on that job right now will make it easier.

Chapter 2

The Military Services
are Workforces

In the last chapter I said that, collectively, the military services are one of the largest, most complex, and least understood workforces in the United States. In this chapter we will look behind that statement to see how this fact may affect you, directly or indirectly, now and in the future.

First of all, you may ask, what is a workforce? As I use the term, a *workforce* is a group of persons organized to carry out a defined set of tasks that contribute to the accomplishment of an overall goal or objective. In the civilian world of work, for example, we may talk about the manufacturing workforce, the agricultural workforce, or the construction workforce. Each of these workforces has its own goals and objectives. Each produces a product or products: automobiles, wheat, or houses, for example.

As we saw in the previous chapter, however, traditions are hard to kill. Thus, a civilian might ask: Even though each of the military services has a role in the common objective to protect and defend the United States, how can it be a workforce? Show me what it produces!

Well, the fact is that the men and women in the military services produce *services*. And for that very reason the widely presumed difference between the military services and the civilian labor force is disappearing. Nowadays the product of more than 80 percent of the men and women who work at civilian jobs is not goods, like the automobiles mentioned above, but *services*. In February 1987, TIME magazine reported that "of the 12.6 million new jobs created since the last recession, in 1982, almost 85 percent have been in the service industries as opposed to goods-producing fields." The Department of Labor predicts that during the period 1984–1995 nine of every ten new jobs created in the civilian labor force will be in service industries.

Another characteristic of a workforce is that it contains a large number of employees who work at jobs that are not defined by the goals of the workforce. Thus, a computer operator may move *laterally* from one workforce to another once or several times during his or her working life. There is no career penalty for this. Those who do

11

move are often applauded as seeking more responsibility along with better pay and other employment benefits.

The automobile industry provides a good example of how these nonunique jobs are organized to support a common goal. Those who perform in nonmanufacturing "service" occupations probably outnumber the men and women on the assembly lines who actually put the vehicles together. Included among these service occupations are: accountants, carpenters, computer operators, electronic technicians, engineers and engineering technicians, environmental health specialists, food service specialists, graphic artists, journalists, lawyers and paralegal assistants, mechanics of all kinds, medical technicians and doctors, nurses, office machine repairers, photographers, plumbers and pipefitters, power plant mechanics, secretaries and stenographers, trainers and educational administrators, and welders. The people who work at these jobs in the automotive industry can just as well do the same kinds of jobs in another workforce. In some cases, of course, they may require some retraining before they can become fully effective in their new jobs with other employers.

Figure 1 illustrates how the similar jobs required by different industries may be distributed in the business sectors of manufacturing and a service industry such as finance, insurance, and real estate. The service industry employs nearly three times as many people in the

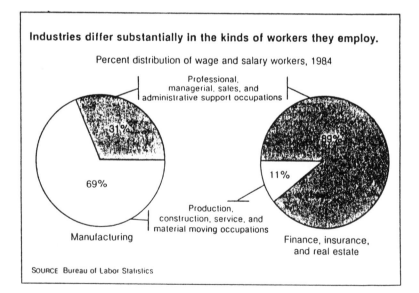

Industries differ substantially in the kinds of workers they employ.

Percent distribution of wage and salary workers, 1984

Professional, managerial, sales, and administrative support occupations

31%

69%

89%

11%

Production, construction, service, and material moving occupations

Manufacturing

Finance, insurance, and real estate

SOURCE Bureau of Labor Statistics

Fig. 1

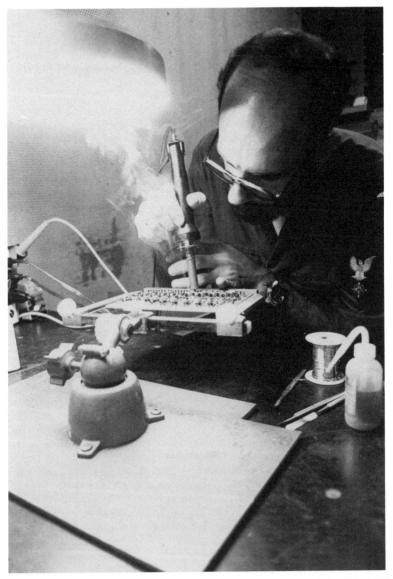

Eighty-seven percent of enlisted military occupations relate to civilian jobs, including many high-tech jobs in the electronics field.

category of "Professional, managerial, sales, and administrative support occupations" as does a typical manufacturing industry. On the other hand a manufacturing industry employs many more people in "Production, construction, maintenance, and material moving." The point is that both categories of jobs exist in the two very different industries.

Compare the list of jobs performed in the automobile industry to the sampling of jobs performed by military personnel at the beginning of Chapter 1, and you will get the picture if you haven't already. Most of the military jobs listed can also be found in Ford, General Motors, or Chrysler.

In fact, about 87 percent of the enlisted men and women—and many officers and warrant officers—who serve in uniform work at jobs that are comparable to, if not identical with, those performed in civilian workforces. Many of these jobs are in the high-tech fields that are in increasing demand in the civilian job market.

Like those who work in the civilian labor force, the men and women in military jobs are organized into work groups, usually according to their specialization or along "task" or program lines. A central data processing center in the military services is not much different from a central data processing center operated by a large civilian business, for example. And in general terms military 'employees" also work under managers who are responsible for work standards and performance, much like managers in the civilian labor force. These military managers are the senior non-commissioned officers, warrant officers, and commissioned officers of each service.

Yes, the military services are workforces. The good news is that the enlisted men and women who make up about 85 percent of the active duty personnel of the armed forces are often able to transfer to the civilian job market the skills and on-the-job experience they have acquired during military service. In some cases, of course, they require some retraining or additional training to fit them for particular jobs. Senior non-commissioned officers, warrant officers, and commissioned officers, for reasons to be discussed later, may find their transition from military service to civilian careers a bit more difficult than those of enlisted men and women.

You may already understand the similarities between the military and civilian workforces, but you may not have thought about them in a framework that includes much more than your own specialty. That is, if you are working as an automobile mechanic in uniform, you know that there are jobs for automobile mechanics in the civilian job market, but that is not enough to get you a job when you leave the service. You must know more about what is going on in the civilian job market. In fact, part of the transition process is to begin to think like a civilian *before* you hang up the uniform.

Enlisted Military Service Provides Job Training

Civilians who are not in tune with developments in the military services often conclude that the youths who enter the armed forces are both poorly educated and otherwise unqualified to do anything else. Worse, this attitude may lead to the conclusion that those who leave military service cannot have learned much and are still unqualified for the civilian labor force. After all, aren't the young men and women who seek employment directly after graduation from high school or college hired because they have marketable job skills?

No!, says Richard Nelson Bolles, author of the job-search manual with the intriguing title *What Color Is Your Parachute?* There are two kinds of employers, he declares. The first hires you for your skills. The second is willing to take a chance on you. The military services belong to the second group of employers, though they do not take chances on everyone who applies any more than do civilian employers. Those who are accepted for military service are trained while they serve.

Prospective recruits who are accepted by the military services without prior job experience must therefore have the potential to master both the rigors of military life and the skills required by the military workforce. Recruitment standards for the all-volunteer services are high. In recent years more than 96 percent of all enlisted recruits have either been high school graduates or qualified by the GED. Tough physical standards, vocational aptitude testing, and other screening devices ensure that only the best of those who apply are accepted.

Basic military training is, in the best sense, a test of the personal potential of each new member of the services: potential to adapt, potential to learn, and potential for leadership, for example, along with the demonstration of (or development of) self-esteem, self-confidence, self-discipline, adaptability, initiative, personal integrity, perseverance, problem-solving abilities, loyalty to the group, and strong personal commitment to accomplishment of the job or task assigned or perceived. Some recruits do not pass the test. For those who do pass, the next step for most enlisted men and women is skill training. The training may be technical school training or on-the-job training.

Not everyone enlists directly from high school, of course. All the services offer better entry grades (and pay) and the lure of accelerated promotions to applicants who have qualifying job experience in some military-related technical field, advanced educational standing, or both. If you entered service under such a program, you may have an advantage over your peers in transition to a civilian career. You may qualify immediately for advanced training in your technical field.

Rapid promotions move you into supervisory roles sooner than your peers.

A few military career fields are open only to those who are already trained and have some experience. They are usually professional fields that have been designated as officer career specialties: law, health services, engineering, and religion are examples. By and large, the work requirements in these fields resemble those common to civilian career fields; reentry into the civilian sector is relatively easy.

Despite the fact that these are officer and warrant officer career fields, opportunities for training in some professional fields are available to qualified enlisted men and women *who have already entered military service*. Moreover, service-supported training in these and other fields is available to some *civilians*; in return for that support, they may be obligated to perform some military service when they complete their training. We will explore some of these opportunities to acquire professional skills in Part II.

Most Enlisted Military Skills Are Marketable

Most of the skills required by the military services are related to those in demand in the civilian job market. But how can you know when you enlist that the job you qualified for (or were assigned in accordance with the "needs of the service") includes one of those skills?

High school guidance counselors and military recruiters have that information, and you probably relied on their advice. After you enlisted, however, the process of orienting yourself to military life, the demands of technical training, and the pressure to perform well in your assigned military specialty probably pushed all thoughts of an eventual civilian career way back in your mind. Right? Or possibly you thought that the job you want was "out there" just waiting while you do your thing in uniform? Wrong!

Despite all the similarities between the military workforces and the civilian labor market, no one in uniform has ever guaranteed that you would get a civilian job of your choice when you left military service. The technical training and job experience you can acquire during your military service may help you get a job when you leave, but getting that job is mostly up to you. So let's look at how enlisted military specialties relate to civilian jobs and how you may be able to get into the one you most want.

The *Military Career Guide*, a publication compiled by the Department of Defense and used largely for recruiting purposes, lists 134 "military occupations" available to enlisted men and women. Of this number, 129 are indeed directly related to civilian occupations. Approximately 87 percent of all enlisted people work in these military occupations. The other five military occupations are combat arms specialties that have no direct civilian equivalents. You will find the entire list of the 129 civilian-job-related military occupations in Appendix A.

The titles of these military occupations do not always describe the duties actually carried out by those who work in them. That is, they seldom match the military specialties used by military career managers: the MOS's of the Army and Marine Corps, the AFSC's of the Air Force, or the "rates" of the Navy and Coast Guard. Most of these "military occupations" are clusters of those military occupational specialties. Nevertheless, you should become familiar with the list of military occupations; it is a device that you can use to help you translate your military training and job experience into terms that civilian employers understand.

Following each military occupation are the code number and title of one or more equivalent civilian jobs, taken from the *Dictionary of Occupational Titles*. This book, known also as the "DOT," is a Department of Labor publication that describes about 20,000 jobs. Appendix A contains only about 400 DOT job codes, but more than half of those codes refer to jobs in which greater than average growth has been forecast by the Department of Labor.

Most enlisted personnel, whether first-termers or confirmed careerists, can find in the list the civilian job code that fits his or her military occupational specialty. The exceptions are combat arms specialties. If you are in one of those specialties, do not despair; we'll have more to say about that situation.

What you can do with this information is one of the subjects covered in Chapter 5. But at this point you may want to turn to Appendix A and find your own military occupation and its civilian job equivalents. When you do, you will see that the list contains other useful information. Relative growth in the number of civilian jobs in each occupational field is shown for the period 1984–1995 by a letter code: "N" stands for average growth; "F" means faster than average growth; "S" stands for slower than average growth. You will also find after some military occupations the code "APP," which indicates that an apprenticeship training program may be available in some subfields of that military occupation.

The Army, the Navy, and the Marine Corps offer opportunities for enlisted members in a number of military occupations to enroll in apprenticeship programs. The programs are arranged by the individual services, but they are approved and supervised by the Bureau of Apprenticeship and Training of the U.S. Department of Labor. Apprenticeship programs usually start after completion of entry-level technical school training. Service standards vary, but you usually remain eligible for such programs through the grade of E-5. Note that these apprenticeship programs are not the same as the Navy and Air Force training levels designated "apprentice," as in "Seaman Apprentice."

Successful completion of an approved apprenticeship program leads to the award of a Journeyman's Certificate that could give you a leg up when you seek civilian employment in your field. Partial completion may also help, since your documented military job experience can be more readily equated to civilian job requirements or credited toward a continuing apprenticeship in the same field after you leave military service.

At this point, it seems important that you be aware that the military technical training that generally follows enlisted basic training may be one of the most important cards in your deck of job qualifications when you are preparing to leave service. Technical training may even be your trump card if you are not planning to make a career of military service.

Do not wait, in any case, until your term of enlistment is up to get some idea of where you stand with respect to a potential civilian occupation. Those who are assigned to combat specialties and men and women who are not satisfied with their current military occupational specialties may have opportunities to move into other fields by applying for another military specialty or by reenlisting for a different specialty.

Furthermore, not all these military occupations are available to entry-level recruits. Assignment in some fields depends upon your grade or years of service or both. Recruiters, trainers, and counselors are a few examples of this kind.

Up to this point we have been concentrating on the technical skills enlisted personnel can acquire during military service. In all services, however, specific MOS's or rates provide for career development, through E-9. In practical terms, this means that the enlisted men and women who receive entry-level training as automobile mechanics are already programmed to move out of the repair shop and into the office, perhaps first as shop supervisors and later as command maintenance managers.

Once you have been promoted to E-5, you will find that the emphasis in your military training changes from acquisition of useful technical skills to advanced professional military development. As you move through the non-commissioned officer grades your supervisory responsibilities will increase; opportunities will appear for assignment as an instructor in your technical specialty or for out-of-specialty tours of duty with a recruiting command, a Reserve unit, or an American Embassy abroad, among other possibilities. Eventually, you become a professional *manager*, and to some extent you may find yourself in the kind of situation that faces many warrant or commissioned officers as they advance in rank: their technical or professional skills may erode with time and disuse. Suggested ways to deal with this common problem as you contemplate separation or retirement are also covered in Part II.

Military Service Trains Officers to Be Managers

Unlike most enlisted personnel, commissioned officers and warrant officers generally qualify for their initial appointment because they have already acquired professional or job-related skills and the advanced education required by the military services. Though many officers may perform in assignments that utilize skills related to the civilian workplace, relatively few of them—aviators are one exception—are given opportunities for the kinds of entry-level vocational or technical school training commonly available to enlisted personnel. The emphasis in the training provided officers is instead on "professional development" and the profession is military service. The role of officers in that profession is essentially to manage the armed forces.

In traditional military usage, of course, commissioned officers have been thought of as leaders rather than specialists. The precommissioning process screens out candidates who lack leadership potential or ability. It is also designed to develop or reinforce such personal traits as adaptability, self-discipline, self-esteem, motivation and initiative, personal integrity, loyalty to the group, commitment to the task assigned or perceived, and problem-solving abilities. If you have noticed that this list of personal qualities resembles that already given for enlisted men and women, that is no coincidence. The objectives are the same though the character development process is more intensive for officers in the precommissioning stages.

The distinction between leaders and specialists is becoming blurred. Officers are being encouraged to specialize to satisfy the demand for high-level technical and professional skills generated by the race for technological superiority over any potential enemy. Even many combat arms or line officers now alternate between traditional command assignments and assignments in their technical specialty.

Warrant officers are by and large already specialists, particularly in such fields as administration, intelligence, law enforcement, maintenance, and logistics. Though warrant officers are generally outside the chain of command, they often serve as senior administrators and supervisors in military occupational fields that are closely related to the enlisted occupational fields listed in Appendix A.

The experience common to officers is that they tend to become skilled managers of people, resources, and programs rather than leaders of men as they advance in grade and responsibility. There is some irony here. While military officers may be classed as "managers," and some assume truly awesome responsibilities at the upper grade levels, "management" is not commonly an entry-level occupational field in the civilian job market.

Meanwhile, the professional skills—especially in engineering, medicine and biology, and the "hard" sciences—that may have helped qualify a person for appointment as a commissioned officer often fall into disuse or become obsolete over time. In our high-tech era, such erosion of skills is almost taken for granted. Civilian engineering, medical, and science professionals are already facing the need for retraining every five years or so. But even professional competence in the less technical military fields becomes stale. A university degree more than five to seven years old may actually damage your chances for a civilian job.

These observations apply in particular to mid-level and senior commissioned officers. Promotion standards above the grade O–4 tend to emphasize personal qualities and managerial potential over performance in a technical skill or professional discipline. These officers become professional members of the military establishment. As such, they also become "generalists": people who can do just about anything that needs doing. The *Dictionary of Occupational Titles*, unfortunately, does not list a job code for "generalist."

When the time comes to make the transition to civilian life, many of these professional military officers have worries and self-doubts about their ability to make the move successfully. "What can I do?" they may wonder. "How will I fit in?" Employers ask the same questions, implicitly or explicitly. As they face the move, therefore, career officers may sense that they are confronting "a riddle wrapped in a mystery inside an enigma," a phrase that Winston Churchill made famous when he was asked to forecast Soviet intentions. Others are sublimely confident that the experience they have gained as managers of complex military projects and programs has qualified them for immediate placement as the chief operating officer of such giant civilian enterprises as General Motors. As usual, the truth lies somewhere in the middle.

Appendix B contains a list of representative career fields available to officers, along with some civilian job equivalents. The list is not service-specific nor is it intended to be comprehensive; in particular, it excludes most combat specialties. Like Appendix A, the list of officer career fields contains information about the relative growth in the number of jobs in the field for the period 1980–1995, based on projections made by the U.S. Department of Labor. Unlike Appendix A, however, no *Dictionary of Occupational Titles* job codes for the equivalent civilian occupations have been included.

What is more important is that six in ten of the civilian job fields shown as counterparts within the military career fields are "fast track" jobs with significantly greater growth than the average. With only a few exceptions, all the others listed are also growing in numbers of civilian jobs. Even most of the fields that show slower job growth can provide opportunities in the future. Most of the civilian equivalents in Appendix B are in the expanding services sector of the civilian economy. Most of them also imply acquisition of *management* skills and experience.

But, you say, you have loaded the deck by eliminating the combat specialties for which there are no civilian equivalents. Not at all. Career transition strategies that will provide equivalent civilian skills do exist. Many commissioned officers and warrant officers can adopt one or another of these strategies *while they are still in uniform*. Moreover, these strategies conform with established career development policies common to the military services. We will come back to them in Part II, where we will examine some of the opportunities for advanced university-level education available to career military officers. But, to repeat a statement made earlier, it may often be advisable to remain in uniform longer than you planned so that you can take advantage of one or more of these career development strategies.

Chapter *3*

Military and Civilian Workforces Compared

Despite the many similarities in *job opportunities* between the military workforce and the civilian workplace, significant differences in objectives, structure, and operational styles can impede the search for civilian jobs by even well-qualified members. Understanding and compensating for these differences is an essential part of the transition process.

The Business of Business is Making Money

Everyone knows that private enterprise exists to make money. But the power of the profit motive that energizes American business is in practice often underestimated, sometimes overlooked, and occasionally ignored by people in military service. The profit motive, nevertheless, remains an essential element of our economy. Anyone who contemplates a transition from military service to civilian employment must adopt it with enthusiasm.

The profit motive is a basic factor in the job market and an inevitable component of the employer-employee relationship. We can go further and say that understanding the importance of the profit motive is essential to a successful transition. You don't become a full-fledged member of the civilian labor force simply by putting on a blue pin-stripe suit or jeans and a hard hat.

In the two previous chapters we attached considerable importance to the fact that you can acquire or sharpen marketable technical and professional skills while you are in military service. True, but the hard fact is that confirmation of technical and professional skills is not the only factor in obtaining civilian employment. Private business creates jobs when something needs to be done that is not being done. In many cases employers train their own employees to fill newly created jobs: American employers spend about $200 billion a year for training, including both on-the-job and formal courses of instruction. On the other hand jobs are eliminated when they no longer contribute to the business objective. Several million men and women who

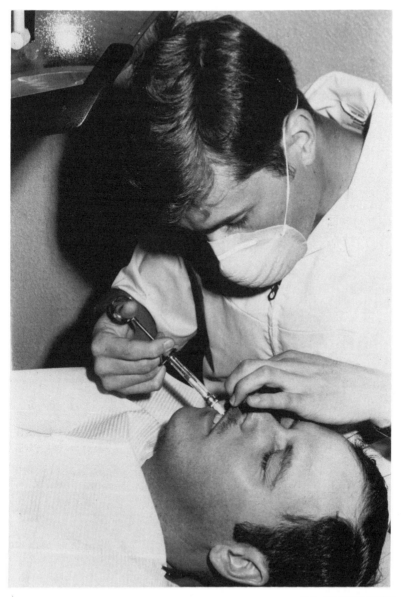

Among civilian professions practiced in the military is dentistry.

have marketable skills are unemployed at any one time, even when the economy is vigorous and expanding. So what else does it take to get a job—and hold it?

The straight-from-the-shoulder answer to the question is that those who are hired to fill vacant jobs must have the qualifications or at least the potential to contribute to the successful operation of the employer. In business terms the only successful operation is a *profitable* operation.

Thus, in the first place, the salary or wages paid civilian employees are not rewards for the experience or the technical and professional skills that they bring with them. Nor are wages and salaries paid in recognition of an employee's economic needs. Rather, an employee's pay represents that portion of the company's expected income that the employer is willing to pay someone to do a job and that will still enable the company to make a profit from its operations.

In the order of things, then, unskilled workers and trainees are at the bottom of the pay scale. Their contributions to a company's profitability are minimal; moreover, they can be replaced easily. Skilled or experienced workers are paid more. Those who are paid most are the managers who coordinate the varied activities of a company and focus the results on profits. Key managers are often paid annual bonuses in proportion to their contributions to the profitability of the enterprise.

This order of things helps account for the huge annual incomes of some senior executives of *Fortune* 500 corporations. The income of $1,700,000 enjoyed by Chrysler Corporation's chairman Lee Iacocca in 1986 is not so much when compared to that year's $1.4 billion profit on corporate sales of $22.6 billion. Iacocca's income for 1986, by the way, included a bonus payment of nearly a million dollars.

But, you may ask, does any one person deserve such a huge income? Well, consider the fact that Lee Iacocca is credited with rescuing Chrysler Corporation from the brink of bankruptcy in the early 1980's. Without him, as one automotive industry analyst has said, "Chrysler would not be around today."

In any event, Iacocca was not the only Chrysler manager to receive a bonus in 1986. According to an Associated Press report, Chrysler's board of directors distributed $76.9 million of the company's $1.4 billion profit to 1,914 executives. Profit-sharing in one form or another is, of course, not limited to Chrysler Corporation. In many other companies, profit-sharing work-incentive plans run from the Chairman of the Board all the way down to the men and women at the bottom of the career ladder.

Successful Employees Need More Than Technical Skills

The skills or experience of particular job applicants do not by themselves assure employers that they will be able to continue and expand

Table 1. Personal Traits Valued by Industry

1. Honesty and dependability
2. Reliability and punctuality
3. Getting along well with people
4. Cooperation with supervisors
5. Ability to accept and handle responsibility
6. Willingness to undergo further skill training
7. Self-esteem, sense of personal worth
8. Good verbal communications skills; ability to listen
9. Ability to work with minimum supervision
10. Ability to solve personal and professional problems
11. *Entry-level job skills/knowledge*
12. Ability to read with understanding
13. Knowledge of required mathematics

profitable operations if any applicant is hired. Each employer also screens prospective employees in an effort to determine whether they have the *personal* attributes that contribute to successful operation of the business. What are those personal characteristics? What do they have to do with making a profit?

Many of the personal attributes that civilian employers look for in employees are the same ones that the military services seek in recruits or officer candidates. Professional military education during service is designed to confirm, develop, and reinforce those attributes. If you skipped over the list in Chapter 2, here they are again: self-confidence, self-discipline, motivation and initiative, adaptability, ability to learn, problem-solving abilities, loyalty to the group, personal commitment to the accomplishment of the job or task assigned or perceived, personal integrity, and leadership.

Examine your own behavior patterns and attitudes toward your military assignments. Can you honestly affirm that you have all, or most, of these qualities? If you can, you may have an advantage over some of the civilian applicants who may be competing with you in the same job market—provided, of course, that you can apply these personal attributes in your new civilian job.

Many studies of employers confirm this statement. One such study in California reported that "employers rate entry-level job skills below ten other traits as a predictor of job success." The thirteen personal traits, or attributes, included in the report are shown above. Not all the terms are identical to the military terms listed, but you should be able to match them up.

Note that the California list includes good communications and interpersonal skills and knowledge of mathematics in addition to the military traits we have mentioned. That translates, more or less, to an emphasis on reading, writing, and arithmetic.

More recently, in the summer of 1986, a group of educators in my hometown of Colorado Springs met with a group of local businessmen to discuss technical training standards for entry-level employees. The educators were surprised when the businessmen reported that they did not want more training in specific *job skills*. What they wanted were employees who are dependable, dedicated, and flexible, who have good interpersonal skills, who are able to follow instructions, who take pride in their work, and who demonstrate initiative, industry, and other positive attitudes. The businessmen put heavy emphasis on preparing students "to become educable rather than educated." Most of them pointed out that, regardless of previous training or experience, new employees are usually given additional training of some sort after being hired.

Since that meeting, one Colorado Springs school district has developed a program to teach vocational students twenty-one attributes of successful employees based on responses of businessmen to a recent nationwide survey. That list is on the facing page.

The good news for men and women in military service is that basic training or precommissioning training, on-the-job training, and professional military education each plays its role in the development of the positive personal traits so sought after by civilian employers.

What we have been dealing with here, in business terms, are the personal and technical skills required for entry-level employment or a first job after high school or college. Interestingly, however, the more demanding the job, the more important the personal skills become. Military retirees and separees who have acquired civilian-related technical skills or professional proficiency *and* who have already developed the personal qualities we have been discussing through experience on the job probably should not have to transfer to the civilian labor force in entry-level positions, though they may need some additional technical training or retraining. On the other hand, many former military personnel who have mastered some or all of these traits while in service may find the transition relatively easy even though they have minimal civilian-related technical skills.

What does all this have to do with making profits? Everything. Undependable workers are not there when you need them: late to work or frequently absent from work, for example. Workers who cannot follow instructions waste time and materials, or produce unsaleable goods, or antagonize customers because of their mistakes. Lack of initiative may cause the waste of time or materials, perpetuate inefficient business methods, or result in the loss of sales. Lack of industry clearly results in underproduction of goods and services.

Time, materials, and support and administrative services all have dollar values in the civilian workplace. Labor costs may account for 70 percent or more of a manufacturer's cost of production of a sale-

Table 2. Twenty-One Attributes for Successful Employability

Dependability
Accuracy in performing operations
Ability to follow instructions
Attendance and punctuality
Shop and laboratory safety
Amount of acceptable work produced
Remembering necessary details
Taking initiative, being resourceful
Appropriate dress and grooming
Working well with others
Physical fitness for the job
Ability to work under pressure
Industry, diligence in task completion
Personality and cheerfulness in the workplace
Neatness and orderliness
Minimal time spent on personal matters
Ability to make quick, accurate decisions
Natural aptitude and attitude for the job
Acceptability of work produced
Ability to organize work; prioritizing
Ability to suggest improvements

Courtesy Harrison School District No. 2, Colorado Springs, Colorado, 1987.

able item; labor costs in service industries may be even greater. In either case, inefficient employees cost employers more than they are worth. In other words, inefficient employees reduce profits.

If you apply the positive personal attributes that you acquired during military service to do your job better and thus increase your employer's profit, you may be given a raise in pay or be promoted to a more responsible position. If, on the other hand, your job performance does not contribute to profitable operation, you will be back on the street very soon. It doesn't matter whether you are an electrician on the maintenance gang, a bookkeeper in the accounting office, a project manager, or the vice president for marketing.

Some insight into the importance of understanding and embracing the profit motive can be gained from considering the field of sales and marketing. Because civilian enterprises generate their profits from the sale of products or services, effective advertising and sound sales management are essential to their very existence. Further, they are two essential factors in business expansion. In general, more sales mean greater profits. Greater profits usually lead to expanded operations. Expanded operations mean more jobs. And around we go.

In 1984 about 10 percent of the civilian labor force was engaged in sales and marketing activities. By 1995 about two million more jobs in sales and marketing are expected. These figures are startling, especially if you are used to grumbling about cashiers, retail sales clerks, telephone solicitors, insurance agents, stockbrokers, and real estate agents, as most of us do.

Few men and women in uniform work in marketing and sales jobs, unless you include recruiters, club managers, commissary managers, and the like. But, oddly enough, many former military people enter sales fields, especially insurance, securities, and real estate. About two out of three fail, often because they have not considered the importance of their job to the continued profitability and expansion of their employer.

All three sales categories mentioned are "commission" sales fields, in which people are paid only when they produce sales. To encourage competition, commission salespeople are often pitted against each other. Sales training is usually provided by the employer, but actual sales guidance may be minimal. This kind of situation makes great demands on such personal traits as initiative, motivation, self-discipline, resourcefulness, problem-solving abilities, and perseverance.

Even though the former military people who seek these jobs see themselves as "go-getters," many become discouraged and quit before they see any return on their investment of time and effort. They are used to being paid to do a job. They have been accustomed to carrying out assignments with precise guidelines, assignments that produce tangible or visible results in a relatively short time. They are used to cooperating to accomplish results, not competing with their peers. They gradually succumb to "rejection syndrome." Being told "No!" several times a day, every day of the week, by prospective customers can rapidly erode self-confidence.

Others who have begun to earn a comfortable income tend to think of their commissions as "salary"; they simply lean back and relax. Military retirees who have all the personal attributes needed to succeed in business nevertheless frequently fall into this behavior pattern. After all, they have their retired pay as an economic "floor"; their supplemental income needs, though urgent, may be modest. Why should they break their backs to make more money? Let's take some time off for golf. Or lunch with old buddies? After all, all work and no play...you know!

They don't last very long, either. Employers do not hire people to satisfy their economic needs. They hire people who will beat the bushes to make more sales this month than last month, and do it month after month, year after year. The employer is willing to pay commissions for sales only because sales increase profits.

The profit motive, then, is the engine that drives private or civilian businesses. The technical skills you have may help you get a job, but you will keep it only if you apply your whole person to the company objective. And the final objective is profit, whatever intermediate objectives lie in the way. Call it product development, increasing market share, new plant development, or improving administrative support, it all adds up to the same thing. The business of business is to make money. If you cannot or do not contribute to that goal, you are out of business.

Business Structure Advances Business Objectives

Structurally, the civilian economy is dynamic, flexible, and amorphous compared to the military services. The old shibboleth from the design world seems to apply: "Form follows function." Sole proprietorships, partnerships, professional corporations, corporations, and —more recently—franchise operations have all developed in response to the business function: making money.

Business ventures and even entire industries grow and flourish, or they may grow old, sick, and die. When old ventures fail, new ones take their place.

Business managers rise and fall in accordance with their ability to keep an enterprise alive, growing, and profitable. They are often forced to borrow money in order to create profits, though that may seem contradictory. Management styles are constantly being examined and revamped in an effort to reduce inefficiency and to produce more profits.

Few constraints of the kind that apply to the military services operate on the civilian economy. The size of each military service is determined by Congress. With few exceptions, military "income" represents the annual allocation of funds by Congress. The accepted military management style is to *spend* those funds as efficiently as possible. Managers are not permitted to make profits or reinvest "savings" in new ventures. In this context, new functions or programs are generally undertaken at the expense of existing ones. The number of military "jobs" remains the same.

Civilian jobs flow to where the money is or seems likely to be. Successful business enterprises create about a million jobs a year, and the jobs are created largely by the four million small businesses that employ about half the national labor force, not by the giant corporations that make up the *Fortune* 500. The official U.S. government definition of a small business, by the way, is one that employs no more than 500 workers.

Another ten million or so small businesses exist in the form of sole proprietorships and personal corporations. They are very small businesses indeed, often limited to one person. Artisans, consultants, and part-time entrepreneurs characterize this group.

Though about half of all new businesses started up each year fail within about eighteen months, the total number of these small businesses continues to grow. They also provide much of the variety and excitement in the business world. They are the high-tech companies that grow like mushrooms—and may die like them; the franchise businesses with total sales of $500 billion a year; and thousands of other new, imaginative ventures. The probability is that your eventual civilian career will involve you with one of these small companies or corporations. You may even start one yourself.

Meanwhile, the dynamism of the civilian economy favors structural change and functional diversity in what were once highly specialized industries. Corporate giants like Ford Motor Co. have abandoned what used to be called "vertical integration" under which they owned or controlled everything that went into an automobile: from the iron ore deposits, to the ships that transported the iron ore to their own steel mills, to the distributors who sold Ford cars and trucks. Most of the components of Ford automobiles and trucks, for example, are produced by small businesses that perform as contractors. This arrangement benefits everybody. It has created a lot of jobs for people in small business enterprises and allowed Ford to pursue interests in situations where the profits seem to be greater. Among other things, Ford is now involved in aerospace activities.

Other examples of restructuring for greater profitability can be seen among the hundreds of business consolidations and acquisitions reported in the press almost daily. Sears, Roebuck & Co. provides one instructive case. Sears remains top dog in the retail trade, but it also owns and operates the real estate firm of Coldwell Banker, the brokerage house of Dean Witter Reynolds Inc. and the Allstate Insurance Co. Recently, Sears has moved into the all-purpose credit card industry in search of more profits. Under Sears management, each of these financial subsidiaries has expanded its share of the market. To repeat, expanding business operations create jobs.

Civilian Job-seekers Must be Flexible and Knowledgeable

Civilian job-seekers must be as flexible as the businesses that create and sustain the job market. As many as twelve million civilian workers are reportedly on the move each year, most of them either seeking better opportunities in their own fields or retraining to qualify for jobs in new fields. Civilian workers change jobs on an average of every four years. More and more men and women are opting for early retirement and starting out on "second careers." The traditional image of the worker who has settled into his or her job to await a genteel retirement thirty or forty years down the road has been shattered.

Some employment counselors believe that this change in the civilian outlook greatly increases the competition as former military men and women begin their job search. Others hold that the constant movement in the civilian labor force presents opportunities for former military personnel. Both views are correct, at least in part. Every civilian worker who leaves a job for another leaves a job vacant. However, as we shall soon see, the practice in private business is to promote from within.

Finding your way around in this dynamic but formless business environment can be very upsetting when you first leave military service. Indeed, some people experience serious disorientation for several years. But there are road signs, traffic controllers, and information centers to help you along the way.

Several thousand business, industry, and professional associations have been formed in the United States precisely to provide some coherence to our highly diversified economy. They range over the entire business landscape. Examples are the American Trucking Association, the National Association of Dental Laboratories, the Associated General Contractors of America, the Air Conditioning and Refrigeration Institute, the Automotive Service Industry Association, the American Society of Travel Agents, the Professional Photographers of America, the American Society of Radiologic Technicians, and the American Society of Civil Engineers. Such associations assist with setting industry standards, including education and training standards for people in their fields. In many cases they provide free career or related information about their industry. Most professional associations offer employment services to their members. We will have more to say about these industry and professional associations later, because they are as important to you as to established civilian workers.

New Entrants to the Workplace Must Also Be Flexible

Whether you are in the enlisted or officer category, you should have recognized by now that career planning involves much more than acquiring technical and professional skills and work experience while still in military service. Because of the economic, political, social, and technological factors that constantly interact in business but barely touch the armed forces, many employers simply reject the notion that anyone who has served in the military could have any relevant skills to offer. And that includes the important personal skills and traits that employers value in their employees. Even highly qualified former members of the military services often find it difficult to display those personal skills in a positive way outside the immediate military environment. Partly as a result of these circumstances, employers tend to hire former military men and women in entry-level jobs.

Others factors common to the business world, however, help to confirm this tendency and justify the practice:

1. Normal business practice is to recruit employees at the "entry" level in any particular occupational field and *to promote employees who are already working in the enterprise.* Even many business managers begin as "management interns," with entry-level pay and probationary status.

2. Even though most "military occupations" have civilian equivalents, the men and women who work in them are often either undertrained or overspecialized by civilian employment standards. They may work, for example, on service-specific equipment that is technologically obsolete by civilian standards. Or they may work according to rigid military task requirements in assignments that limit the scope of their work experience. Military aviation mechanics are the greatest source of mechanics for the civilian aviation industry, for example, but most need additional training to meet FAA standards. As you move toward "transition," you must understand what a future civilian employer may expect of you. Otherwise you may build up unrealistic expectations.

3. Postemployment training, whether in formal classes or on the job, is an essential function of civilian personnel management—which, incidentally, is now widely known as Human Resource Management or Human Resource Development. This in-house training is designed as much to familiarize new employees with the company, its operating procedures, its objectives, and its work ethic as it is to train them in specific job techniques and procedures. The process may vary in time from a few days to a year or more. Until it is completed, however, new employees are on probation, subject to dismissal if they do not prove that they identify with and can contribute to the company's goals and objectives.

Most private businesses, then, resist pressures to hire new, untried employees at other than the entry level simply because they must preserve the integrity and continuity of their business operations. In principle, the business objectives in this situation resemble those of the military services incorporated in enlisted recruit training and officer procurement. "New hires" in the business world who prove themselves during their probationary employment are generally given pay raises and placed on permanent status. Those who demonstrate outstanding technical skills and personal potential may be singled out for rapid promotion.

Exceptions to this situation exist, of course. Earlier we said that business *creates* jobs when something needs to be done that is not already being done. Many of these new jobs are at the management level. In general, they are filled by promoting eligible employees with high potential and a proven "track record." If no employee in-house is considered eligible, however, the company may recruit qualified employees from other sources—though they do not always advertise these positions publicly.

A similar situation may occur when an established employee leaves a company for a job elsewhere. The vacant job is usually filled from the ranks of other eligible employees, without public advertising.

The prevailing business practice of promoting from within serves to create "the hidden job market." Most job search consultants concentrate on techniques designed to break through the barriers that each company erects and penetrate that institution. We will come back to this important subject in Part III.

One final note about the differences between the military workforce and the civilian workplace: Hardly anyone out there is hiring Marine Corps Gunnery Sergeants or Army Lieutenant Colonels simply because they held those ranks while they were in uniform. The Mr. Smith who interviews you for your first civilian job may be a former draftee who only made it to E-4, but he has since earned an MBA and racked up fifteen years as a manager with XYZ Corporation. If you want the job, you have to sell him on your qualifications—on his terms. He wants to know what or how you can contribute to the success of XYZ Corporation.

There are few permanent personal ranks in the civilian workplace to match those that motivate military people to achieve. By personal rank I mean the military grade that each individual carries around inside his or her head—and that is, of course, also a visible part of the uniform. The person who holds it is a Gunnery Sergeant or a Colonel, or whatever, regardless of what he or she is doing. The pay received each month is according to the rank held, *not the job held*. Of course, we all know that the nature of military assignments often depends upon promotion to a certain rank. In general terms, the grade or rank itself certifies to prior experience, education, and professional qualifications. If you have made it into the senior enlisted or officer ranks, you can be justly proud of yourself.

When you leave military service, however, you hang up the rank with your uniform. Once you are outside a military service, you are just another "Mister" or "Ms." Whatever title you may have is functional. The Chairman of the Board of Chrysler Corporation is still only "Mr." Iacocca.

Some fomer military personnel, particularly retirees in the senior grades, may undergo severe identity crises because this lack of recognition seems to ignore past accomplishments. The situation has to be anticipated and managed with grace. The people who need to know do know: your "résumé" is the civilian counterpart of your service record. In particular, have the grace to refrain from suggestions that begin: "Now, when I was in the service we approached that problem this way..." Your new colleagues will know that you haven't gotten the message.

When you hang up your uniform, frame your medals, certificates, celebrity photos, and other memorabilia of your military service. They will comfort you and help you preserve your identity. But hang them up at home, in your den or wherever, not in your new office. If you are going to hang anything in your office or other place of work, let it be a diploma from college or graduate school or some pictures of the wife and kids with the family dog. Your new colleagues will applaud; they care more about who you are than who you were. And so should you.

In the final analysis, you become a valuable employee of a private business enterprise not because of who you *were* but because of what you can contribute from your accumulated training, education, and experience to the profitability of its operations. The more you contribute, the more you will be recognized for who you *are*. When that happens, ironically enough, you are bound to overhear someone say, "By George, the Old Colonel has become a great member of the team, after all!"

Chapter 4

Getting in Touch with Your Future

We have all grown up in a world that is changing so rapidly that we take it for granted. To a large extent we choose the new ideas or things that appeal to us—remote-controlled solid-state TV's and stereos fed by satellite dishes; sleek automobiles constructed of fiberglass and equipped with lightweight fuel-injection engines, electronic ignitions, and computers; pocket calculators operated by solar power; watches that run for a year or two on tiny batteries; electronic toys for the kids; and instant-replay, pocket-sized video cameras to record and preserve memories of the latest family outing. We ignore or reject the rest. As a result, few of us have "the big picture."

Most of us have only superficial ideas about the extent to which the whole world is changing around us. The fact is that the things we take for granted today, those listed above and thousands of other consumer items that incorporate the latest technology, did not exist ten or fifteen years ago. Or, if they did exist, they were available only to laboratory researchers and the select few who could afford to pay outrageous prices for them.

Everyone tends to be egocentric or self-centered. While we are all really inhabitants of a global village, each of us tries to select some comfortable little corner that we can call our own. When we venture away from that corner, we often find ourselves alone, bewildered, and—sometimes—frightened. We may have the feeling that we have been overtaken by events or simply passed by.

Some people in this situation are energized and try hard to catch up with whatever they think left them behind. Others reject whatever is new or different; if that feeling is strong enough, they won't venture out of their corners willingly. Often these comfortable quarters are equipped with the latest electronic gadgets, though they may be furnished with reproductions of Early American or Victorian antiques and personal memorabilia. The people who live in them tend to cling to the familiar and turn their backs on the tremendous variety and excitement of the present. "Cocooning" is the current buzzword for the behavior of people in this category.

Career military service affects most people this way, including many who may not know it. Even those who serve in uniform for only

35

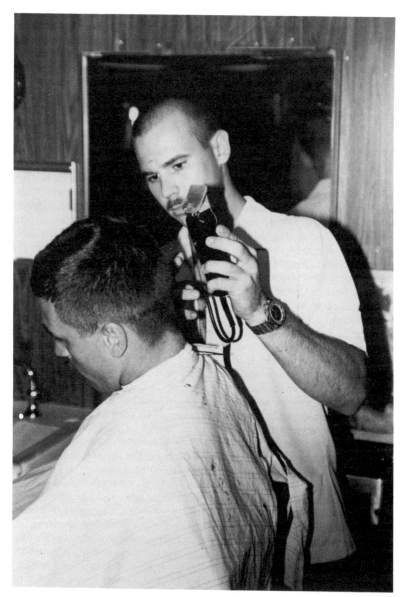

U.S. MARINE CORPS PHOTO

Military barbers can use their skills in the civilian job market but may need additional training.

relatively short periods can experience disorientation or withdrawal. The more they feel that the "present" beyond the fences of military installations is out of control, the more likely they are to reject or ignore the future.

That is to say, they are apt to behave as though everything beyond the gate of the base is just the way it was when they entered military service. No way. Even if you go back to the small town from which you entered service, just about everything and everybody will have changed, though some changes may be less obvious than others. The likelihood is, however, that you will not go back "home" at all but to a totally new and strange environment.

Almost everyone who leaves the relative comfort of military service experiences to some degree what is commonly called "culture shock." Culture shock occurs when you move from a familiar environment to one that is unknown. It involves frustration and sometimes angry emotional and physical rejection of or retreat from the unknown environment.

If you have been assigned to a foreign country during your service, you have probably already experienced culture shock twice: the first time when you arrived for duty in the foreign country, and the second when you returned to the United States three or four years later. I still have vivid memories of complete frustration when I arrived at Kennedy International Ariport, in New York, after a long assignment overseas. In the first place, the airport hadn't been built when I left the United States. But the reason I became angry and frustrated was that I couldn't turn on the water faucet when I tried to wash my hands in the men's room! Faucet technology had left me behind. I finally solved the problem by asking someone to help.

In many respects you enter a foreign culture when you leave military service. Everyone who faces a move from military service to a civilian career must be prepared to understand and overcome the debilitating effects of culture shock. Unfortunately, no acceptable alternative to civilian society is available to you. You may be able to reenlist or volunteer for another tour of duty as an officer and escape for a while. You may be able to secure a civil service job in your former military field and continue to work in a familiar environment. But these options only postpone the ultimate problem.

Another factor needs to be considered here, then: Our work lives stretch out ahead of us, down an unknown path. If you leave the service after a single tour of duty, for example, you have something like forty years of productive work life ahead of you. If you retire with twenty years of service or leave the service in mid-career, you have twenty-five to thirty-five years in which to carve out a civilian career that will ensure your economic, social, and emotional survival. Even if you retire after thirty years of service, you can anticipate having to earn an income for another ten to fifteen years unless you live very frugally or have done some pretty shrewd estate planning and can augment your retirement pay with investment income.

When all that is said, another problem faces you. How can you be sure that the considerable skills or professional background and work experience you have accumulated during military service will be useful or "marketable" over the long period of time remaining in your life?

If you have not done so already, you must get in touch—and stay in touch—with the broader implications of the present in order to prepare yourself for your own future. The long-term implications of this are to ensure your personal and economic survival in a rapidly changing world. In the short-term view, this is an essential step toward determining a realistic career objective for your inevitable transition to civilian life.

The Path to the Future Lies Through the Present

Some of the forces that are changing the world around us are the subject of a fascinating and gratifyingly short book called *Megatrends*. Author John Naisbitt's principal contribution in this book has been to identify key trends that are transforming society. His basic premise is simple: "The most reliable way to anticipate the future is by understanding the present."

Naisbitt is one of the country's top authorities on social, economic, political, and technological movements. The material for his book was developed by subjecting newspapers from around the country to content analysis, a military intelligence technique only occasionally used in civilian research. What he has to say is both revealing and important to you and your future. If you have not already read the book, I urge you to get it and read it now.

Ten prevailing long-term trends discussed by Naisbitt point to a "restructuring of America [that] is already changing our inner and outer lives." Most of the trends that he identifies may be expected to have an explicit or implicit impact on jobs in the future. The broad statement of the trends identified by Naisbitt is, in brief:

1. Our declining industrial society is being replaced by "an economy based on the creation and distribution of information."
2. "High tech" is being matched by a concern for human needs and responses; Naisbitt's phrase for this is "high touch."
3. Our formerly self-sufficient national economic system is changing as it becomes part of a global economy.
4. Approaches to economic, political, and social problems have become longer-term than we have been used to.

5. The effectiveness of grassroots movements has been redis-covered.

6. "We are shifting from institutional help to more self-reliance in all aspects of our lives."

7. Traditional forms of representative democracy are becoming obsolete in an age of instant communications.

8. Traditional hierarchical structures are giving away to informal "networks."

9. Population is moving out of the old industrial Northeast and into the South and West.

10. The scope of personal choice is expanding as we abandon traditional "either/or" thought patterns.

Naisbitt's book was published in 1982 and many of the trends discussed have become quite obvious; others are still evolving in ways we cannot always recognize. As Naisbitt wrote in the Introduction, however, "This book focuses on the megatrends or broad outlines that will define the new society.... Attempts to describe it in detail are the stuff of science fiction and futuristic guessing games that often prove inaccurate or annoying." If you are already familiar with *Megatrends*, you may want to read the annual updates from the same publisher.

Another thought-provoking book is Alvin Toffler's *Future Shock*. The title of this seminal book has, not incidentally, entered the language as a same-society alternative to "culture shock."

Toffler's principal theme is that the pace of technological change in our time has become so accelerated that it has left many people bewildered and insecure. Some have lost their jobs as obsolescence has overtaken their industry; others face the loss of jobs in the future. In a broader sense, rapid technological change not only influences every aspect of our individual lives but exerts enormous pressures on society as a whole. The dizzying pace of technological development continues to accelerate. We ignore it at our peril.

In my opinion, no one who is even thinking about entering the civilian labor force after military service can afford not to have read *Future Shock*. Although the book was first published in 1970, a reading at this time should have the immediate effect of putting you into the "big picture" of the present. In the context of this book, more-over, familiarity with the works of Alvin Toffler and John Naisbitt, or others in their category such as Norman Feingold, should help you formulate a realistic career objective.

Once you have established a base for understanding the present by reading these books, you must work to keep up with what is going on in the world "out there." Regular reading of one or more of the weekly newsmagazines (*Time*, *Newsweek*, *U.S. News*) is essential, but don't stop with them. You should also be scanning publications in your own field of interest, as well as others such as *The Wall Street Journal, Business Week, Fortune*, and *Forbes* for articles that deal with new developments and emerging trends. It is from sources like these that the editors of the news magazines and TV newscasts get many of their own leads for articles about what is happening. You might as well get there first with the original source.

Forecasting Near-Term Employment Prospects

While the work of the forecasters and futurists provides a lot of food for thought and should be familiar to anyone who has begun transition planning, most people in military service are justifiably concerned about civilian employment prospects in the near-term future. In general usage, "near-term" means the period of time that extends about three years beyond today. Unfortunately, no one can afford to be that nearsighted these days.

As it happens, the most readily available and reliable forecasts of the changing civilian job market are to be found in a publication of the U.S. Department of Labor, the *Occupational Outlook Handbook*. The current *Handbook* uses 1984 as a base year and projects growth and other characteristics of the labor force to the year 1995. This time span offers a useful and workable framework for career planning for several reasons.

First, we are already several years into the period and thus can get some feel for the reliability of the forecasts. Second, the period extends far enough ahead to allow you to make adjustments to career planning that can compensate for unfavorable trends or permit you to take advantage of favorable trends. Third, the final year of the forecast period approaches the end of the century, by which time we can expect to see most of the major trends identified by independent forecasters pretty well confirmed or modified, or even decisively repudiated.

The employment forecasts in the *Handbook* are based on hard statistical data but softened by consideration of economic and social trends. Some of the considerations and conclusions that influence its forecasts may also influence both your selection of a career objective and the courses of action you develop that will help you to reach it:

- Fewer young people will be available to enter the labor force because of the low birth rate during the 1960's and 1970's. By 1995 about three fourths of the workers will be in the age group 25–54.
- A direct relationship exists between high unemployment rates and low levels of education.

- In 1984 about half the workers age 25–34 had completed at least one year of college; a quarter had completed four or more years of college. This is a marked increase in education level since the 1970's. The upward trend is expected to continue.
- The number of workers in age group 55–64 will decline, partly because of the low birth rate during the Depression and partly because of trends toward early retirement—often followed by "second careers." Demand for recreational services will increase.
- By 1995 women will make up three fifths of the labor force. Increasing numbers of women will take jobs and offset the shortages of young workers and those in age group 55–64.
- A sharp increase in the number of adults age 65 and older will result from extended life expectancy. Though many older workers will remain in the labor force, the demand for recreational services and health services should increase.
- Population movement to the South and West will continue. By 1995 these two regions should account for 60 percent of the population of the country. The population in the West will be considerably younger than the national average. Demand for public services, consumer services, and construction will increase, but the influx of large numbers of people looking for employment in these fast growth areas will result in greater competition for jobs in other occupations.

Overall about 16 million jobs are expected to be added to the economy between 1984 and 1995. This figure represents growth in employment somewhat slower than that experienced during the period 1974–85. The predictions for slower growth are based on demographic factors, social trends, economic restructuring, the continuation of foreign competition, and other factors. Figure 2 shows projected growth in the number of jobs by major industry. About fourteen million new jobs are forecast in the service-producing industries by 1995, representing about nine of every ten new jobs created in the economy.

The fastest growing sector in the service industries is the catch-all category of "services." The number of jobs in this category is expected to increase by about 30 percent, about twice the national rate. This group includes hotels, hospitals, business services (accounting, data processing, building maintenance, and temporary help agencies, for example), professional services, and small shops (barbershops, appliance repair shops, automobile repair shops, and so on). The fastest growing member of this group is expected to be business services, though expanding demand for recreational services, health care services, and professional services (engineering, legal, and social)

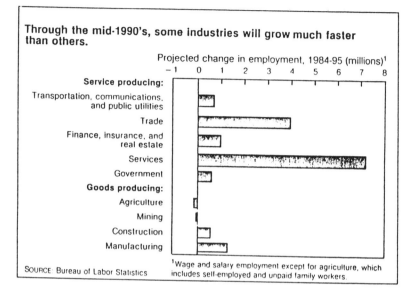

Through the mid-1990's, some industries will grow much faster than others.

Projected change in employment, 1984-95 (millions)[1]

Service producing:
- Transportation, communications, and public utilities
- Trade
- Finance, insurance, and real estate
- Services
- Government

Goods producing:
- Agriculture
- Mining
- Construction
- Manufacturing

SOURCE: Bureau of Labor Statistics

[1]Wage and salary employment except for agriculture, which includes self-employed and unpaid family workers.

Fig. 2

should also result in substantial increases in the number of jobs in those fields.

Employment in the wholesale and retail trades will also grow considerably over the period 1984–1995, especially in the restaurant trade. In the retail sector, large increases are expected in the number of new jobs in department stores, supermarkets, and automobile dealerships. Increases in the wholesale sector are seen in companies that handle machinery, electrical and electronic goods, and motor vehicles. Employment overall is expected to grow by 16 percent. Some kinds of jobs in the trade sector may decline in number, however, because of widespread use of computerized inventory systems and automated warehousing techniques.

The number of jobs in the category of finance, insurance, and real estate is also expected to grow by 17 percent, a rate just above the national average, and continue the growth phase started in the 1970's. New marketing techniques, the development of new banking techniques, and the introduction of new services combine to make this sector of the services industry a dynamic one.

The most rapid growth in the transportation, communications, and public utilities sector is anticipated in the field of communications. In the transportation category, the greatest increase in jobs is expected in transportation services (travel agencies), local transit, and trucking; a trend toward self-employed truckers is expected in the trucking industry. Jobs in railroads are expected to decline in number. Growth in airline employment is expected to slow. Public utility jobs will increase to keep pace with increasing demands for power, gas, water, and sanitary services as the population and industry grow.

The government sector of the economy is expected to grow relatively slowly. The greatest number of jobs created will be in state and local governments. About three of every seven new jobs added at the state and local levels will be in the field of public education. Jobs in elementary education are expected to increase faster than those in secondary schools through the period, though this trend may reverse itself after 1995.

The goods-producing industries are expected to show little overall growth. In agriculture, higher productivity is expected to permit increased output with fewer jobs. Some jobs in the mining sector will also disappear in the face of improvements in mining technology, declining demand for coal, stabilization of domestic petroleum production, and foreign competition from metals suppliers.

Improvement in the outlook for the construction industry can be expected, however, partly as a result of the tax reforms of 1986, but particularly after 1990 when the commercial building glut has been digested. Continued construction of residential housing is indicated to compensate for low production when home mortgage rates were high. On the other hand, rising prices, rising home mortgage loan rates, and a decline in the number of youths of marriagable age may all have adverse effects on the construction industry.

The growth of employment in the manufacturing sector is expected to be modest, at a rate about half the national average of 15 percent. Within the sector, the greatest increases will be in the industries that produce computers, electronic equipment, industrial controls, and materials handling equipment. The automobile and steel industries are expected to post only modest gains in employment, partly because of the installation of automated equipment and manufacturing processes and partly because of continued foreign competition in the marketplace. Employment in the nondurable goods sector (food, textiles, clothing) is expected to decline.

Two of the factors influencing a forecast for below average growth of employment in manufacturing are: (1) increased reliance on computer-assisted manufacturing (CAM) techniques to improve productivity, and (2) a tendency to reduce direct labor costs by contracting for service-type functions formerly handled internally by employees: janitorial services, maintenance, food services, data processing, accounting services, engineering design services, and the manufacture of subassemblies, for example. The loss of these manufacturing jobs should, of course, result in an increase in the number of jobs in the service-producing industries.

To summarize, the places to look for a civilian career are the growing business sectors in which employment is expanding faster than the national average. These are the fields of computers and electronics, health care, high technology, leisure and recreation services, printing and publishing, banking and financial services, tele-communications, and retailing. Much slower than average growth in employment is anticipated in the manufacturing sector, except for the manufacture of electronics equipment; job losses are predicted in the manufacture of textiles and automobiles and in the food processing industry. A general decline in the number of jobs available is expected in two major sectors of the economy: mining and agriculture.

A word of caution is necessary here. The *Handbook* forecasts deal with employment and not with the growth or decline of individual industries. Some industries will continue to grow but will produce more goods or services with fewer employees—or with different kinds of employees. Even in industries that are said to be declining, older workers must be replaced or new jobs may be created as a result of new technology or changing patterns of supply and demand. Those business sectors not specifically mentioned above are not standing still, either. But it is well to know that employment is much more competitive in the business sectors where the numbers of job are growing slowly.

On the whole, the *Occupational Outlook Handbook* provides the most reliable forecasts available, but it does not represent itself as infallible. Forecasting social change is always difficult because society is made up of people, and people can change or be changed in unpredictable ways. In some cases, a "forecast" may of itself influence behavior to such an extent that it becomes a self-fulfilling prophecy. In other cases, forces external to the business community may directly or indirectly influence social and economic change. Government budget and fiscal policies, tax legislation, unexpected or unexplained economic recessions, and international trade policies and strategies all influence the business environment and affect individual and business decisions.

The Department of Labor is aware of these factors that influence its employment forecasts. Particular aspects of the job market are examined in quarterly supplements to the *Handbook*, for example. The entire *Handbook* is updated every five years; the next revision should extend the employment outlook to the end of the century.

All that is great. You know where the jobs are likely to be now. What you really want to know is how to get *your* job. That problem is one that only you can solve. The next few chapters will, however, help you to evaluate your own skills and personal assets, to chart some courses of action, and to apply yourself to the task ahead in an intelligent and informed way.

PART I. SUGGESTED READING

Marvin Cetron (with Marcia Appel). *Jobs of the Future: The 500 Best Jobs—Where They'll Be and How to Get Them.* New York: McGraw-Hill Book Co., 1984.

Norman Feingold and Norma Reno Miller. *Emerging Careers: New Occupations for the Year 2,000 and Beyond.* Garrett Park, MD: Garrett Park Press, 1983.

John Naisbitt. *Megatrends: Ten New Directions Transforming Our Lives.* New York: Warner Books, 1982.

Tom Peters and Nancy Austin. *A Passion for Excellence: The Leadership Difference.* New York: Warner Books, 1986 (paperback edition).

Tom Peters and Robert H. Waterman, Jr. *In Search of Excellence: Lessons from America's Best-Run Companies.* New York: Harper and Row, Publishers, 1982.

Alvin Toffler. *Future Shock.* New York: William Morrow, 1970.

Alvin Toffler. *Previews and Premises.* New York: William Morrow, 1983.

U.S. Department of Labor. *Occupational Outlook Handbook: 1986–87 Edition*, Washington, DC: Government Printing Office, 1986.

Transition Planning: Tactics and Strategies

Chapter 5

Evaluating Your
Military Experience

The four chapters of Part I should help you to understand
better the obstacles that you can encounter as you prepare to launch
yourself into a civilian career after you have completed your military
service. You will also have an appreciation of the ways in which your
military service can help you overcome some of those obstacles.
Some insights you may have gained into the civilian economy may be
particularly important. The necessity of keeping up-to-date with what
is going on in the world cannot be ignored, particularly since it is the
only means of getting in touch with your future. With all this behind
you, you are about ready to take a first step down the road that leads
to a successful transition to a civilian career.

The fact that business employment practices tend to discount the
importance of military technical training and on-the-job experience
means that anyone who is considering that transition from military
service to a civilian career has to make a special effort to meet civilian
job-training standards and to understand civilian recruiting and employment practices. In this chapter, we shall concentrate on the first
requirement. You can determine for yourself what those civilian job
standards are and then "translate" your military experience. An
essential step in the process is, of course, to "war game" your skills
and experience against the standards to confirm assets and locate
deficiencies.

What Civilian Career?

Much of our emphasis until now has been on gaining a better understanding of the world in which you will live after you leave military
service. Now it is time to focus on what you might want to do in that
world where *not* to work is a luxury few can afford.

The first steps in the transition process are similar for everyone:
establish an objective, inventory the skills and personal resources
that will help you meet that objective, set up alternative courses of
action to reach the objective, and then decide on the course of action
that offers the best possibility of reaching the objective.

Military auto mechanics can improve their chances of civilian employment by taking off-duty courses at local community colleges.

If that reads a bit like a tactical "estimate of the situation," it is supposed to. There is no reason why you should abandon the problem-solving techniques you have learned during military service just because you are leaving the military environment for another one. Those techniques can work for you wherever you go. Don't ever forget that a valuable personal asset on the job is your ability to solve problems. The first evidence of that ability is how you set about launching your civilian career.

In the final analysis, you are the only one who can solve the problems involved in your own transition. Guidelines can be provided. Sources of assistance can be pointed out. But before you are ready to hang up that uniform for the last time, you have a lot of work ahead of you.

What problems are involved in the transition process? They are problems centered around the development of realistic career objectives, problems that are more easily stated than solved. For example:

1. *Objective*:
   - What do I want to do for the rest of my life?
   - In what industry or business should I seek a job?
   - How much time do I need to prepare myself? Do I have?
2. *Skills, Personal Resources, Other Factors*:
   - What skills are required for employment?
   - What skills or experience do I already have?
   - What favorable personal traits do I have?
   - What personal assets and liabilities (financial status, education, family, geographical location, physical condition, etc.) can or will influence my objective?
   - What physical conditions am I likely to encounter on the job? (Heat, cold, dust, noise, health hazards, etc.)
3. *Some Possible Courses of Action*:
   - Leave service as soon as eligible; seek immediate employment in specialty field in which already trained.
   - Remain in service (reenlist/extend tour, if necessary); seek advanced training, education, and experience required for civilian employment in my current occupational field.
   - Leave service; abandon military specialty; seek retraining in civilian institution to prepare for job.
   - Remain in service (reenlist/extend tour); seek new MOS or military specialization; acquire advanced training and improve general educational level.

Which of the possible courses of action you may eventually pursue depends on you. You may develop others, in fact, to suit your own

---

Table 3. Fast-Track Occupations with Future Growth

Accountant/Auditor	Electronic Technician
Advertising	Elementary School Teacher
Avionics Technician	Employment Interviewer
Architect	Engineering Aide
Attorney	Facilities Manager
Auto-body Repairer	Genetic Engineer
Automobile Mechanic	Geriatric Social Worker
Baker	Graphic Designer
Bank Officer and Administrator	Hazardous Waste Disposal Technician
Battery Technician	Home Electronics Systems Technician
Biomedical Engineer	Housing Rehabilitation Technician
Blue-collar Supervisor	Illustrator
Bricklayer/Stonemason	Industrial Engineer
Broadcast Technician	Industrial Laser Technician
Cable TV Installer	Industrial Truck Mechanic
Cardiopulmonary Technician	Legal Secretary
Carpenter	Licensed Practical Nurse
City Manager	Materials Utilization Technician
Civil Engineer	Mechanical Engineer
Computer Operator	Medical Laboratory Technician
Computer Programmer	Medical Record Technician
Computer Repair Technician	Meteorologist
Computer Systems Analyst	Nuclear Medicine Technician
Construction Laborer	Office Machine Repairer
Cook	Paralegal Assistant
Correctional Officer	Photographer
Dental Assistant	Photoprocessing Technician
Dental Laboratory Technician	Physical Therapist
Diesel Mechanic	Physicians Assistant
Dietitian	Retail Sales Clerk
Dry-wall Technician	Robotics Technician
Economist	Security Guard
Editor, Writer, and Reporter	Social Worker/Counselor
Electrical Engineer	Telemarketing Salesperson
Electrician	Truck Driver
Electronic Engineer	Waiter/Waitress

Sources: BLS; Cetron, *Jobs of the Future.*

---

circumstances. One course of action you should not even consider: "Leave service as soon as I can; I'll find *something, somewhere.*" Forget it! Employers, you may recall, want employees who are highly motivated and who enthusiastically identify with the employer's objectives. That brings you right back to the beginning: What is your career objective? If you do not have an objective, it is time to think about one.

More than seventy civilian occupational fields in which the number of jobs is growing faster than the national average are listed in the accompanying table. You may be surprised to find such occupations as automobile mechanic, cook and baker, construction worker, and geriatric social worker listed along with the expected high-tech occupations. If you are surprised, you should reread the last section of Chapter 4. As you will discover, furthermore, many of these "fast-track" civilian occupations have military counterparts; you can find them listed in Appendices A and B.

In looking over the list of rapidly growing occupations, do not make the mistake of concluding that the numbers of jobs in all other civilian occupations are on the decline. Some occupational fields that are growing only slowly may generate more employment opportunities each year than those that are growing more rapidly.

Figure 3 illustrates this situation by showing the percent (*relative*) growth and the numerical (*absolute*) growth in employment opportunities in two occupational fields: paralegal assistants and secretaries. The number of jobs for paralegal assistants will almost double by 1995, with a relative growth rate of about 95 percent. Jobs for secretaries are increasing much more slowly, at the rate of 10 percent. However, the slower growing secretary field is expected to produce many more new jobs between 1984 and 1995 than the faster moving

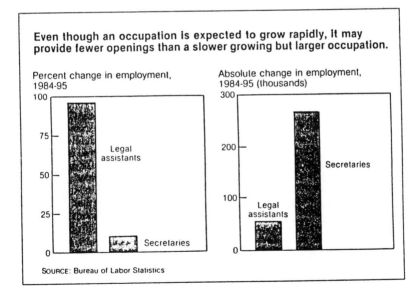

Even though an occupation is expected to grow rapidly, it may provide fewer openings than a slower growing but larger occupation.

Percent change in employment, 1984-95

Absolute change in employment, 1984-95 (thousands)

Legal assistants

Secretaries

Secretaries

Legal assistants

SOURCE: Bureau of Labor Statistics

Fig. 3

paralegal assistant field. The explanation, of course, is that in 1984 the entire economy employed about 2,800,000 secretaries; even the growth rate of 10 percent will result in 280,000 new jobs. By contrast, only about 53,000 paralegal assistants were employed in 1984. Even the very high growth rate of 95 percent can produce only about 50,000 new jobs by 1995.

As you work through your transition planning you should keep these factors in mind. As a general rule, the *competition* for jobs in a slow-growing occupation is greater than in a field that is growing faster than the average. Conversely, the *average pay* in the slow-growing occupational field may be lower than in the field that is growing faster, in accordance with the economic law of supply and demand.

The "fast-track" occupations in the table are the fields in which the numbers of new jobs are expected to grow faster than the national average and to continue to grow in the future. If you are already trained and working in one of these fields in military service, you are probably ahead of the game. If you are not, you may want to give serious consideration to preparing yourself for one of them while you are still in service, for they are the jobs of the future.

That does not mean, of course, that there will be no other opportunities for employment. Heed, however, the plight of the young apprentice buggymaker at the turn of the century when automobiles were just appearing. He not only had to adjust to an environment changing rapidly because of the new technology that he had good reason to hate, but he had to change his occupation in mid-life. Still, thousands of jobs in a couple of hundred occupational fields are not really endangered. Many of those that have military equivalents are also listed in Appendices A and B.

The "correct" career objective will vary from person to person, but the alternatives boil down to two: (1) keep on doing what you are doing, or (2) start over. In Part III we will consider some refinements of these two alternatives under the headings of "lateral entry" (making your military experience work for you) and "retreading" (developing a different career). I might observe here that even if you decide to keep on doing what you have been doing in military service, you may not continue in that activity for the rest of your life—or at least you may change the *form* in which you do it. For example, you may start out as an employee and end up as a business owner or consultant.

How to Evaluate Your Military Training and Experience

One of the most useful places to begin researching the marketability of your military training and experience is the *Occupational Outlook Handbook*. You can find the *Handbook* in the reference section of the library at most military bases and in almost any public library; you may also find that your base Education Center has a copy. If you can't find a copy on the base, ask the librarian or the Education Center director to order one. Or order a copy yourself from the Government Printing Office. The publication sells for around twenty dollars, but the price is well worth paying.

The *Handbook* contains detailed descriptions of about 200 civilian occupations or career fields that provide employment for about 60 percent of the civilian labor force. They include about 90 percent of the technician and professional specialties, the career fields that are expected to provide increasing employment opportunities during the period 1984–1995 and probably beyond. Briefer comments on 200 other career fields are included in an appendix. Job opportunities in many, but not all, of the career fields listed in the appendix are growing only slowly or are actually expected to decline in number. How can you use the *Handbook* to help you evaluate your future employment prospects?

As we have already indicated, Appendix A of this book lists more than 400 civilian job titles, based on the *Dictionary of Occupational Titles*, that are related to 129 enlisted "military occupations." Representative officer career fields are listed in Appendix B, together with their equivalent civilian occupations but without *DOT* job titles or codes.

After each such civilian job title (Appendix A) or civilian occupational field (Appendix B) you will find a notation about the forecast for growth in that field: "F" indicates faster than average growth in employment opportunities; "N" stands for average growth; "S" stands for slower than average growth.

You will also find after each job title a code that indicates whether that job title is included in the *Handbook*. More than 75 percent of the more than 400 job titles listed in Appendix A are accounted for, along with most of the job fields listed in Appendix B. The code "HBK" means that the job title or job field is included in the narrative discussions in the main part of the *Handbook*. The code "SUM" means that it is discussed only in summary or in an appendix to the *Handbook*. The symbol (?) after a job title in Appendix A indicates that no discussion of that occupation is included in the *Handbook* and no information is available on the growth trends in it, though some informed guesses have been made, as you will see.

Remember that the main purpose of the *Occupational Outlook Handbook* is to discuss the occupational fields in which about 60 percent of the members of the civilian workforce work. It is of some interest, then, to note that about 58 percent of the DOT job titles attributed to enlisted military occupations are included in that section.

Another 19 percent are included in the summary appendix of the

Handbook; these titles deal with various clerical jobs, boat operators, blasters (demolition experts), seamen, shipfitters, shipping and receiving clerks, and stock and inventory specialists. That leaves about a quarter of the DOT job titles unaccounted for, but they are largely concerned with such military specialties as intelligence, emergency management, electronic weapon repairers, and ordnance specialties that have bona fide civilian counterparts but do not occupy a significant portion of the civilian workforce. (Jobs of these kinds are most likely to be found in the federal civil service or among defense contractors.)

Military members who are in the job fields not included in the main body of the *Handbook* can find details of the civilian jobs in their fields in the *Dictionary of Occupational Titles*, which includes training requirements.

The narrative descriptions of the two hundred or so occupational fields in the *Handbook* are invaluable as an introduction to civilian training standards and work requirements, whether you are an E-4 automobile mechanic or an O–5 combat commander rounding out twenty years of military service.

The information in the *Handbook* is especially valuable to career combat arms officers and enlisted men who are considering alternate military specialties or changing MOS's. Given the opportunity, why not select a new military specialty that may later help you to move into a civilian occupation? Others may simply want to evaluate their own accumulated military training and experience, professional military education, or civilian education against the standards the *Handbook* provides for civilian occupations. A timely review of this kind could permit them to take action to remedy deficiencies while still in service by taking advantage of opportunities for training, education, and assignments that might otherwise be overlooked.

Case Study: Researching Civilian Employment Standards

Jim is an Army E-4 who enlisted after graduating from high school with a General Diploma. He has been working for about a year and a half as a light vehicle auto mechanic gaining on-the-job training after completing an entry-level Army techical school at the top of his class. Recently he has begun to specialize in transmissions. He enjoys the work and is good as it, but he really wants to leave the Army in about a year, when his enlistment is up. Jim's high school sweetheart is waiting for him.

> *Jim's Objective:* To get a good job as a transmission mechanic, work hard to get ahead; advance to Service Manager; eventually set up my own shop; settle down to raise a family.

Jim's Possible Courses of Action:

1. Leave Army when enlistment expires; find job as transmission mechanic. (Marry Jean!)
2. Leave Army when enlistment expires; seek job. (Marry Jean?)
3. Reenlist in Army; seek advanced technical training; master skills; become shop supervisor. (What about Jean?)

Jim wonders what kind of job he might be able to get in the automotive field with the training and experience he will have at the end of his three-year enlistment. He starts by looking up the military occupation of automobile mechanic in Appendix A.

There Jim finds four DOT job classifications under the "military occupation" of *Automobile Mechanics*:

620261010	Automobile Mechanic	F	HBK
620281034	Carburetor Mechanic	F	HBK
620281034	Transmission Mechanic	F	HBK
620381010	Automobile Radiator Mechanic	F	HBK

According to the letter codes, all four jobs are on the fast track. The *Handbook* includes some discussion of all these DOT occupations. But where does he find the one he wants in the 500-plus page *Handbook*?

At the back of the *Handbook* is the "Index of Occupations." Jim looks under the "T's" to find the page number for the discussion of "Transmission Mechanic." When he turns to the page, he finds that "Transmission Mechanic" is included in a general discussion of "Automotive and Motorcycle Mechanics." It is important at this point to understand that the *Handbook* narratives describe occupational fields, not *jobs* in the narrow sense of the term.

Jim also discovers that each narrative description of a civilian occupation in the *Handbook* has the same organization, with these subject headings and content:

Nature of the Work: What you are expected to do; what you are expected to know.

Working Conditions: Environmental considerations (indoors/outdoors, noise levels, temperatures), physical requirements, health hazards, safety considerations, etc.

Employment: How many people work in the field; where they are employed.

Training, Other Qualifications, and Advancement: Training standards, certification procedures, essential personal traits, opportunities for promotion.

Job Outlook: Relative growth in number of jobs in the occupational field; economic or social factors that influence growth.

Earnings: Average earnings at various skill levels, special pay arrangements (commissions, for example), labor unions in the field, etc. (Local pay rates may vary.)

Related Occupations: Jobs closely related to the main occupation may suggest alternatives for career choices.

Sources of Additional Information: Where to go or write for career information, training requirements, certification standards, and related information. Very important for follow-up purposes.

What did Jim learn? First of all, he found out that he did not realize how many automobile mechanics there were: almost a million! And he really didn't know what it meant to be a paid mechanic working full time in an automotive repair shop. Oh, sure, he had puttered around cars ever since he was old enough to know a torque wrench from an Allen wrench. But he found that he needed a lot more information before deciding to leave the Army and put his future in the hands of a civilian employer.

What he found out from reading the *Handbook* raised doubts in his mind about his career objective. As he read the section on Automobile Mechanics, he took notes, underlining important points or things about which he had questions:

- *Good employment outlook*. More job openings for auto mechanics than for most occupations. Auto repair business *not greatly affected by changing economic conditions*. During economic slumps *employers may be reluctant to hire trainees*.
- *Army training and experience* qualifies for *entry-level trainee job. Additional OJT: 3–5 years. Factory training needed. Trainee pay: $9.31 an hour, national average*.
- *Good mechanics* make *quick and accurate diagnoses* of mechanical problems.
- *Associate degree* becoming important. Courses suggested: electronics, physics, chemistry, math, and hydraulics.
- *Service Managers*: senior mechanics who *show leadership*.
- *Customer Service Reps*: mechanics who *get along well with people*.
- Mechanics who set up independent shops need *money*.
- *Certification* as transmission specialist: minimum two years' experience plus written test. *Write to*: National Institute for Automotive Service Excellence, Washington, D.C.
- *Write for information about training and work conditions*: Motor and Equipment Manufacturers Association, Automotive Service Industry Association, Automotive Service Councils, Inc., Motor Vehicle Manufacturers Association of the U.S.

Clearly he had a quick fix on the situation. He was a little upset because his Army training would only qualify him for entry-level employment, with lots of OJT ahead. But the pay looked good, and he would be just twenty-one years old when he got out of the Army. He went through his notes point by point and made notes of his own qualifications: "High school grad, General Diploma (not much math or science, but enjoyed what I had). Two years' experience as transmission mechanic possible by time I leave Army. Good diagnostic skills. Good leadership and communications skills; already a team leader training new tech school grads. No money!"

He was pretty optimistic, but he knew he needed to do some investigating on his own: Certification standards, for example. Associate degree? Factory training? Jim's investigation reads like a classic case, but that is a story for later chapters.

Taking the Statistical Approach

Right now, we should look at another Department of Labor publication that is published each year as a statistical supplement to the *Occupational Outlook Handbook*. The title is *Occupational Projections and Training Data*. You may be able to find a copy at a base Education Center or a good public library; or you may be able to talk your Base Librarian into ordering a copy for the reference collection.

Occupational Projections and Training Data contains brief statistical summaries that augment the narrative material about the occupational fields included in the *Handbook*. It is full of statistics but fairly easy to work with. Short descriptive sections are included, but they are not as useful as the detailed narratives in the *Handbook*. These statistical summaries provide useful information that can help you decide on your career moves. The amount of information varies by occupational field, but a typical summary includes:

EMPLOYMENT PROFILE: Total employment, Selected characteristics of workers (sex, race, age, part-time employees), Unemployment rate, Industry concentration of workers, Projected employment (to 1995), Employment growth, and Annual separation rate (per cent of employees leaving their jobs). *Note:* Projected jobs is given in three categories: Low, Moderate, High. This is the Department of Labor's way of hedging for possible recessions or economic slowdowns. "Moderate Growth" is the category used by most people who attempt to predict future employment.

SUPPLY PROFILE: Entry and training requirements, Training completions (numbers of students who completed training in various kinds of institutions), and Characteristics of entrants.

Note that this publication contains details and numbers that supplement the descriptive sections in the *Handbook*. The table, for example, shows where automobile mechanics work as percent

---

Table 4. Sample Occupational Statistical Supplement

Automotive and Motorcycle Mechanics
EMPLOYMENT PROFILE:
Total Employment, 1984 922,000
Selected Characteristics of Workers, 1984:
    Percent female.. 0.8
    Percent black 8.1
    Age distribution (percent):
        16–24 years 24.5
        25–54 years 67.1
        55 and older 8.4
    Percent employed part time, total 7.5
    Percent employed part time, voluntary 3.3
Unemployment rate .... About average
Industry concentration of workers, 1984 (percent):
    Motor vehicle dealers (new and used) 27.0
    Automobile repair shops 15.3
    Gasoline service stations 10.1
    Auto and home supply stores 6.0
    Machinery, equipment, supplies wholesalers 5.9

	Low	Moderate	High
Projected jobs, 1995	1,052,000	1,107,000	1,154,000
Percent change, 1984–95	14.2	20.1	25.2

Employment growth.................................... Faster than average
Annual separation rate (percent) 13.8

SUPPLY PROFILE:
Usual Entry and Training Requirements. Employers prefer entrants with mechanical aptitude and knowledge of automotive or motorcycle technology. Skills may be acquired through work experience as a helper or lubrication worker, but completion of a formal training program in automotive or motorcycle mechanics is increasingly preferred to experience alone. Such programs are offered by high schools and postsecondary vocational schools and community and junior colleges. For those without experience, training acquired while helping friends or through working on automobiles or motorcycles as a hobby can be helpful in getting a job.

Training completions:
Public vocational secondary and postsecondary, 1983:
    Automotive mechanics, automotive technology, and small engine repair .. 84,113
Private noncollegiate postsecondary, 1981:
    Auto mechanic 13,862
Associate degrees and other awards below baccalaureate, 1983:
    Automotive technology, automotive mechanics, and small engine repair .. 8,776
Characteristics of entrants. The majority of entrants have not been working—most have been in a formal training program, or were experienced mechanics who had been laid off between jobs. The remainder have been working in another, related occupation. Most entrants are high school graduates.

Source: BLS Bulletin 2251 (1986).

of the total number employed; the *Handbook* merely states where they work. This kind of information should help job-seekers target a particular industry or business. The annual separation rate of 13.8 percent suggests lots of mobility in the occupation, with many vacant jobs at any one time. The number of entry-level auto mechanics with Associate degrees was already about 9 percent of the training completions for 1983—and according to the *Handbook* the number is increasing.

Summing Up

Understanding the process of "translating" your military training and experience into the civilian frame of reference is critical in transition to a civilian career. In most cases you must do this yourself by finding out what civilian employers expect of you in training, education, and work experience and then comparing your own qualifications. If you come up on the short end you must do something about the situation. The two Department of Labor publications we have discussed are invaluable tools in that process. In fact, there are no readily available alternatives to them.

The career projections and statistics that appear in the many existing "career" books are largely based on these and other publications of the Department of Labor. The advantage of going to the sources yourself is that they are revised and republished every year. Many so-called career books are seldom if ever revised; if you are not careful, you can acquire and act on a lot of stale information.

Moreover, everything you do for yourself while you are still in uniform will put you ahead of the pack. If you wait until you are separated or retired, you could pay large sums of money to professional career counselors and résumé writers to do what you have been reading about in this chapter. Aside from the unnecessary expense, waiting means that it will usually be too late to make any real improvement in your qualifications. Getting to work on your civilian career while you are still in uniform often means that you can improve your qualifications by taking advantage of many free and low-cost opportunities for advanced skill training, advanced education in civilian disciplines, and even assignments that will smooth the transition process.

The procedures for using these two publications can benefit anyone planning for or already in the career transition process. The examples in this chapter are intended only to be illustrative. The two publications, when used in conjunction with Appendix A and Appendix B to this book—or with the list of fast-track occupations earlier in this chapter—can help you to formulate a career objective and develop a realistic course of action leading to it. No matter whether you want to continue to work in your military specialty, change to another military specialty, or forget all about your military specialty and become a sculptor.

That is, they are jump-off points for your career plan. Besides conveniently packaged basic information, they provide clues for remedial action and further research. They provide the names and addresses of organizations that will send you, free, much of the detailed information you will need to perfect your plan.

If you have trouble making sense of all this, talk it over with someone now, before you leave military service—perhaps your in-service career counselor or one of the professionals at your base Education Center.

One of the most persuasive pieces of information that emerges from even a casual look at the *Occupational Outlook Handbook* is that the level of general education required in most "fast-track" civilian occupations is steadily increasing, largely in response to rapid technological change. The general educational level of the civilian labor force has increased dramatically since the mid-1970's. In Chapter 7 we discuss what the educational opportunities offered by the military services can mean to you as you plan your transition to a civilian career.

Chapter 6

Romancing the Objective

Now that you have established some sort of objective for an eventual civilian career, investigated training and other standards for civilian employment, and translated your military skills into terms that civilian employers can appreciate, are you finished with your career plans? Of course not. You have a lot of work ahead of you to determine the course of action that will best help you accomplish your objective. How much you do and how long it will take depends on your own abilities and circumstances; one important factor is how much time you have before you leave military service. What you can do and how to do it can, however, be set out in what might be thought of as "Standard Operating Procedure for Career Transition."

Because each of us is a unique human being, no one can tell you exactly what you should do to succeed at anything you undertake. However, one of the advantages almost anyone should have obtained from military service is knowing how to "plug into" existing guidelines, procedures, and formulas for effective action. Among other things, the military process requires dedication to the mission or objective, varying amounts of thought, the ability to sift the wheat from the chaff while handling quantities of unorganized information, techniques for collecting additional information, willingness to adapt to changing circumstances, a sense of urgency, personal integrity, and considerable personal energy.

The techniques and personal qualities needed to "plug into" military planning guidelines or standard operating procedures can and should also be applied to developing your own civilian career transition plan. In military terms, poor planning may lead to failure to reach the objective and result in forfeiting the mission, whether it is to seize and occupy a piece of terrain or to complete an essential report on time. In civilian terms, poor planning leads to the same unacceptable results, but the difference is that it is the rest of your life that is involved. Knowing what to do, therefore, can improve the effectiveness of your transition planning. But only you can make the procedures work.

Radio and television specialists have good opportunities for civilian jobs.

How Much Time Do You Need?

An important factor in any planning process is, of course, the time available to the planner. From the beginning an important consideration in the development of this book has been to encourage readers to plan ahead with some sense of urgency. How far ahead you should plan depends on your own abilities and your career objectives. Most observers of the process, however, urge that transition planning begin at least one year before your proposed or actual separation from service.

In practice, that means that you should begin your planning *more* than a year ahead of your ETS. Only in that way can you hope to take advantage of the many career transition opportunities available to you while you are still in uniform, including advanced technical training, MOS changes, and opportunities to improve your educational standing. In some cases preliminary or provisional planning for a career transition may stretch over several years or even throughout an entire service career.

No one, of course, should neglect military duties during transition planning. Rather, the career planning tactics and strategies suggested in this book are entirely consistent with established military policies and procedures. Much of the pretransition investigation and follow-up will be done on your own time and some of it must be done off the military base. Keep in mind that the time and effort you spend on this phase of your transition planning is an investment in your future. At the same time, however, the information you gather and the personal contacts you make will often contribute to your effectiveness in your current or future military job or assignment.

The time factor involved in transition planning varies considerably for military personnel in different categories. No iron-clad rules apply, but the three categories presented below appear to suffice for purposes of discussion.

Category A. Short-termers. Anyone who has entered military service for a tour of three to four years or less probably should have begun career preplanning *before* entering on active duty. This applies in particular to men who enter combat arms specialties, for which there are no civilian counterparts. In general, neither enlisted personnel nor officers who enter military service for three years or less— Army enlistments can be as short as two years—can expect to acquire sufficient technical or professional skills to qualify for more than entry-level employment in the same occupational field unless they brought skills with them from civilian life. (Examples: those who enlisted for programs that provide advanced training because they were already skill-qualified by military standards; commissioned health services professionals who had already earned professional degrees.) The emphasis in transition planning should probably be on (1) improving general educational levels while in uniform, or (2) planning for postseparation technical or professional training to qualify for civilian employment in jobs not necessarily related to the in-service military specialty.

Many young men and women who enter military service on short-term enlistments have no post-service career goals; or, if they do, the goals are vague or unrealistic or both. The men and women in Category A will therefore need to explore and exploit in-service avenues to post-service civilian careers as soon as possible after they enter military service.

Category B. Midterm noncareerists. Officers and enlisted personnel who serve on active duty for five to ten years can acquire advanced technical and professional training and job skills while in uniform. Although they will be aging and maturing during their military service, both good assets for mid-level employment, the dynamic civilian job market will also be moving along in its own peculiar ways without them. "Keeping in touch" is essential. Technical and professional training obtained in earlier years, whether in or outside military service, must be updated. The civilian jobs that were "hot" when they entered military service may have "cooled off." New career opportunities are constantly emerging.

These people should probably begin serious transition planning at least two years in advance of their ETS date, if not sooner, to be sure that they get the right kind of advanced military training, make informed changes in MOS or officer specialty, or allow necessary time to complete an appropriate postsecondary educational program. Some experts advise people in this category to extend their service commitment, if necessary, to provide more time for completing transition planning actions.

Category C. Career-minded personnel. Officers and enlisted members with eleven or more years of active duty will be moving out of narrow technical specialties and into the broader field of professional military development as they advance in rank. Senior noncommissioned officers (E-6 to E-9), warrant officers, and officers (O-4 and up) are generally faced with such alternatives as keeping up with their original technical or professional field, changing transition goals to exploit their advanced training in the management of people, resources, and programs, or formulating an entirely new career objective.

Men and women in this category also face the possibility of involuntary release before qualifying for retirement or of mandatory retirement as soon as they do quality. Some are confronted with personal or family problems so severe that they can only be handled by leaving military service. No one really plans for such contingencies, but they exist. Early and continuous planning for a transition career can soften the blow if it comes or improve your civilian prospects if it does not.

Category C people are those who are most apt to experience difficulty with their career transition. Career service tends to foster expectations of upper-level civilian jobs that are generally disappointed. Moreover, almost anyone who has been out of the civilian labor force for twenty years or more—or, more likely, has never held a significant civilian job—can expect to have been overtaken by events unless he or she has done very good transition planning over a long period of time. For everyone in this category, then, early and continuous contingency planning is essential. That planning will be climaxed and confirmed by a period of intensive activity for six months to a year prior to the anticipated ETS. But this is not the time to be scrambling for tractical or strategic advantage. Rather, assuming that the earlier planning has been done well, this last phase can concentrate on perfecting job-search strategies and the techniques needed to carry them to a successful conclusion.

What Should You Be Doing?

Chapter 5 suggested resources and procedures for translating your military training and experience (or your nonmilitary qualifications and personal preferences or traits) into civilian occupational terms. If you follow the procedures, you will almost certainly develop a list of questions that need answering and a set of tasks that need doing to confirm your career objective. *Research* is a common term for these activities. *Networking* is also involved.

Both terms are used here to describe processes for gathering information: information to augment that available from the resources described in Chapter 5; information that will confirm, challenge, or deny what you read in those resources; information about where to go for more information. Sources for some of the information can be found in this book; other information you will have to dig out for yourself.

How do you begin your research, and what do you do with the information you have gathered? The two questions are interrelated, and the answer to the second is that you use the information to test, to confirm, or to reformulate your career objective and the tentative courses of action you have developed. Then, obviously, you pursue the most likely course of action.

The research begins with the questions you have after you have done your "translating" exercise. In general, they will involve such things as Training, Education, Experience, Personal attributes and qualifications, and Pay or salary. The *Occupational Outlook Handbook* gives you some information about all these topics; but in most cases, three basic questions arise:

1. Do I have enough?
2. Do I need more?
3. How can I get more?

The *Handbook* also provides information about the industry or industries where the work is done and what kinds of people or how many they employ. The figures apply to the entire national labor force. You will want to know where to concentrate your attack, perhaps. *Question*: Which industry should I target, and why?

You will develop other questions as you read the *Handbook* and the training and statistical supplement. Questions arise when you do not have enough information or, perhaps, when you doubt the truth of information someone presents to you as fact. When you read the *Handbook* or any other publication, keep pencil and paper handy and make notes about things that you want to know more about. Eventually you are going to ask the big question: How do I get answers to my questions?

The information you need comes from two basic sources: books (and other publications) and people, and you must learn to use both effectively if you are to succeed. The books and other publications you will need are in libraries, by and large, though you may have to investigate other sources that we will discuss. The people, at least in the beginning, are the librarians, counselors, and people you work with. Later, as you start networking, you will meet people you never dreamed of meeting. There will be side benefits to all this activity, by the way: You will sharpen your communication skills as you read, take notes, talk, listen, and write letters. Remember that employers seek employees who have good communication skills.

The research suggested need not be a chore. Indeed, if approached in a positive way, research can be a very satisfying and rewarding activity. But research is not an end in itself. I can assure you, for instance, that the research phase of this book was a lot more fun than the writing phase. I learned a lot by reading books, magazines, newspapers, and other publications. I met dozens of interesting people and listened to their stories or milked them for information. I talked by telephone and corresponded with dozens of other involved men and women. But I had to keep in mind while I was doing the research that the real objective was to write this book. As you start on your own research, keep your objective in mind.

Case Study: Researching the Objective

Jim, the Army automobile mechanic we met in the last chapter, did a pretty good job with his career research. So let's see how he handled the questions he developed from reading the *Handbook*. These are some of the things he did over a period of several weeks:

- He talked to his shop supervisor. Results: (1) he got the name of a former staff sergeant who had once worked in his shop and was then was working in town at an AAMCO transmission shop; (2) the supervisor recommended that Jim visit the base Education Center and talk to a counselor about enrolling in a community college program; and (3) factory training? Possible in an advanced tech training program, but Jim would have to reenlist.
- Jim wrote to all the associations listed in the *Handbook* to explain his situation and to request information.
- He met the ex-staff sergeant one evening after work. They had a good talk; afterward the old "Sarge" invited Jim to visit the AAMCO shop to talk to the lead mechanic and the service manager.
- Jim visited the AAMCO shop but made sure that everybody knew he was not looking for a job. No, he was merely seeking good advice. But he kept his eyes open as he was being shown around. Jim noticed that the shop was clean, well lighted, and airy. There was even a small lunchroom for the staff. While they were having coffee, one of the mechanics took Jim aside and suggested that he look up a pal who was working in an independent transmission shop. "Just tell him Bill from AAMCO sent you," he told Jim.
- When he visited the mechanic, the man turned out to be sour on the Army and wouldn't talk to him. "You ain't gonna get my job, sonny!" he said. "No way. I worked too hard and too long to get where I am." Jim took a look around the dark, greasy shop and decided that the mechanic didn't have to worry about him.
- The service manager unexpectedly invited Jim to his home for a barbecue that weekend. Among other things, he confirmed what Jim had already been hearing: He could figure that it took about ten years to become a transmission rebuilder. Jim's Army training and experience would be useful, but he would only qualify as an advanced trainee. To get ahead, what he really needed was factory training, because AAMCO worked on all kinds of transmissions, American and foreign. The service manager said he like Jim's attitude and would be glad to have him as a trainee, except that business was slow and he wasn't hiring: "Maybe in a

year, after you are discharged, things will be better," he sighed. "Look me up then, if you are still interested."

- Jim looked in the Yellow Pages and found that there were other transmission shops in town; he visited some of them to talk about what it took to become a transmission specialist. He got the same story, more or less, about a long period of on-the-job training and factory training. The one thing he heard wherever he went was that business was off; nobody was hiring trainees. Glad I have another year in the Army, Jim said to himself.

- He heard about another association: the Automatic Transmission Rebuilders Association, but he had no address. A buddy suggested that he go to the base library and ask for help. The reference librarian found the name and address for him in the *Encyclopedia of Associations*. Before he left the library, Jim learned that the association conducted advanced training sessions for mechanics who worked for its member companies. He wrote for information.

- He found that the replies to the letters he had written for information included references to books and publications that he wanted to look at. The base library didn't have all of them, but the librarian was able to find them in the public library and have some of them sent over, under an agreement between the two libraries. The others were reference books, and Jim found himself driving to town to work at the public library on several evenings. Jim had never been much for visiting libraries, but the librarians were helpful and he soon felt comfortable doing his own research.

- Jim went home on leave for a week. His uncle introduced him to the service manager at the local Ford dealership. Not much came of that: Transmission work was pretty much limited to replacing damaged transmissions with new or rebuilt ones. The service manager did send Jim over to see Steve, the owner of the local transmission rebuild shop. "Tell him that Jack at the Ford agency sent you," he told Jim when they parted.

- Jim's next visit was encouraging. In the shop he found a plaque that said the shop was a member of the Automatic Transmission Rebuilders Association. He also saw that the shop was new, well laid out, and clean. Steve laid it on the line for him: Army training and experience was helpful, but several more years of on-the-job training and some factory training would be required before he could qualify as a transmission rebuilder. Steve thought Jim might qualify as an advanced trainee, skipping over the R&R phase right into helping rebuilders. He explained with a laugh that R&R meant "remove and replace"; that was the job done by beginning trainees.

- Jim asked about the transmission rebuilders association. Steve said that an association training team was due in that week and invited him to attend the session on an advanced Toyota transmission. During the session Jim found that he could follow it easily. He already knew the principles involved and quickly picked up the new points. Steve was impressed when they discussed the session. As Jim left the shop, Steve gave him his business card and said, "Keep in touch, Jim. Bill, my chief rebuilder, is talking about retiring in a year or so. I'll be looking for someone to fill out the team."

- Jim found one of his high school buddies working as a trainee mechanic in another auto repair shop. The two of them compared notes and talked shop over a pizza. Jim had to pay; his buddy said he was dead broke until payday. "Can't hardly live alone on four-fifty an hour," he said. "Don't know when Jane and I can ever get married. You got it made in the Army, Jim." Jim grunted something cheerful but thought back to that "average wage" for trainees he had read about in the *Handbook*: $9.31 an hour, he recalled. Something to look into, he thought to himself.

- He went back to a couple of shops before leaving town and talked some more to the mechanics he had met. He found out that his hometown was noted for its low wages. The wives of all the mechanic trainees were out working as soon as they could leave the kids; but the more experienced men were making living wages. So, he asked himself, what else is new? Anyway, Jean was finishing up a computer program at the county community college; she had already been promised a job. They weren't planning children right away.

- Jim visited the Education Center when he returned to the base and told a counselor what he had been doing and what he had learned. The counselor listened for a while and then he let Jim have it. The facts, that is. But that is another story.

Standard Operating Procedure for Career Transition

The case study that we are using is a fairly simple one, but it does illustrate how one relatively naive young man found ways to solve his transition planning problems. Along the way, Jim accidentally bumped into what amounts to a Standard Operating Procedure (SOP) for career transition planning in general. While it is impossible to tell you exactly what to do, it is possible to show you how to do it by looking more closely at what Jim did.

The actions that Jim took along the way can be lumped together in three categories:

1. Library research;
2. Field research; and,
3. Networking.

Let's examine each category and establish a general procedure for transition career planning.

1. *Library Research.* Library research starts with looking up your career objective in the *Occupational Outlook Handbook*. The questions that you develop form the initial agenda for continuing your research. You should include here the collection of names and addresses of organizations that can provide further information about your occupation of choice. Write to them as soon as possible, but don't stop everything until you receive the replies.

For one thing, you can look into "career" books. Most of them are written for entry-level high school students; you are not likely to find many at the library at your military base. If that is the case, you can either join a local public library or talk to your librarian about getting what you want on an interlibrary loan. You may find some of these books in your base Education Center. However you get them, career books provide useful information about such subjects as recommended or required training, education, personal attributes, work characteristics, working conditions, and career advancement. They will help you round out the skeleton information you have obtained from the *Handbook* and its statistical supplement. They will also provide references to other books and publications, along with more names and addresses of agencies and organizations that can give you additional information. You can keep busy finding and reading (or scanning) the other books and publications. You should also write to the agencies and organizations you have found for the information they can provide.

Most good libraries maintain clipping and pamphlet files on a wide range of topics, including careers, career education, and small business. Ask the librarian to steer you to the "vertical files" and browse through them. They are usually a gold mine of easily absorbed information. But be a little careful: Many of the pamphlets are sent to the library free of charge by groups that represent a special interest or are pushing some program or other.

Get acquainted with the reference section of the library. Many noncirculating books and pamphlets are kept there, along with all kinds of encyclopedias and directories that can be useful. For example, if Jim had looked further in the listing for the Automatic Transmission Rebuilders Association in the *Encyclopedia of Associations*, he would have found that the association publishes a list of its member companies. You can find the same kind of information for associations in your career or occupational field in that encyclopedia.

Having such a list will help you locate potential employers in various parts of the country, for example. Industry associations often establish training and performance standards for their members; member companies may therefore be more desirable employers than others in the same industry.

Some consultants recommend targeting particular corporations or companies for a job search. Some of the more progressive corporations are listed in Tom Peters' book *A Passion for Excellence*. The information you will need about individual companies is available from business, trade, and financial directories. Several are listed at the end of Part II.

The reference section is also home for the guides to higher educational institutions and college catalogs that may be useful to you as you pursue your research.

Last, but not least, familiarize yourself with the periodical collection. There you can usually find national newspapers like the *Wall Street Journal* and the *New York Times*, along with some or all of the national news weeklies and business magazines. Some libraries maintain back issues in restricted areas; some subscribe to microfilm or microfiche services to save room. Subject indexes to magazines and newspapers are usually available.

2. *Field Research.* At some time or other you will have to get out of the library, and off the base, to visit actual employers. When you do this, as Jim did in our case study, you go as someone seeking *information* and not as a job-seeker. The information you seek will be based on questions that have been generated by your library research. Seeing is believing: You can observe work conditions, employees at work (and play), facilities for employees; you can observe equipment and machinery; you can observe production techniques or other aspects of the company's business activity. This kind of field research may reveal, for example, that the ABC Corporation you targeted is using an advanced computer of a kind that you as a computer operator are unfamiliar with. You may also learn that all new employees in the data processing facility are trained in-house; or that none are: Only applicants with training in the ABC Corporation's system need apply. Observations of this kind should lead to necessary action to improve your job qualifications.

As another example, do not restrict your off-post adventures to consuming the products of local bars, fast-food emporia, and convenience stores. Befriend a bartender or a waitress and find out how they got their job and what training they needed. Bartending and waitering/waitressing are occupations that can give you a substantial part-time income while you are attending school or between jobs; these fields may also lead to permanent careers in food-service management. Or approach the manager of a fast-food store and ask about the company's management training program; McDonald's has an excellent one. Convenience stores like Seven-Eleven are often owned and operated under a franchise system, but the franchiser conducts management training programs for local managers and for field representatives who work within a sales district and help train local employees or assist with store management problems.

J.C. Penney and Montgomery Ward have outstanding management training programs; stop by some day (or telephone ahead) and talk to the store manager about what it takes to enter such a program. I have had a number of frank conversations with senior people in sales jobs in retail stores, stock brokerage houses, and real estate offices, for example, without ceremony—though you should probably call ahead to make an appointment. Most people like to talk about themselves and their experiences as long as you do not ask for anything more than information and advice. One essential tip: Don't show up in uniform; wear civilian clothes appropriate to the level of the proposed meeting. That means a conservative suit, white shirt, and a tie in most cases.

Visitor access to private companies like ABC Corporation may be restricted, so the question is: How do you get inside the gate or main entrance? You can call ahead, find out the name of the manager of the department in which you are interested, and arrange an appointment with him or her. Restrict your conversation to information gathering and say nothing about possible employment. Before you go to the meeting, of course, you should gather all the information you can about ABC Corporation and what it does. Another way is to go with a group of some sort, possibly one arranged by the base Public Affairs Office, the Recreational Services Office, or even the Education Center. If there are no such tours, be creative. Suggest to the Public Affairs Office or the Education Center that a tour of ABC Corporation would interest a lot of men and women on the base who are considering civilian careers but who have never seen the inside of a business corporation; besides, wouldn't it be great for community relations? Before you launch the suggestion, be sure you have lined up some friends or colleagues who would join the tour!

Another excellent approach to field research is to do what Jim did: engage in networking.

3. *Networking.* As you will recall, up to this point Jim had done a pretty good job on his own. His initial talk with his own shop supervisor had led him to a meeting with a working mechanic who had been in the Army and was willing to tell it like it was. The old "Sarge" introduced Jim to other working mechanics and his own customer service representative and service manager. Jim picked up new information at each stage, including information that led to more research as well as firsthand knowledge of working conditions, training, wages, and so on.

While on leave Jim followed the same process, starting with his uncle and ending with the owner of an independent transmission rebuild shop. Before he left town he had a tentative job offer. What Jim was doing was networking.

Networking is usually thought of as part of the job-search process, something to do *after* leaving military service, but it should also be considered an important part of pretransition planning and research *while you are in uniform*. In many cases, of course, networking is also the device by which you can penetrate the hidden job market during an actual job-search—or even before, as Jim did.

The objective of networking at this stage, however, is to develop the information you need from a succession of personal contacts of increasing importance. The process permits you to bypass the "gate-keepers"—the secretaries and screening interviewers, for example—who prevent applicants for employment from ever seeing anyone important.

As you move through your own developing network, you become more and more familiar with the targeted civilian work scene and the forces that animate it, the people who populate it, and those who manage it. You acquire information that you can use in later personal contacts to demonstrate your interest in, enthusiasm for, and knowledge of the occupation or the place of employment, or both. But you never ask for a job. Stick to information.

How do you start? Jim's starting places were his shop supervisor and his uncle. You can start with almost anyone you know; but do be on the alert for people you may meet for the first time, perhaps at a social event or on an airplane. Americans typically exchange information on their occupations at first meeting. Don't be shy about asking —just be careful that your new acquaintance doesn't get carried away with talking about his or her career. Jump in when you can with something like this: "As you can see (if you are in uniform), I am in the service right now, but I am considering getting out to follow a civilian career in —." You have to watch this one; your new acquaintance may just murmur, "How interesting," and keep on talking about his or her career.

On the other hand, if your opening arouses some interest on the part of your new aquaintance, your ploy is about as follows: "Oh, yes, I am a trained computer programmer. I've been working in computers for eight years now. I don't know much about computer-based businesses in this town; in fact, I have never been inside a data processing center that wasn't a military one. Maybe you know someone who could help me make up my mind?" Your first contact may not, but you keep trying until you find someone who does.

You talk to someone who has a friend whose wife is an electronic assembler at ABC Corporation—the very company you have targeted. You meet the friend and his wife and chat about this and that while you steer the conversation around to the ABC Corporation and its computers. Chances are that the wife will know someone who is a computer operator. Your new friends offer to arrange for you to meet that someone. When you do, you say you have always wanted to see a civilian data processing center because all your computer experience has been in military service. Would it be possible to visit ABC Corporation some day?

Before you know it the visit is laid on, and you arrive at ABC Corporation dressed in a conservative suit, white shirt, and a quiet necktie. Very businesslike. After you are introduced to the Data Center manager, you chat a bit. Ask him about his own background and training; he will be pleased, and you may find some talking points in common. Then he proudly tours you through his whole operation while you ask questions that show you are a real professional. You make opportunities to tell him something about yourself: your training, your assignment as an instructor at a service school, the operational improvements you made in your own data processing center and the award you received. Ask him if he knows about an informal group or club of people involved with the kind of computers that the ABC Corporation uses. Chances are that there is one and that he will invite you to a meeting. When you leave, you thank him very much for his time and courtesy.

After you get back to the base, you write a short note of thanks to the Center manager. In it you may suggest having lunch or an after-work drink to go over other questions about your career objectives, confirm your interest in attending the computer club meeting, or send him a copy of a program you have just written on a topic of mutual interest—whatever fits the occasion. Meanwhile you have a lot of firsthand information about ABC Corporation that you can use for advanced planning.

That's the way networking should work, and you can make it work and have an interesting time doing it. The problem for many military people is bridging the gap between the base and the community. Well, you are going to have to do it some day; why not now? One key to the process is to join something in the community near your military base and to get involved as a member. A church or a synagogue, perhaps, is a good start, especially if you are young and single: You will meet new friends, improve your social life, and have a handle on a network. But there are many other ways to get started. Even the smallest town has dozens of organizations that you can join, depending on your circumstances:

- Service organizations (Rotary, Lions, Kiwanis, Junior Chamber of Commerce, and the good old PTA, if you live in the community and have children in school).

- Service agencies (YMCA/YWCA, Boy Scouts/Girl Scouts, Campfire Girls; become a den or troop leader and meet parents and the business people who serve as volunteers on the Council).
- Professional associations (Medical Society, Dental Society, Press Club, Engineering Society, Business Management Association, Banking Association, and so on).
- Fraternal organizations (Masons, Knights of Columbus, Moose, Elks, and their ladies' auxiliaries).
- Hobby and craft organizations of all kinds.
- Military-related and veterans organizations (you don't have to be out of the service in most cases; if you do, go as a guest of someone who is).

You can take it from here. Local newspapers usually report extensively on the activities of these organizations. Or you can look in the telephone directory for addresses and telephone numbers and make your own first contacts.

Whatever the organization, the networking process is the same. And the bottom line is another old saw: "It's not what you know, but who you know." No need to be shy, coy, or embarrassed. Networking is an established institution in the civilian society from which you came and to which you are planning to return. In fact, if you are not too far into a military career, the folks you left at home already constitute a network: family, relatives, friends, neighbors, teachers, religious leaders, among others.

If age and rank are gaining on you and you are in for the long haul, consider the importance of joining and taking an active role in a military professional organization. You will find a long list of them in Appendix D. The Association of the United States Army, the NCO Association, and the Retired Officers Association come readily to mind. They all have committees on which you can serve and projects in which you can participate; many of them will help you interface with the civilian community. Most have chapters scattered around the country, typically near military bases with retired military populations; join and be *active*. They all produce professional publications, and they usually have annual regional or national conventions where you can meet members who know someone you want to know or civilians who are out scouting for potential employees. The key word, however, is *involvement*. If yours is just another name on a membership roster, you might as well not bother.

And there you have it. A trail already reconnoitered and cleared of mines that can lead you from a military specialty to a rewarding civilian career. The suggestions in this chapter should start you down the path with some confidence of success. You may feel that this transition process means a lot of work, and it does, but it can be rewarding in many ways. The bottom line, however, is that a great deal of the necessary research can be done while you are still in service—while you are still earning an income and have the time to take any corrective actions necessary to confirm your qualifications for your post-service career objective.

Chapter 7

Gaining an Educational Advantage

The importance of educational advancement and retraining to the career transition process can hardly be overestimated. The pace of technological change has become so rapid that postsecondary education is a virtual necessity for even some entry-level employment that has traditionally hired high school graduates and trained them on the job. Many people in civilian engineering, medical, and scientific professions already require retraining about every five years. Graduate degrees are almost a prerequisite for military separees and retirees whose career transition objectives include employment somewhere above entry level and who aspire to rapid promotion to managerial status. These are obvious and compelling reasons for advancing your educational standing while you serve in uniform. But, as we shall see, they are not the only reasons.

The military services operate or support a wide variety of free or inexpensive in-service educational programs that range from correspondence courses to postgraduate programs in civilian or service institutions—the latter with full pay and allowances. Some college credit can be awarded upon completion of certain phases of military training, beginning with basic training and continuing with military technical schools and professional military educational (PME) courses and programs. Military service can also be a pathway to a college degree—and officer status—for enlisted men and women. And, of course, the various forms of the GI Bill, old and new, can help both career and noncareer enlisted military members to advance educational qualifications after they leave active duty. Subsequent service in the reserve forces offers many of the same opportunities available to active duty military personnel.

The existence of these opportunities is generally known throughout the military services as a result of intensive recruiting efforts and in-service publicity. But these means often do not spark a sense of urgency or offer direction. Rather, they offer *opportunities*.

No service will stand in the way of your personal educational advancement, though the "needs of the service" may dictate circum-

U.S. ARMY PHOTO

Military Education Centers provide space for classes and shop courses conducted by civilian institutions.

stances. On the contrary, all services encourge participation in advanced educational programs precisely for the reason that better educated service people—whether in the enlisted or officer ranks—contribute more to the performance of their mission. The Army has even adopted the slogan, "Education does make good soldiers better." In that sense, the military services are in full agreement with civilian employers.

The Importance of Higher Education in the Labor Market

"Anyone who stops his or her education after high school is committing occupational suicide," according to Marvin Cetron, president of Forecasting International and co-author of the book *Jobs of the Future*. Cetron and other experts in the field of civilian career development who agreed on the importance of continuing study as a prerequisite to a climb up the career ladder were quoted in an issue of *U.S. News and World Report* devoted to "Jobs of the Future" (December 23, 1985).

"Low-skill repetitive jobs are being replaced by robots and flexible machine systems in the U.S. and by cheaper labor abroad," observed Stephen Bradley, a professor at the Harvard Business School. At the other end of the scale, a manager of Professional Recruiting for the General Electric Company pointed out that he looks for engineers and computer scientists who are willing "to be stretched out, people who can think, learn, and grow beyond the specialized knowledge they bring to the job from academia." A vocational education expert from North Carolina declared, "Technology is equalizing the workplace and is even giving women the edge in some cases." As evidence, she pointed to the number of women who are entering engineering and other professions that they have traditionally avoided.

These observations about the civilian labor force are as valid today as they were when they were first reported. And the policies of the military services point in the same direction for much the same reasons. They encourage posthigh school education for enlisted members. Some services already require completion of an associate (junior college) degree for promotion to senior non-commissioned officer grades, and they are moving toward a requirement for a baccalaureate degree for promotion to E-7 and above. The services are tightening educational prerequisites for both commissioned and warrant officer candidates. Postgraduate study is almost routine in the officer corps and encouraged for enlisted members.

What is happening, in both the civilian and military environments, is that the most valuable employees are those who have useful skills *and* can think beyond the requirements of the job at hand. Both seek employees who, as the General Electric recruiter put it, can "think, learn, and grow beyond the specialized knowledge they bring to the job..." No one who is contemplating leaving military service for a civilian career can ignore this situation.

The net effect of the increasing emphasis on postsecondary education in the civilian labor force is apparent from Figure 4. Between 1970 and 1984 the number of employees with four or more years of college education increased by nearly 70 percent. The number of those with one to three years of college increased by nearly 50 percent. By 1984, 41 percent of all the members of the civilian labor force between the ages of 18 and 64 belonged to one of these two categories, compared to 26 percent in 1970.

These impressive gains are expected to continue into the 1990's as older, less-educated workers leave the labor force and younger, better-educated workers join it. Another contributing factor is that younger, less-educated workers are twice as likely to be laid off as their better-educated peers.

One problem with this situation should be recognized: Having a college degree does not guarantee you a better job or even a job at all. What Figure 4 does not show is that about one of every five college graduates in the civilian labor force in 1984 worked at a job that did not require that level of education. The Department of Labor, in fact, predicts an oversupply of college graduates through

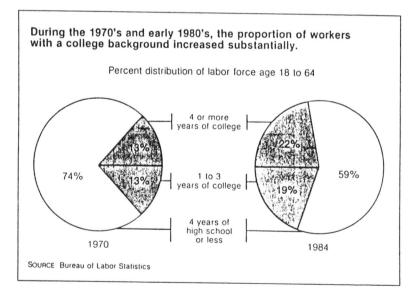

During the 1970's and early 1980's, the proportion of workers with a college background increased substantially.

Percent distribution of labor force age 18 to 64

4 or more years of college

1 to 3 years of college

4 years of high school or less

74%   13%   13%   1970

22%   19%   59%   1984

SOURCE Bureau of Labor Statistics

Fig. 4

the 1990's. These are gross figures, of course, that do not provide information about the quality of education, kinds of college degrees, economic and business conditions, age, sex, personality traits, and personal choice. Much of the oversupply is at entry level—young college graduates seeking their first job. To some extent, the reported figure may result from the fact that many people accept employment at a lower level than that for which they are qualified while they wait for the "big chance." Others may simply be happy working where they are.

What you should be concerned with here, however, is getting the advanced education, consistent with your long-term career objectives, that will permit you to hold a job and facilitate your climb up the career ladder. Do not overlook the fact that your postmilitary career may be longer than your military career!

The moral of the story, so far as this book is concerned, is to take advantage of the educational opportunities available from the military services while you are still in uniform. You may have to stretch yourself a bit, spend a lot of your otherwise free time in classrooms and libraries, sweat over correspondence courses in your room or billet, and sacrifice some immediate goals. The reward, as much as anything, is in the effort you expend: Evidence of successful completion of advanced academic studies is generally recognized by employers as proof of an applicant's potential to learn and to grow on the job.

Postsecondary Education Is Not Vocational Training

Advanced education should not be confused with vocational training. *Education*, in the traditional sense, has always involved training students to think, to communicate effectively, and to function intelligently in whatever career they may choose. A common concept has been that education serves to insure the continuity of the prevailing culture, though many people reject that view today because it implies cultural domination by those who have historically controlled the institutions that shape the culture itself.

For reasons that are not well understood, the vast body of shared common knowledge that in the past ensured easy, effective communication of ideas between individuals and groups has eroded in recent years. Furthermore, in our age of high-tech, high-speed communications the national literacy rate is declining. The two events are thought to be related: Even many people who are functionally literate (able to read or "decode" words in print) are unable to understand the *idea* that a series of words and sentences is intended to convey. The problem is most often found among the young, from high school age into the thirties, and seems to be directly related to a decline in the quantity and quality of shared information or common culture.

If this seems a bit academic, it is not. Business leaders are already expressing concern about the lack of communication skills, both written and spoken, in their junior executives—deficiencies that inevitably influence the ability of their companies to remain competitive and profitable. At a lower level, as E. D. Hirsch, Jr. comments, the ability to read the technical literature in one's field is not true literacy. Regarding vocational training, he writes:

> ". . . a directly practical drawback of such narrow training is that it does not prepare anyone for technological change. Narrow vocational training in one state of a technology will not enable a person to read manuals that explain new developments in the same technology. In modern life we need general knowledge that enables us to deal with new ideas, events, and challenges."

Dr. Hirsch has stirred up something of a controversy with the publication of his book *Cultural Literacy: What Every American Needs to Know*. In an appendix he includes a list of more than four thousand dates, keywords, song titles, literary titles, names of people, slogans and folk sayings, and names of places that should be familiar to everyone who would consider himself "culturally literate." *Familiar* is, in fact, not quite the right word. What is intended is that anyone who is "culturally literate" should know what is behind each word; that is, should know what the use of that word or phrase conveys to others.

Critics may argue with Dr. Hirsch about the choice of entries in his appendix, which requires sixty-three pages, but his idea has great appeal. Men and women in military service whose formal education may have stopped with high school should find the book particularly interesting, but everyone who serves in the military should be aware of the concept that Hirsch exposes. Harvard sociologist Orlando Patterson commented:

> "Industrialized society [imposes] a growing cultural and structural complexity that requires persons to have a broad grasp of what Professor Hirsch has called cultural literacy: a deep understanding of mainstream culture, which no longer has anything to do with white Anglo-Saxon Protestants, but with the imperatives of industrial civilization. It is the need for cultural literacy, a profound conception of the whole civilization, which is often neglected in talk about literacy."

> Hirsch, *Cultural Literacy*, p. 10

As I read the tea leaves, so to speak, Lee Iacocca at Chrysler Corporation and his counterparts in the *Fortune* 500—or even in the

INC 500, the five hundred fastest growing *small* companies—should be cheering on the sidelines. Few chief operating officers of important businesses are MBA's. Successful senior executives who do hold this graduate degree have somewhere along the way acquired that "deep understanding of mainstream culture."

Cultural literacy requires more than the acquisition of an unorganized mass of information that will help you star in your next friendly game of Trivial Pursuit—though anyone who is truly culturally literate can easily star in that game. Rather, Professor Hirsch refers to Martin Luther King's well-known "I Have a Dream" speech. There King projected his view of a society where men and women could deal with each other as equals and judge each other on the basis of character and achievements. "Like Thomas Jefferson," Hirsch writes, "[Martin Luther King] had a dream of a society founded not on race or class but on personal merit." He then goes on to say:

> "Putting aside for the moment the practical arguments about the economic uses of literacy, we can contemplate the even more basic principle that underlies our national system of education in the first place—that people in a democracy can be entrusted to decide all important matters for themselves because they can deliberate and communicate with one another."

Hirsch's brief book makes a compelling case for the importance of educating yourself beyond the literacy required by a specific task. But his arguments are older than the Republic. They stand behind the traditional high school course in "civics," for example. They are the basis for collegiate "core" curricula" that are now back in fashion, following the nihilism of the 1960's. No one who aspires to be a participating—and contributing—member of our unique American society can afford to be counted as a cultural illiterate.

It is, however, an unfortunate fact that, in their highly commendable devotion to duty in pursuit of task-oriented goals and missions, members of the military services often minimize the importance of their own role as members of the greater society. Longer-term career members may immerse themselves completely in the military subculture, with its own rather limited goals, its own patterns of thinking about those goals, and its own jargon. When they complete military service, they are often unable to function effectively as citizens for extended lengths of time because the values, issues, and objectives—even the terms of reference—of the greater society are not fully understood or accepted.

This important consideration leads to the very use of the term *transition* to describe the process of moving from the military environment to the civilian one, a process that may take as long as three to five years to complete. It is this situation more than any other that gives truth to the advice that I heard a retired senior military officer urge on a group of young Army men and women who were beginning their official transition processing. "You have to *civilianize* yourselves," he told them.

If you are already enrolled in an advanced education program on base, or elsewhere, you must keep these ideas in mind. Sign up willingly and put everything you have into those required courses in English composition, public speaking, and literature, history, science, economics, government, art appreciation, or whatever.

In passing, you should know that all the service academies require cadets and midshipmen to succeed in their "core curriculum" courses. At West Point the core curriculum of thirty-two courses includes fourteen required courses and two electives in the fields of English (composition and literature), history, political science, constitutional law, international relations, economics, philosophy, psychology, foreign language, and computer science. Most of the remaining courses are math, science, and engineering, regardless of the "major" field of study. In the jargon of educational theory, Academy graduates are being "prepared for life." Can you afford to do less?

If you are working toward or already have an associate or bachelor's degree, you may do yourself a good turn by getting a copy of Hirsch's book and checking yourself. Then you can either restructure your academic program to emphasize core subjects earlier rather than later or "bone up" on the topics that fail to ring a bell.

Reading ability is, of course, essential to accumulating information rapidly. If you are considering extracurricular work to improve your own cultural literacy, start with a good encyclopedia. In a few minutes you can acquire a great deal of basic information. Biographies of famous people let you slip easily into the total environment in which a historic figure lived and worked—and they are certainly more interesting to read than college textbooks.

But other kinds of learning experiences are also valuable. Drop a record on your turntable or slip a tape into your tapedeck and listen to music by a composer you have been reading about. Attend a play by a well-known playwright. Check your local newspaper or *TV Guide* for relevant TV programs on the Public Broadcasting System channels—especially science programs—and take the time to watch them.

Other opportunities will occur spontaneously or can be tracked to develop your own cultural literacy. Travel, for instance, can be broadening but only if you understand what you are seeing as you travel. Visit Paris, by all means, but read into the problem beforehand. Memorize common greetings and some useful phrases in French, if you do not already know the language; they will help you breach the cultural barrier. Familiarize yourself with a map of the city. Take time to visit the world-renowned museums and monuments before you hit Harry's Bar for that first Martini, taxi to the *Folies Bergère*, and finish the evening with dinner at Maxime's followed by some disco at Regine's. It's all "culture," in a manner of speaking, but some sticks with you for life and some will just leave a hole in your bank account. You do not have to treat this kind of activity as a chore or a bore. Indeed, if you persist, you will find much that is exciting, challenging, and personally rewarding.

Educational Strategies and Tactics

A pretty tight case can be made for the necessity of advanced education to the transition planning. Your personal objectives, circumstances, and abilities will influence what you do and when you do it. But three basic strategies seem to apply to almost anyone in military service:

1. Whatever your *level* of education, take advantage of every opportunity to improve it *while you are in uniform*.

2. Whatever the *focus* of your previous education, consider broadening or changing it *while you are in uniform*.

3. If you have educational goals that cannot be met while you are in service, take advantage of every opportunity *while you are in uniform* to prepare yourself to accomplish those goals quickly after you leave military service.

Each of the three strategies is feasible and can work for anyone, though tactics may vary with individual post-service career objectives and from service to service. In some cases you may find that two or all of the strategies may blend into one course of action as you mature over the period of your service career. For now, let's examine each strategy separately.

1. *Improving the level of education* can work for everyone from the enlisted recruit to the senior officer. The strategy simply involves moving up a rung on the educational ladder, depending on where you start. Initially, advanced educational standing will have a positive influence on your military career. But the long-term effect of *not* improving your educational standing while still in uniform can influence your entire adult life. Leaving military service at the same educational level at which you entered will almost certainly put you at a disadvantage in the job market.

Under this strategy a high school graduate should consider an educational program leading to an associate degree. The degree field is not particularly important at this level, with the possible exception of Category A short-termers. A more important consequence may well be to demonstrate an ability to learn at that higher level of study. You will have to muster considerable initiative, self-discipline, and perseverance once you start.

Furthermore, the more you study, the more proficient you become at learning. Good study techniques work almost without regard to the subject matter. Of course, if you have been "a poor student" you may simply have poor study habits or need to improve your basic skills in reading, writing, and arithmetic. A visit to your base Education Center or unit Educational Services Officer is, in any case, an essential first step along the road to advanced education for anyone in this basic category.

Once you have acquired a recognized level of advanced education, the same strategy can be continued. That is, most men and women who have achieved the associate degree should consider enrolling in a program that leads to the bachelor's degree. The associate degree, incidentally, is not a *terminal* degree. It may satisfy entry-level requirements for many technician jobs, but remember that an entry-level civilian job should not be the final objective of your career transition strategy. On the other hand, if you have earned an associate degree in uniform during a short-term enlistment, you will already have the basic credentials needed for acceptance in a full-scale bachelor's degree program after you leave military service.

If you already have a bachelor's degree, consider working toward a master's degree, but be sure to consider the importance of Strategy 2, below.

Strategy 1 does not necessarily lead remorselessly beyond the master's degree to the doctorate or to postdoctoral study, though that possibility should not be overlooked. Service-related study at the doctoral and postdoctoral levels is available only to a few highly qualified or highly selected officers as part of their professional military development.

For most men and women in uniform, the pursuit of a doctorate is too time-consuming, difficult to complete on a part-time basis while moving around in military service, and has little relevance to career objectives. Most business enterprises prefer employees who have combined a good educational background, up to the master's degree, with solid field experience. Of course, exceptions must be made for those whose career goals include university teaching or a profession in which a doctorate serves as a "union card": physicians, dentists, economists, scientists, and consultants of various kinds.

The most desirable course for military personnel who have already acquired a master's degree is to adopt the second strategy: broaden or change the focus of the educational effort.

2. *Broadening or changing the focus* of your educational effort may be equivalent in academic terms to changing your major field of study. This is a common occurrence in civilian academic life. In many cases such changes result from increased maturity and self-confidence or heightened interest in a field of study that had not earlier been of great importance to the student.

In other cases the shift may be less dramatic: Elective courses may be included in a defined study program to provide added scope. Some career consultants, for example, insist that everyone seeking employment work to develop a high level of communication skills and a basic knowledge of computer science. Anyone aiming for a management career should have a basic understanding of accounting principles, if only to help them read sales or financial reports intelligently.

Shifts in field of study are often fairly obvious. An enlisted member who has earned an associate degree in electronics from the Community College of the Air Force may, for example, decide to work toward a bachelor's degree in Industrial Engineering, a widely available in-service degree program. An officer who holds a bachelor of science degree in Electronic Engineering, on the other hand, may elect to study for a master's in Business Administration. As suggested above, most who have the master's degree should shift their focus and seek a second master's in another field rather than pursue a doctorate in the same field. In each case, of course, a carefully evaluated career transition is assumed.

A few combination degree programs are of fairly obvious utility in transition planning. The combination of almost any undergraduate degree with an MBA can work for you. It may be worth mentioning here that liberal arts graduates are now being recruited for management training programs, sometimes in preference to MBA's. Liberal arts graduates tend to have deep, broad educational experiences and well-developed communication skills, the assets that industry executives now seek in employees. In another switch, recruiting for hospital administrators is said to be focusing on MBA's rather than the traditional graduates in the field of hospital administration, as health services become more and more industry-oriented.

Someone with an undergraduate degree in Economics, Political Science, or International Relations might consider study toward a graduate degree in Finance and Banking—two of the fastest-growing sectors of the services industry, by the way. Other such shifts depend on individual career objectives and are too numerous to discuss here. But solid preparation in two or more academic fields is very much in vogue these days. In the job market, your options are greater.

Broadening the scope of your educational background does not always take the form of study for a degree. Nondegree study to sharpen communication skills and to gain computer literacy has already been mentioned, but there are more imaginative approaches.

One appealing example is that of a journalism graduate who, on her own, studied everything available about hospital administration and its problems. She then targeted a successful job search to employment as a public relations officer with a hospital-operating company.

With a little thought and imagination, almost anyone can pursue that kind of career transition by redirecting a solid base of educational accomplishment and related work experience gained in military service toward a new career objective. Taking the reverse approach, an experienced medical technician might study journalism or public relations while in uniform and accomplish the same kind of transition. Or a skilled military technician who has well-developed communication skills, basic computer knowledge, and a good feel for business operations—all of which can be acquired under an associate degree program in business while in uniform—might seek employment as a field service or sales representative rather than continue to work at the bench. Advanced education can increase your options.

Do not overlook related military career strategies when you are considering Strategy 2. Longer terms of service give enlisted members opportunities for changing military occupational specialties that can lead to technical training in a new field closer to their transition career objective. Officers can elect alternate specializations with the same result; in some cases an alternate specialization may lead to opportunities for graduate training at a civilian university that would not otherwise be available.

Finally, no one should overlook opportunities to attend the numerous "short courses" in military subjects related to his or her career transition objective. Years ago, a short course in Army Financial Management taught me enough about accounting and program planning and budgeting to facilitate my own transition from military service to become a successful business executive. Later I was able to utilize the same instruction in the capacity of "expert" consultant when another government agency installed a program planning and budgeting system.

Some officers (and some senior enlisted members) may have opportunities to be assigned in various capacities to work in industry. Seek them out. Your service would not offer such assignments if it didn't believe that your military performance and career prospects would be enhanced. Meanwhile, you can experience what it means to work in a civilian environment while you are still in uniform.

3. *If educational goals cannot be met while in uniform*, take advantage of alternative opportunities before leaving service. The objective is to smooth the way to the accomplishment of those goals after you leave. Very often this strategy applies to relative short-termers, both enlisted and officer members, who do not have time to complete a formal degree program, to change MOS, or to qualify for an advanced military program. In other cases the educational goals are not possible in the framework of programs available during military service: medical and legal training, for example, or undergraduate engineering and scientific studies that require extensive laboratory facilities. (Some exceptions to this general rule do exist: Army and

Air Force officers on active duty can obtain law and medical degrees under fully funded programs, for example. Officers and enlisted members of all services can qualify for "bootstrap" programs that provide for resident study at civilian colleges and universities.)

The obvious tactic here is to do what you can while you are qualified for educational benefits. Suppose your objective is an undergraduate degree in Business Administration but you enlisted in the Army for only three years right after graduating from high school. Some things you can do:

a. Be sure you are eligible for New GI Bill benefits. (You are unless you rejected the program at your processing center. If you enlisted for certain MOS's, you may also be eligible for the Army College Fund.)

b. Convert eligible military training (basic training, technical school courses) to college credits through the base Education Center (joint agreement between the Department of Defense and the American Council on Education). I know a young man who was kept from graduating from a community college because he had not satisfied the Physical Education requirement. You can obtain some or all of the necessary credit for that requirement for an associate degree as a result of completing basic training.

c. Enroll in whatever junior college or college courses you can while you are in service. If the degree program does not fit your objective, do it anyway, but concentrate on core subjects such as English, history, and math. Your Education Counselor can advise you, or you can consult college catalogs to find out what required courses in your own degree field can be satisfied while you are in uniform. Under the Servicemembers Opportunity College program, the college credits you earn, wherever you are, can be consolidated on a single "transcript" that charts your educational progress and will provide transferable credits when you leave the service and enroll in a civilian institution. The more credits you can earn while in uniform, the sooner you can reach your educational goal—and the lower the cost to you.

d. Have the Education Center administer occupational interest or occupational aptitude tests. Favorable test scores may influence a later application to a civilian college.

e. Find out the schedule for the Scholastic Aptitude Test (SAT) at your Education Center; most four-year colleges require that SAT scores be submitted as part of the application process. Take the SAT early, if you can. If you do not do well at first, you can take it again after some "prepping," without penalty. Only the last scores need go to the college(s) you seek to enter. (Community colleges generally operate on an open enrollment basis and do not require the SAT.)

f. Ask your Education Counselor to help you select a suitable college (or community college) and prepare the application. If you are going to return to your home of record, consider nearby community colleges and state colleges where tuition fees are lower for residents. Keep in mind that four-year colleges have "seasons" or deadlines for applications. (Community colleges have less formal procedures; you can register at the beginning of any semester or quarter.)

g. Finally, while you are in uniform, investigate the advantages of serving in the Selected Reserve after you leave active duty. Reservists are entitled to a version of the New GI Bill. The Army Continuing Education System (ACES) has been extended to the Army Reserve. You may also be able to qualify for an ROTC scholarship (but may lose the use of the New GI Bill) or the Army Reserve "simultaneous membership program."

Service members with advanced educational standing can use much the same approach. Those who are planning to attend graduate school can also generally take the required qualifying exam, such as the Graduate Record Examination (GRE), at or through base Education Centers. Service members who lack some prerequisites for graduate study in their field of choice can often remedy deficiencies through courses in on-base educational programs.

In some areas state universities or university extension programs are convenient to military bases; they may offer wider choices in courses than on-base educational programs. Some offer courses in the evening or on weekends. Members of the uniformed services on active duty qualify for resident tuition rates at most state universities, a fact that can be important even if your military service provides tuition assistance. A source of graduate fellowships is included in the reading list at the end of Part II.

Educational Centers operated by most services can also provide or arrange for professional and technical certification in certain fields, taking into account training and work experience acquired during military service.

Finally, do not overlook the adult education courses available in most communities, the continuing education programs offered by most state colleges and universities (and others), and the "open universities" found in many metropolitan areas. While these courses usually do not carry credit, they can often fill a void in your educational background or provide information you need in other phases of your transition planning, such as personal financial planning. Moreover, they cost very little and are usually offered in the evening or on weekends.

How you pursue any of the suggested basic strategies depends to a great extent on where you are beginning, on your own learning abilities, and on the resources available through your military service. In general, however, the resources and programs offered to eligible active duty personnel are sufficient to satisfy most needs. They include opportunities for enlisted men and women to be appointed to the service academies, to acquire the bachelor's degree under "bootstrap" programs and enlisted commissioning programs, or even to qualify for medical school training while in uniform. Officer programs include postgraduate study in civilian or service-operated institutions, including studying for a law or medical degree while in uniform. A list of these programs is included in Appendix C.

Educational programs change from time to time, and Appendix C does not necessarily include every possible program of all five military services. Your Education Center or Career Counselor can probably best advise you on your eligibility for these and other programs. A list of official offices where you can obtain current information is also included in Appendix C.

Special Educational Situations: Military-Related Programs

Other military educational programs are available to former military personnel, either as a result of their active duty service or in augmentation of it. Those mentioned below may be particularly interesting to younger short-termers who have not had time to complete (or compete for) in-service programs leading to academic degrees. Some of the programs require an undergraduate degree for entry. Some generate obligations for additional military service in return for financial and other assistance. Most also have age limitations.

1. The Reserve Officers Training Corps (ROTC) programs of the Army, Air Force, and Navy (with a Marine Corps option) offer scholarships of two to four years that cover the cost of tuition, laboratory and incidental fees, and books at colleges and universities across the country. The choice of major fields of study may be restricted.

Prior military service usually qualifies applicants for the two-year Senior ROTC program. Senior ROTC cadets are paid stipends of one hundred dollars a month during the school year; uniforms are provided free. They are paid at the grade of E-5 during required summer training. Graduates are commissioned O-1's in the appropriate service Reserve component. Scholarship recipients may be required to serve on active duty for up to four years (or longer if Air Force, Navy, or Marine Corps aviation options are elected), but this requirement varies with the "needs of the service."

Former service members interested in this kind of program should probably have completed the associate degree while in service and be accepted or enrolled in an eligible college program. GI Bill benefits cannot be used by scholarship recipients. Contact the nearest ROTC unit, usually located at a state university, or see Appendix C.

2. The Army's unique "simultaneous membership program" combines service in the Army Reserve with enrollment in an Army Senior ROTC program. Participants serve in the Active Reserve as officer candidates (pay of E-5); they may be commissioned as early as the end of the sophomore year and continue to serve in the Army Reserve (pay of O-1) while they complete degree studies. Upon graduation they remain in their Army Reserve unit, though they usually serve limited tours of active duty to attend their Branch Basic Course. Contact an Army Reserve recruiter.

3. ROTC training is also available to qualified applicants on a non-scholarship basis with no restrictions on major field of study. Prior military service usually qualifies applicants for entry in the Senior ROTC category, where they are paid the same stipend as other cadets/midshipmen during the academic year and during summer training. Graduates are commissioned in grade O–1, but there is no active duty obligation. GI Bill entitlements may be used. This is an excellent opportunity to complete a college degree at minimum cost, assuming you already have earned the associate degree and that you enroll in a state college or university where tuition charges are manageable. Contact the nearest ROTC unit, a Reserve recruiter, or see Appendix C.

4. Appointments to the military academies (Army, Air Force, and Navy) are available to members of the Active Reserve components, who form a special category in the selection procedures. You must meet all prerequisites, the most important of which may be that you be under twenty-one years of age. Contact your Reserve recruiter or the Director of Admissions at your service's academy (see Appendix C).

5. National Apprenticeship Programs are available to enlisted members of the Army, Navy, and Marine Corps, supervised by the U.S. Department of Labor. Programs begin during active duty (entry possible through grade E-5) and cover a wide variety of skilled trades (see Appendix A). Records of military technical training and a log book, in which are recorded military on-the-job training or performance, are maintained for each person. From 4,000 to 6,000 OJT hours are required for certification to journeyman status. However, enlisted members who enroll in these programs and do not complete them before they leave active service are given their records when they are discharged. These records can facilitate advanced standing in an apprenticeship program conducted by a labor union or a private employer. They can also document your military training and experience in connection with other employment. Contact your Education Center or Educational Services Officer.

6. Assistance for students in legal, medical, health services, and chaplaincy fields is provided by the Army, Navy, and Air Force (unless otherwise stated). All are commissioning programs and require varied periods of active duty. See Appendix C for details.

   a. Armed Forces Health Professions Scholarship Program (full scholarship in civilian medical schools).
   b. Uniformed Services University of Health Sciences (fully funded; requires active duty while a student).
   c. Medical Internship or Residency.
   d. Air Force ROTC Nurse Program.
   e. Air Force ROTC Pre-Health Professions Program.
   e. Army and Navy Early Commissioning Program (medical, osteopathic, and dental students).
   g. General Practice Dental Residency.
   h. Army Early Commission Program (sanitary engineers, social workers, optometrists, podiatrists, and psychology students).
   i. Army and Air Force Dietetic Internships.
   k. Army Occupational Therapy Clinical Affiliation.
   l. Army Clinical Psychology Internship.
   m. Chaplain Candidate Program.

In summary, overwhelming evidence exists for the usefulness of advanced education to transition planning. Advanced education can improve your communication skills, enhance your cultural literacy and your self-confidence, and ease your movement from the military environment to a civilian one. The ranks of the unemployed are full of men and women who have not advanced their education.

The military services offer a wide variety of free or low-cost programs that can assist you to acquire a higher level of education while you are still in uniform and in some cases even after you leave active duty. These opportunities can contribute to your own post-service career goals and help to minimize personal and economic stress after you hang up your uniform. The process requires initiative, motivation, and self-discipline. These are all qualities that will improve your military performance while you remain in service and that employers look for in prospective employees.

Chapter 8

Focusing Your Career Objective

So far in Part II we have been concerned with how you can find out where you stand in qualifications for a future civilian career and how you can improve your qualifications by research and advanced education or military training. The career objective has been mentioned as an important part of the process, and the emphasis in this chapter and the next will be on the tactical means of approaching the objective in the more concrete terms of your eventual search for a job that can lead to a career. Keep in mind that the final objective is not an entry-level job, though some separated or retired military personnel may have to accept such a position at first. The transition planning strategies and tactics advocated in this book are intended to help you prepare for a *career* in your chosen occupational field.

It may be well to digress a bit to put into perspective the somewhat vague distinction between entry-level job and career. Though the terms are used both in the military services and in the civilian job market, they may have different meanings to different people.

In the military services, a recruit who has completed basic training and a Class A or basic technical school course in auto mechanics, for example, is qualified for an entry-level assignment as an auto mechanic, working under the supervision of experienced mechanics. But that entry-level mechanic is also launched into a "career" pattern that has been designed to fit the hierarchical environment of the military services. The career pattern provides for advancement in grade (and pay), assignment to more complex tasks, advanced technical training, and eventual promotion to a supervisory role. The entry-level mechanic who confirms his aptitude and abilities during on-the-job training progresses along the career path to become a first-line supervisor.

Beyond that point the *military* aspect of the automotive mechanic career development program begins to take priority over the *technical* aspect. The technical training emphasized in the earlier years is replaced by professional military education (PME), and the emphasis is on the development of leadership and management attributes. Opportunities arise for assignments "out of specialty." At the upper

Military aircraft mechanics find jobs with civilian airlines, but they may need added training to qualify them for FAA licenses.

enlisted grades, the automotive mechanic career field may have little resemblance to the original entry-level assignment. Senior NCO's may be primarily involved with training, command readiness, and/or plans and operations on a command staff. Every military occupational specialty, including those for officers, follows a similar career development pattern.

In the transition process, the career development systems common to the military services may put the military technician or officer specialist at a disadvantage during the job search because it can lead to unrealistic expectations. A non-commissioned officer in the grade of E-5 or above (or an officer in the grade of O-4 or above) will probably already have begun to shift away from training in a technical specialty toward an emphasis on leadership and management. By civilian standards, however, the person may be considered technically undertrained or overspecialized (or both). At the same time, the management training and experience, though valuable, is not likely to result in a job offer. The civilian pattern, you will recall, is to promote seasoned company employees to management positions.

Civilian employers do not routinely provide career planning and counseling services to employees. In fact, the very term "career" is relatively new outside the professions and business management. Does a civilian auto mechanic have a career? Not in the traditional sense of the term. In civilian terms, automotive mechanics is a "trade." Anyone in that trade is expected to "follow" it and become as skilled as possible.

A civilian automobile mechanic may be hired as a trainee, progress through an apprenticeship, be certified as a journeyman mechanic, and eventually qualify for certification as a master mechanic. And that is the end of the line. Pay raises recognize the achievement of higher skill levels, but promotions to successively higher levels of performance and responsibility (service manager, instructor, maintenance supervisor, field representative, district training manager, for example) are not part of the employment pattern. The best qualified mechanic in the shop may be designated "lead mechanic," supervise new trainees, or assume the duties of shop foreman, but he is first and last an auto mechanic and is likely to remain one until he retires.

This traditional system imposed a stability in the workplace that is nowadays becoming less important. Where it still exists, upward mobility for new hires is restricted because each mechanic who is junior to the lead mechanic has his own "seniority." The only way to advance may be to leave the shop and find another job as an auto mechanic—or leave the automotive field for another.

Thus, some career transition advisers shun the term "entry-level job." The recommended job-search technique is to reject any employment opportunity that does not match the qualifications and experience of the job-seeker—no matter how long it takes to find a job. The principle seems to be based on the traditional skill-and-seniority system. The advice is, however, difficult to justify as a general job-search principle because standard business practice is to hire at the bottom and promote from within. Exceptions exist, of course, in which the recommended strategy is indicated—especially in the case of senior NCO's and officers, but it requires the job-seeker to crack the "hidden job" barrier that the standard business practice creates. We will have more to say about that when we discuss job-search techniques. Meanwhile, you should be aware that in certain circumstances an entry-level job may be a dead-end job.

As used in this book, however, the term "entry-level" job describes the lowest level at which employers customarily hire new employees *according to skill categories and the employer's needs.* And it is the employer, not the prospective employee, who decides whether the skills are adequate to his needs. Thus, the term does not imply that you have to start off as a janitor. It may apply to management or sales employees (hired as "trainees"), or to a highly qualified military surgeon whose transition leads to a job on the staff of a health maintenance organization, as well as to an automobile mechanic. Almost invariably, new employees are subjected to company orientation, company-specific job training, and continual evaluation of their personal qualifications before they are confirmed in their job.

Of course, you may have established an overall career objective for planning purposes. Jim, for example, decided that he wanted to pursue a career as an automotive mechanic. In his case the career plan extended far into the future. He really had several objectives: (1) to become a qualified transmission mechanic; (2) to progress to service manager in a transmission rebuild shop; and (3) eventually to establish his own transmission rebuild business. In military terms, Jim's eventual goal was the "final objective"; his first two goals can be thought of as "intermediate objectives."

Like Jim's, your career planning should not end when you find your first job after leaving military service. What we want to do in this chapter, then, is to introduce some considerations involved in defining, refining, or redefining your final career transition objective, however tentative it is. Because career planning and counseling services are not provided by civilian employers, you have to do your own.

Your choice of a final career objective requires consideration of the planning factors already discussed: prior military training and experience, evaluation of your personal attributes, your educational level (or your plans to upgrade it), the entry job requirements in your occupational field, and as much information as you can gather about the qualifications you will need to turn a job into a career. These factors help you prepare yourself for *what* you want to do. You still need to take another couple of steps to determine *where* and *how* you can do what you want to do.

Refining Your Career Objective

One of the most important steps in your self-evaluation is to go beyond *what* you want to do after you leave military service to determine *where* you want to do it. In this sense, *where* means in what kind of a work environment.

A decision about where you want to work after you leave military service sounds easier than it is. What is required is gathering information about where the jobs in your career field actually are. An immediate but rather general source of this information is the statistical supplement to the *Occupational Outlook Handbook*. In Chapter 5 is a sample page from this publication, *Occupational Projections and Training Data*, which contains information on about 200 career fields.

The information in the supplement is only a starting point. Like all statistical data, it is based on what the situation was, not on what it is. Moreover, the statistics do not give information about *trends within industries* that may influence job prospects. The gasoline service station industry, for example, is undergoing changes that have already resulted in the reduction of automobile repair services traditionally available from "service stations." A current trend involves sale of automotive fuels in association with franchised convenience stores like Seven-Eleven or "minimarts" of the kind now often found at ARCO and CONOCO gas stations. Self-service fuel facilities are also widely available. Station employees are becoming retail clerks, cashiers, and sales managers.

Another well-developed trend is the rapid specialization of automotive maintenance and repair under the guidance of national franchisers. Franchised transmission shops, muffler shops, tune-up shops, front-end and brake shops, automotive electronic shops, ten-minute lube and oil-change establishments, and car-wash facilities have begun to dominate the scene. The old neighborhood "garage" has almost disappeared. In a few years, the "service station" may be as outmoded as the livery stable it replaced when the "horseless carriage" first appeared.

Obviously, we cannot discuss the changes in every business environment that may influence your decision of where to seek your post-service career. The burden is on you, and you cannot afford to overlook the fact that the industry environment "out there" is changing rapidly. If your service separation date is off in the future, the career objective you select now may no longer be valid by the time you leave military service. On the other hand, if your ETS date is coming up fast, your final career objective may have to be revised or redefined within a few years of your separation. In the case study that we have been following, Jim's final objective of owning and operating his own transmission shop may have to be redefined to buying a franchise operation.

Thus, you have to go beyond the statistical data to discover the industry trends and how they may influence your choice of where you want to pursue your post-service career. This means more library research in your chosen career field. You may supplement that by field research within the limits of your free time and the location of your current military assignment. But you simply cannot get away without being able to read effectively.

The *Occupational Outlook Handbook* provides some of the information that you will need. Other useful sources are the *Encyclopedia of Second Careers* and *Jobs! What They Are, Where They Are, and What They Pay* (Snelling and Snelling, Inc.). All these publications, however, report only on trends that existed or were evident at the time they were published. You may be able to obtain more up-to-date information from the organizations listed at the end of the narrative discussions.

The most readily available sources of the kind of information suggested are the general press (business section), television, the financial press (*The Wall Street Journal, Forbes, Fortune,* for example), magazines like *Changing Times,* and trade or professional journals. If you are inclined to ignore the financial press as too specialized, I can only hope that you will change your mind. Industry trends are "hot" topics in these publications because they influence profits, or profitability; financial and industry analysts have to be on top of things.

You may scan a lot of newspapers and magazines before you find anything related to your own career objective, but don't give up. Meanwhile, you will have picked up a lot of good information about the state of business and the economy that may influence your transition planning in direction or timing. Be sure, incidentally, to scan the advertisements for employment opportunities and for new equipment or services. Both can provide a lot of clues to what is going on.

Technical, professional, and trade association magazines and newsletters are good sources of information about industry and employment trends. The *Encyclopedia of Associations* has information on thousands of these organizations. One index to this three-volume encyclopedia is arranged by subjects, a device that will help you locate the associations in your field of interest. Many associations of professionals and technicians operate job placement services. Look for these associations and join them.

This kind of research will also help you identify specific employers in your field and enable you to track their progress or lack of progress. Career consultants are divided in their opinions on targeting specific companies during your job search, but if you do so you will want to go beyond the periodical literature and consult business and trade directories to learn everything you can about whatever company you target. Consult your base or post library first, but you will probably have to go to a public library to find directories such as *Thomas' Register, Moody's Industrials*, and the Dun and Bradstreet reports.

The *College Placement Annual* provides brief narrative descriptions of hundreds of private businesses. Another recent nonstatistical survey of fifty-nine prestige American employers in seventeen industries is *Inside Track: How to Get Into and Succeed in America's Prestige Companies*, by Ross and Kathryn Petras. A valuable feature of the book is the inclusion of seventeen industry surveys. Further, the book reports on what it is like to work for each of the companies included, from AT&T to Xerox Corporation.

Approaching the "How" Factor

Most books about job-search techniques are addressed to civilians, predominantly those in professional and managerial fields, who have a track record and are already moving up the career ladder. Their main problem is *where* to seek the next job. The transition process for those who leave military service and seek employment in the civilian labor force, usually in their first civilian job, imposes different requirements and career-changing tactics.

For these people, *how* they will function in the civilian work environment is just as important as *where* that environment may be. The "how" factor concerns the way you perceive your career objective and, more specifically, what role you will assume.

Looking out from the service environment, you may think that you will be satisfied simply to relax in a comfortable job as an automobile mechanic for the next twenty-five years or so. No more PME, no more promotion boards, no more hassles about assignments. But, if you have been paying attention, you should know that this is not likely in the face of rapid technological change and fundamental management and organizational changes in the automobile repair industry. You are more likely to be caught between the two trends and, as in military service, be forced up or out.

Many career options are available to most men and women who leave military service. An automotive mechanic, for example, may aim for a future job as a service manager, a service representative or instructor for an automobile repair service franchiser, an instructor in a vocational training institution, a service representative for a major automobile manufacturer, or a sales representative for an automobile parts manufacturer or distributor. A final career move may be into management as a district or national manager of services, sales, or training. Similar career options are, of course, available to a great many other people who are now, or will be, trained technicians.

Moves of this kind are not "programmed." There are no career counselors or career managers in the business world. You have to keep your eyes and ears open and be alert to opportunities as they occur. In some cases, you may have a chance to make them occur. Many jobs have been created because an employee recognized a need to do something that was not being done and sold the idea to a manager. Either way, you can see that any career move of this kind means that you need to expand your transition research and planning beyond your immediate first-job goal.

Aside from progressively more challenging *employment* in your field, you may decide that you eventually want to go into business for yourself. The possibilities in the automotive field alone are almost endless: own your own automobile repair shop, buy a franchise automotive specialty shop, set up an automotive parts distributorship, or establish a parts manufacturing or rebuild company, for example.

Even the glimmering of an idea that you may want to move up to management or get into your own business means that you have to do even more comprehensive research. You may also include as part of your transition planning academic courses that will improve your communication skills and at least introductory courses in accounting, management, and computer operations. Be ready when opportunity knocks!

Typical Career Transition Strategies

Thoughtful consideration of where and how you want to work will help you determine the kind of career transition you can make, either long-term or short-term. The discussion to this point has been concerned largely with two general career transition strategies: (1) civilian employment in the occupational field in which you have been training and working during military service, which we will call "lateral entry"; and (2) working for yourself. A third strategy is to seek a civilian career in a different field; that strategy is called "retreading."

We will look at each of the three career transition options separately in the next two chapters, but it will soon be clear that career strategies can be and often are changed or merged over time and in individual situations.

Before we turn to these career strategies, however, let us look at some often neglected aspects of transition planning: financial and family planning.

The Role of Personal Planning in Setting Your Objective

Gearing up for a transition to a civilian career involves other considerations than how you can best prepare yourself for that first job and the career you want to pursue. Financial planning is important to ensure a smooth transition; it is essential if you have a family. Where (and how) you are going to live after you leave military service can be a critical factor in your planning.

The first and most obvious consideration is that you are going to have a reduced income or possibly no income at all when you leave military service. The latter situation is more or less self-evident: those who leave military service before they are eligible for retirement receive no benefits of any kind when they are discharged. The case of retirees is considerably better, but even that leaves something to be desired.

Financial planners generally recommend that family income after retirement should equal between 70 and 80 percent of preretirement income in order to maintain the same standard of living. No military member can anticipate that kind of income at retirement unless he or she has a second source of income. Thus the importance of financial planning to the transition objective.

Military members who serve a minimum of twenty years on active duty are eligible for retired pay that is calculated from their base pay. Under current regulations, retired pay for someone who has served on active duty for twenty years amounts of about one half (2.5% × 20 years = 50%) of base pay.

Military personnel who began their active duty service after August 1, 1986, however, are subject to a penalty of 1 percent for each year of active service less than thirty. The intent of Public Law 99–348, passed by Congress in 1986, was to encourage military personnel to remain on active duty for longer periods of service. Beginning in 2006, therefore, a member of the military services who retires with twenty years of service will be entitled to retirement pay of only 40 percent of his or her "high three" base pay. The penalty is to be eliminated at age 62, and retired pay in this illustration will be boosted to the level of 50 percent of the member's "high three" base pay.

The impact of these calculations on those who entered military service after August 1, 1986, is obvious. A service member who plans to retire during or after 2006 with less than thirty years of service will need a carefully constructed transition career plan. He or she should expect to work at a civilian job for upwards of twenty-four years—longer, that is, than the original military career.

Even those who entered service before August 1, 1986, however, will find that the comfortable "half-pay" they expect to receive upon retirement shrinks to about 37 percent of preretirement income after corrections for the loss of housing, subsistence, and other allowances —all of which are nontaxable while they are in uniform.

The average current gross (before taxes) income of an E-7 with twenty years of service is about $27,850 a year, or $2,320 a month. Upon retirement, the same E-7 will be entitled to retired pay of about $10,200 a year, or $850 a month, all of which is subject to federal and state taxes. Clearly, even a senior NCO who retires in 1987 with twenty years of service is going to be at or below the poverty level unless he or she has given serious thought to family financial planning over a period of years.

Moreover, financial planners recommend that anyone at any time have enough savings (or investments) to support a customary style of living for at least six months in case of emergency—losing a job or becoming disabled, for example. By coincidence, the average job search for former military members in the transition process is about six months. Do you have sufficient savings to keep you and your family afloat for six months while you are seeking civilian employment? If you do not, you had better begin to set aside as much of your income as you can afford or even more, even if it means going without that new car and cutting out expenditures for some things that you think you or your family can't live without. While you still have an assured income, pay off or reduce the credit card accounts and consumer loans that are draining off your "spendable" income. Then destroy the credit cards!

An old adage that is worth heeding is to "pay yourself first." To put it another way, set aside some portion of your income as savings before you pay your bills or spend everything you earn. Regular savings that you can leave untouched can grow rapidly at compound interest; that is, you receive interest on the interest your savings earn. If you don't know where to put your savings, you can probably find courses on financial planning on base or in a nearby community. Adult education programs, university or college schools of continuing education, "open universities," and many investment and brokerage houses offer such courses in the evening or on weekends.

Taking "temporary" employment to tide you over until you find a real job is not an answer to your financial needs after you leave military service. Career counselors point out that you have to consider any job search to be a full-time occupation. A temporary job may be necessary to help keep you afloat, but it will also occupy the daytime hours that you need to search for that career job. All too often, the "temporary" job becomes permanent.

Solid pretransition career planning can reduce the time required for an effective job search. In the civilian world, time saved is money earned.

In these days of two-income families, the role of your spouse may become important to the transition process in unexpected ways. Perhaps your spouse has been working on the base or in the local community. Does he or she work because of need or because work is a diversion? Can he or she get a job in the new community where you will be living? If your spouse is not working, is he or she willing to go to work to supplement family income? How is your spouse going to react when he or she leaves for work every morning and you are sitting at home writing résumés and filling out job applications? What will be your domestic situation when you are still searching for a job after three months? Six months? A year? (Don't expect a lot of tender loving care!)

The estimates of monthly living expenses that are necessary to calculate how large a reserve fund you need are particularly tricky. Retirees will have at least some income available for such fixed living expenses as rent or mortgage payments, food, and clothing. Others may have no income at all, with the exception of possible unemployment benefits. How much more you need each month can be estimated in advance by comparing your current household expenses with a postretirement household budget that you can develop yourself. Standard forms for household budgets are widely available at stationery stores; you may have to modify one to suit your circumstances.

Expenses for housing and food are probably the two largest items in any budget. For many military families, the loss of housing allowances and daily subsistence allowances can come as an unpleasant surprise. How much will you have to pay for rent where you are planning to live? If you plan to buy a house, how much will the mortgage payments, taxes, insurance, utilities, and maintenance cost each month? If you no longer have commissary and exchange privileges, or if you have the privileges but cannot use them where you will live, you can add probably add 25 to 30 percent to your usual monthly expenses for food and clothing.

Leaving active military service also requires you to consider extra expenses that may be involved in medical and health care, life insurance, health insurance, a wardrobe suitable to your new situation, travel and recreation, fuel and service for your car, sales and income taxes, tax and legal advice, and even meals taken in restaurants. The cost of college education for children who are still in school has to be considered.

Where you will live certainly plays an important role in career transition planning; moreover, it may determine how you live. The implications of your current situation as they affect your future mobility have to be considered: Do you live in government quarters, rent an apartment or a house, or own a home—perhaps one that you have designated as a place to live when you retire? Those who live in quarters or who rent have certain advantages: They can pick up and move almost anywhere at government expense.

Those who own a home may have the advantage of known housing costs that will remain relatively stable, unlike rent. They are also acquiring at least some cash value or equity that can be converted to cash, either by selling the home, refinancing, or negotiating a second mortgage or an equity loan.

Career transition may create disadvantages for home owners, on the other hand, especially if the career goal focuses on a job that is not available where the home is located and the home has to be sold or rented. Unplanned moves can bring heavy expenses for temporary lodging or result in a distress sale.

In some cases family ties—especially when there are school-age children—may militate against moving anywhere. The jobseeker may have to accept otherwise unacceptable job-search limits.

The selection of a geographical location in which to live and work may greatly influence a job search, or vice versa. Many retirees try to locate or relocate in areas where the military benefits of retirement can be realized: access to commissaries and exchange systems, medical facilities, officer and NCO clubs, and recreational facilities. But are job opportunities available?

Decisions about location may also be influenced by state taxes (or absence of state taxes) on income, the availability of employment for a spouse, the quality of public education for the children, the availability of state universities and colleges for advanced education, and, not least of all, medical needs.

In 1984 a little more than half of the 1.5 million military retirees lived in ten states. Listed by numbers of retirees, the states were California, Texas, Florida, Virginia, Georgia, Washington, North Carolina, Pennsylvania, South Carolina, and New York. If we add Alabama, Arizona, Colorado, Maryland, and Ohio, we can account for two thirds of all the military retires in 1984. Assuming no major retiree population shifts since that time, some interesting observations can be drawn from the figures:

- Nine of the fifteen states listed are among the ten states with the largest active duty military populations (and many military installations).
- Nine of the states are among the Sun Belt states. About 40 percent of all military retirees lived in these states.
- About 18 percent of all retirees lived in the West Coast states of California and Washington. (If retirees in Oregon are added, the West Coast retiree population was about 19 percent of the total.)
- About 7 percent of all retirees lived in the East Coast states of

Maryland, New York, and Pennsylvania. (When Delaware, New Jersey, and the New England states are added, the retiree population in Northeast states was about 13 percent of the total, or just a bit less than the West Coast retiree population.)

- Among the ten states with the largest retiree populations, Texas and Florida, with about 270,000 retirees or about 18 percent of the total, have no personal income tax law. Another of these states, Pennsylvania (with 39,000 military retirees), does not tax retirement income.

- The fifteen states where two thirds of all military retirees resided in 1984 also were the locations of two thirds of the approximately 940,000 civilian jobs under Department of Defense control. About six in ten of these jobs were in five states: California, Virginia, Texas, Pennsylvania, and Maryland. We will have more to say on that subject in the next chapter.

- Most of the fifteen states have excellent public school systems, and all provide abundant opportunities for advanced education through community colleges and state university systems—for you, your children, or both.

Whether you decide to stay where you are, move to another area for personal reasons, or are offered a job in an area that is relatively unknown, it is a good idea to do some investigation of long-term trends. Many retired and former military personnel have been attracted to the Sun Belt states, but economic growth is slowing in the region; unemployment is well above the national average. In 1987 pivotal cities like Houston, Phoenix, and Denver were experiencing hard times. Meanwhile, the Northeast and the West Coast had recovered from some of their economic problems and were experiencing labor shortages. Watch economic (and political) trends carefully as you go about your transition planning. A Presidential election, in particular, can have an important impact on the national economic scene.

A general pattern applies to this kind of investigation, even if you do not plan to move very far when you are discharged:

- Contact the Chamber of Commerce for a list of businesses, business publications (newspapers and magazines), and general information about the target town or city and the region it serves: the economic climate, the educational system, the cultural scene, religious life, historical background, recreational assets (and weather or climate)—everything. I was surprised to learn that Colorado Springs has more than 7,500 employers and at least one important business weekly, and I live there.

- Look for articles in magazines and tourist guides at your library.

Many cities have given their name to a monthly magazine that covers the local scene; ask your librarian to help identify the ones you may want to read.

- Subscribe to the local newspaper and find out what is going on, what interests residents. Scan the employment ads *and* the real estate ads; note the names and addresses of some of the realtors.
- Write to the executive director of the Chamber of Commerce, tell him or her what you are doing, and ask for an appointment.
- Write also to several companies you have targeted and ask for appointments to discuss trends in their business and ways to confirm a career in your occupational field.

Next arrange to visit the area, on leave while you are still in military service. Make it a family affair if possible, but be sure to take along your spouse. Visit the Chamber of Commerce and similar organizations (economic development agencies?); set up some appointments with bankers and business executives (you are only looking for information, remember).

While you are doing that, your spouse can be checking on schools for the kids; researching downtown stores, supermarkets, and suburban shopping malls; visiting museums, galleries, and cultural centers; looking over residential neighborhoods or apartment complexes with a real estate agent (they usually know a lot about what is going on in town, what businesses are up or down, where the best schools are, and who is who; and whatever else goes with "casing the place"—including job prospects for the spouse. By all means, get out of the motel in the evenings and sample the night life, however you define it.

The investigative process suggested here will take some time, but before you leave town you will know more than some of the residents. More important, you will know whether you want to live and work there. If you do, be sure to write letters of thanks to everyone you or your spouse talked to. You might even enclose a copy of your résumé when writing to your business contacts. There are many cases on record of persons who have received firm job offers as a result of such visits.

Financial and family planning guidance is available from such sources as banks, stockbrokers, and insurance companies. A trade association, the International Society of Pre-Retirement Planners (see *Encyclopedia of Associations*), may be able to help in finding expert assistance. Of particular interest to military families are several pamphlets published by the Retired Officers Association (see Reading List). Each pamphlet is written by a retired officer who has been through the transition process. Single copies are available free of charge to members of the association; nonmembers can obtain copies at a nominal charge. The address of the Retired Officers Association is given in Appendix D.

A more comprehensive discussion of family planning is given in *Transition from Military to Civilian Life*. Though the focus of the book is on retirees, much of the information is applicable to other transitioning men and women.

PART II. REFERENCES AND SUGGESTED READING

The Career Guide: 1987 Dun's Employment Opportunities Directory. Dun's Marketing Services.

Daniel J. Cassidy. *The Scholarship Book* (Undergraduate). Englewood Cliffs, NJ: Prentice-Hall, 1984.

College Placement Annual. Merle Dethlefsen and James B. Canfield. *Transition from Military to Civilian Life*. Harrisburg, PA: Stackpole Books, 1984.

Dun and Bradstreet Reports. Roy W. Durgen (ed.). *Women in the Workplace: A Guide for Women Entering or Re-Entering the Workforce*. Toledo, OH: Resource Directories, 1985.

Encyclopedia of Associations. Detroit: Gale Research Co. (annual).

Peter B. Farrell. *Planning for Military Retirement*. Alexandria, VA: The Retired Officers Association, 1985.

S. Norman Feingold. *Scholarships, Fellowships, and Loans* (Graduate). Arlington, MA: Bellman Publishing Co., 1982.

S.Norman Feingold and Avis Nicholson. *The Professional and Trade Association Job Finder*. Garrett Park, MD: Garrett Park Press, 1983.

Anita Gates. *90 Most Promising Promising Careers for the 80's*. New York: Monarch Press, 1982. (Good career profiles, many useful addresses for additional information.)

Sol Gordon (ed.). *Retired Military Almanac*. Uniformed Services Almanac, Inc., P.O. Box 76, Washington, DC 20044 (Revised annually). (Excellent planning handbook for any transitioning military member.)

Len Griffin. *Financial Planning Guide*. Alexandria, VA: Retired Officers Association, n.d. (Purchase from TROA.)

Edward S. Gryczynski and Lewis J. Tolleson. *Help Your Widow While She Is Still Your Wife*. Alexandria, VA: Retired Officers Association, 1986.

Gene R. Hawes. *The Encyclopedia of Second Careers*. New York: Facts on File Publications, 1984.

E.D. Hirsch, Jr., *Cultural Literacy: What Every American Should Know*. Boston: Houghton Mifflin Co., 1987.

William E. Hopke (ed.). *Encyclopedia of Careers and Vocational Guidance* (3 vol.). Chicago: J. G. Ferguson, 1984.

Moody's Industrials.

Occupational Outlook Handbook. (U.S. Department of Labor Bulletin 2250). Washington, DC: USGPO.

Occupational Projections Training Data. (U.S. Department of Labor Bulletin 2251). Washington, DC: USGPO.

Ross Petras and Kathryn Petras. *Inside Track: How to Get Into and Succeed in America's Prestige Companies*. New York: Vintage Books (Random House), 1986.

John J. Russell (ed.). *National Trade and Professional Associations of the United States*. Washington, DC: Columbia Books.

Thomas' Register.

Part III

Transition Planning: Preparing to Make the Move

Chapter 9

Surveying the Job Market: Lateral Entry

One of the benefits of looking at industry trends is that you begin to get a feel for where the jobs are or are likely to be when you take the final steps toward your transition to a civilian career. In this chapter we go behind the scenes to explore the kinds of transition moves that you may want to consider. In Chapter 8 we labeled them lateral entry, retreading, and working for yourself. This chapter focuses on lateral entry opportunities.

Lateral Entry as a Transition Strategy

Lateral entry involves making your military training and job experience work for you as you move directly from your active duty MOS or specialty to a civilian job in the same field or a closely related field. Appendix A (for enlisted members) and Appendix B (for officers) will help you to identify occupations in which such opportunities exist. This strategy is especially appropriate to enlisted members who have been trained in military occupational specialties that have the word *technician* in their title. The strategy should also appeal to officers who have been working in professional fields: medicine and health services, law, and engineering, for example.

According to Department of Labor statistics, about 1.9 million members of the civilian labor force in 1984 had received training in military service that provided them with some or all of the skills they needed to get their jobs. About one third of those workers were in the precision production, craft, and repair occupations. They were employed largely as electricians, automobile mechanics, aircraft engine mechanics, electronic repairers, diesel and heavy equipment mechanics, telephone installers and repairers, construction workers, and blue-collar supervisors.

Administrative, managerial, and executive occupations accounted for another 17 percent of employees in this category. They included accountants and auditors, personnel and training specialists and managers, public administrators (government), managers in the fields

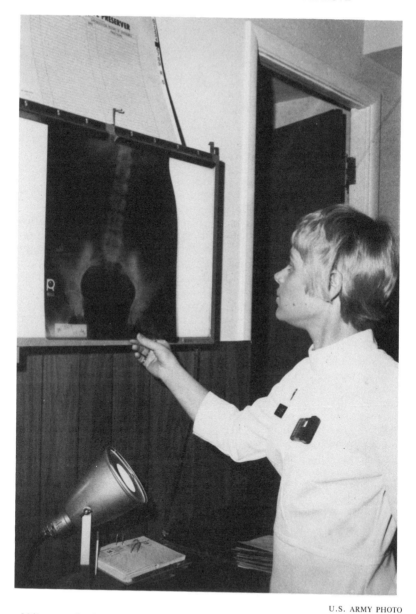

Military medical technicians can acquire transferable job skills as X-ray specialists during service training.

of advertising, public relations, and marketing, inspectors of various kinds, and management analysts.

About 15 percent of all workers who qualified for their jobs as a result of military training worked in such professional specialties as engineering, teaching, computer science, nursing, medicine and dentistry, and the writing crafts.

Other large groups of civilian workers who qualified for their jobs because of their military training were security guards, police and detectives, sheriffs, and other law enforcement officers; sales representatives and sales managers; electrical and electronic technicians; and heavy truck drivers.

Smaller but important groups of military-trained workers were stock and inventory specialists, cooks, secretaries, investigators, office managers, and computer operators.

The range of the jobs and occupations represented in this survey is encouraging. But the situation is even better than it looks because the Department of Labor information accounts for only about 65 percent of the employees who obtained their jobs as a direct result of their military experience. That means that 35 percent of this group of civilian employees were working in occupations that employed fewer workers overall. Airline pilots, demolition experts, divers, seamen, and transportation agents are some of the military occupations in which relatively few civilian workers are employed.

Thus, if your military specialty is not among those listed above, you should not conclude that there is no civilian job market in that occupational field. On the other hand, if there is less demand for your specialty, you will probably have to target your job search somewhat more carefully.

Overall, lateral entry may be the easiest kind of career transition to make. The actual job search will focus on three kinds of employers: private business, nonprofit organizations, and government agencies (federal, state, and local).

Private Industry

Most people in the civilian labor force work for the hundreds of thousands of private companies. You will certainly want to include that category of employers in your eventual job search. Keep in mind that, although the *Fortune* 500 companies get much of the publicity, most of the jobs and much of the action are in the "small business" sector—companies that employ up to five hundred workers. Small business industry representatives claim that they create 80 percent of the new jobs in the civilian job market. Because small businesses tend to be aggressive and expansionist, they can also provide exceptional opportunities for career growth. First-job employment opportunities in private companies are often, but not always, at the entry level for reasons already discussed.

The kind of private business you target for your job search may be heavily influenced by industry trends, some of which have already been mentioned. These trends are sparking changes in management techniques, business structure, and job opportunities.

You do not have to be a farmer to work in agribusiness, for example. There are jobs for mechanics, electronic technicians, engineers, meteorologists, helicopter pilots, truck drivers, computer operators, logistics managers, lawyers, accountants, laboratory technicians, and packaging specialists, among others.

The traditionally conservative banking, finance, and insurance industries have moved into the high-tech era, opening up many new jobs for electronic technicians and computer scientists. Aggressive banking, securities, and insurance marketing programs utilize MBA's, public relations experts, and advertising specialists. Rapidly expanding facilities generate demand for specialized space and facilities managers, along with increasingly complex security techniques— including protection of the computer systems that handle financial transactions.

High tech is also leading to dramatic changes in health care techniques, while health care services are being converted to business enterprises operated by hospital corporations and health maintenance organizations (HMO's) or to group practices and professional corporations. Many physicians, surgeons, and dentists are forgoing the traditional private practice and working on salary. Medical and health insurance has become big business.

Nurses are specializing in such new fields as laser technology. Trauma centers are changing concepts of medical treatment. Aerial MEDEVAC techniques are firmly established and growing. A tendency toward increased utilization of physician assistants is expanding paramedical job opportunities. Meanwhile, the number of hospital jobs for medical assistants and lab technicians is declining as hospital operating companies shave labor costs. (But the jobs are moving to private clinics, physician's offices, and central medical laboratories.)

It is not possible to detail changes in every industry sector, but these few examples should start you thinking about the "where" in your job search strategy—as well as the "how." Military medical technicians (or assistants), for example, who have been trained in a hospital environment will probably have to look elsewhere for employment if they wish to remain in their occupational field. Some medical technicians will want to upgrade themselves to qualify as licensed practical nurses or physician assistants.

Going to work for a private company may mean working under

contract for a defense contractor who needs both your technical expertise and your military background. The kinds of jobs available from defense contractors may not be available in the general workforce: space technicians, aerospace engineers, electronics weapons specialists, and similar specialties more or less unique to the military services. Opportunities for military-trained project and program managers also exist.

There are advantages to this kind of lateral-entry transition. For one thing, you may simply pick up your discharge papers and go to work in civilian clothes, doing very much the same job you had been doing in uniform. Many of your colleagues will also be former members of the military services; you will feel comfortable in your new work environment.

Do not overlook the long-term prospects, however. Contracts are contracts; when they are completed, you may not have a job. Sometimes contracts are canceled before they are completed. In either case you will face all the problems of a real transition to a civilian career as a member of the floating corps of the unemployed.

About the only sensible way to approach employment with a defense contractor is to be hired as a member of the permanent staff, with stated employment rights and privileges. For career military officers that prospect is controlled by DOD policies that impose a "cooling-off" period. Although this policy does not extend to contract employees of defense contractors, you should be aware of the observations made above. Despite solemn promises that you will be converted to permanent status after the "cooling-off" period, by the time you complete your contract the contractor may also have cooled off—on you. What then?

Former enlisted men and women are under no such restrictions, on the other hand, and may be able to find satisfying permanent employment in a wide range of jobs, military-related and others.

Nonprofit Organizations

In addition to the private schools, colleges, universities, and churches that most people think of when the term "nonprofit organization" is mentioned, thousands of trade and industry associations, labor unions, fraternal organizations, professional and technical associations, military-related and veterans' associations such as those listed in Appendix D, public advocacy groups, foundations, educational associations, service agencies, institutes, and research organizations—some of which are military-related—employ hundreds of thousands of people in almost every occupational field or discipline. You can find information about most of these organizations in the *Encyclopedia of Associations*.

The encyclopedia will give you the name, address, and telephone number of each organization, the names of principal officers, the number of employees, the number of members, publications, and the kinds of programs it supports. Such nonprofit organizations as United Way, the American Association of Retired Persons, and the Disabled American Veterans employ large staffs. On the other hand, many nonprofit organizations operate with paid staffs of only two or three people; some of them augment the staff with volunteers.

The term "nonprofit" is somewhat misleading when used to describe these organizations. The laws under which they are organized exempt them from paying taxes because they do not seek to make a profit from their operations but to perform some function related to the greater good of the community. Originally this meant that they were engaged in educational activities or the search for knowledge, supported charitable activities, or ministered to the religious needs of the people. Today, however, the scope of the term includes all kinds of activities, from schools and religious groups to political action committees.

While nonprofit organizations do not seek to make profits, they do not seek to lose money. That has come to mean that they spend every year all the money that they collect from membership fees, donations, endowments, grants, and other sources. Program budgeting and management are obviously very important to the continued operation of these organizations. Some of them operate or control profit-making businesses to generate income for programs, but the federal government is taking a dim view of this kind of situation. In the future, then, sound management and more effective fund-raising will become even more important.

Nonprofit fund-raising and membership drives require specialists in public relations, advertising, computers, tax law, accounting, and financial planning, among other fields.

Operational programs may involve writers and editors, layout artists, TV and motion picture technicians and producers, photographers, counselors, grant and contract specialists, all kinds of technical and professional specialists, and computer programmers and systems analysts.

Support for operational programs requires secretaries, word processor operators, personnel administrators, payroll specialists, legal advisers, librarians, maintenance and repair technicians, nurses and medical technologists, security guards, travel and transportation specialists, computer operators, printing specialists, facilities managers, food and beverage specialists, and many others.

Nonprofit organizations are profitable sources of well-paid jobs that should not be overlooked but often are. A few years ago Catholic University, in Washington, D.C., had such problems finding qualified staff employees that it mounted a campaign to publicize employment opportunities in nonacademic areas, including providing a "hot line" for job-seekers. Most nonprofit organizations, however, tend to fill jobs from within, including recruiting members or alumni, as the situation may apply.

New jobs are advertised publicly, in accordance with rules that govern all Equal Employment Opportunity employers, but the jobs are most likely to be filled as a result of in-house recruiting and net-working. A discreet bulletin that focuses on opportunities for association executives circulates around the Washington area, where two or three thousand important nonprofit organizations have headquarters. Many former senior military officers (and some senior NCO's) are working as executive directors and other key executives in these organizations. Many former military men and women find work in military-related organizations like the Reserve Officers Association and the Air Force Association; others work for veterans' organizations such as the American Legion and the Veterans of Foreign Wars. Do not overlook these and others as potential employers (see Appendix D).

Working for Government

More than eight million civilian workers are government employees; most of them are employed by state, county, and local governments. Many retired or former military members are among them; in some cases they qualify for veteran's preference that may give them an advantage when they apply for jobs or retention rights when reductions in force occur.

You will probably be most familiar with the federal Civil Service establishment, which employs about 1.5 million workers in non-DOD positions and another million or so in DOD positions, at home and abroad. Federal Civil Service jobs cover a wide range of occupations and careers, but the federal ranks are being thinned or are expanding only slowly, whereas the number of state and local government workers is expected to grow more rapidly over the next decade or so.

Some of the more attractive aspects of federal Civil Service employment are the following:

- The Civil Service is, by law, an Equal Employment Opportunity employer that cannot turn you down on the basis of race, religion, sex, or age.
- The Civil Service is a hierarchical organization, much like the military services. It also has standardized job descriptions, grades, pay scales, performance evaluations, and career development patterns. Once you have become a Civil Service worker,

you know where you are and—usually—where you can go with your career.

- The Civil Service offers opportunities to enter at almost any grade level, depending on your qualifications for a particular job.
- All applications for employment are screened for eligibility and then evaluated against objective standards for qualifying education, training, and experience; in most cases, applicable experience can be substituted for some of the educational requirement. You are not forced to get by personnel "gatekeepers" and screeners to get a hearing. Entry-level written qualifying examinations are not required, but you may be subject to a security investigation for certain jobs.
- Interviews are arranged only after your application has been evaluated and a grade or score assigned that puts you among the top few contenders for any particular job; if your application is rejected or assigned a low score, you will be notified. (If you are very close to the top of the eligibility list, you may also be called for an interview at some future time or your name will remain on a register to be considered for future openings in the same job classification.)
- You can apply for as many different jobs as you think you are qualified for and to as many locations, in the United States and abroad, as you want; no one keeps track of anything but your standard application form. If you are turned down for a job at one location, you may be top scorer at another.
- Federal Job Information Centers are operated in cities across the country. The Centers are listed in most telephone books under United States Government; a nationwide list of job centers can be obtained from the Office of Personnel Management, Federal Job Information Center, 1900 E Street NW, Washington, DC, 20415. You do not, and should not, pay anyone to help you find a Civil Service job.

Department of Defense Employment

The Department of the Army has a policy of assisting separating soldiers to qualify for federal Civil Service jobs in its own departmental branch of the Civil Service. Similar opportunities are afforded separating military members by the other services. Career military officers who seek employment with a DOD Civil Service agency may be subject to a "cooling-off" period under DOD policies.

DOD Civil Service jobs can offer easy transition from uniform to three-piece suit (or jeans, as the case may be) because they often involve skills and/or experience that are technically in the civilian area but are military-unique. Tank mechanics, electronic weapons repairers, and military intelligence analysts and counterintelligence agents are a few examples. Uniquely military training and experience in supply, logistics, maintenance, operations, nuclear power, personnel administration, procurement and contracting, and finance and accounting may often be converted to DOD Civil Service careers.

Your base or station Civil Service Office can help you identify fields of employment and job opportunities with DOD agencies on-base, across the country, and even around the world. Nearly a million civilians work for the Department of Defense in the United States. Some idea of where the jobs are (but not what they are) is provided in the accompanying table. Do not wait until you need a job, however. An early contact can help you determine the qualifications needed for employment in various jobs, any restrictions that apply, and application procedures.

Table 5. Distribution of DOD Civilian Workers
(September 30, 1984)

State	Army	Navy/ Marines	USAF	Other DOD	DOD Total
Alabama	23,480	10	3,110	470	27,070
Alaska	2,480	160	1,740	40	4,420
Arizona	5,295	470	3,890	360	10,015
Arkansas	3,115	10	1,400	60	4,585
California	18,215	78,475	29,435	7,650	133,800
Colorado	5,605	15	8,425	445	14,490
Connecticut	575	2,870	425	770	4,640
Delaware	225	—	1,505	20	1,750
District of Columbia	6,550	7,810	1,065	610	16,035
Florida	1,675	18,900	9,325	1,125	31,025
Georgia	16,435	3,385	16,580	1,070	37,470
Hawaii	4,860	13,225	2,605	110	20,800
Idaho	410	30	760	15	1,215
Illinois	13,530	2,340	5,215	1,240	22,325
Indiana	6,600	6,135	1,220	425	14,380
Iowa	855	10	485	120	1,470
Kansas	5,080	180	1,330	190	6,780
Kentucky	10,720	2,525	280	330	13,855
Louisiana	4,925	1,770	2,145	290	9,130
Maine	290	905	805	70	2,070
Maryland	16,985	15,515	3,340	5,475	41,315
Massachusetts	5,210	890	4,185	1,660	11,945
Michigan	7,640	95	2,275	2,065	12,075
Minnesota	1,385	115	850	365	2,715
Mississippi	4,415	2,745	3,440	145	10,745

State	Army	Navy/ Marines	USAF	Other DOD	DOD Total
Missouri	13,055	1,300	1,240	4,770	20,365
Montana	395	—	720	15	1,130
Nebraska	1,690	10	2,015	45	3,760
Nevada	255	290	1,350	40	1,935
New Hampshire	535	8,745	720	135	10,135
New Jersey	18,350	6,425	2,390	1,090	28,255
New Mexico	4,685	185	4,265	410	9,545
New York	10,555	1,050	5,390	2,045	19,040
North Carolina	6,315	7,920	1,180	265	15,680
North Dakota	345	—	1,280	30	1,655
Ohio	1,915	1,630	20,860	8,750	33,155
Oklahoma	6,075	75	18,825	230	25,205
Oregon	2,440	40	465	50	2,995
Pennsylvania	18,605	25,565	1,500	8,180	53,850
Rhode Island	270	3,540	255	300	4,365
South Carolina	3,190	14,170	2,560	125	20,045
South Dakota	475	—	750	15	1,240
Tennessee	2,610	1,045	945	2,840	7,440
Texas	28,610	2,230	31,400	2,215	64,455
Utah	5,210	90	15,025	2,125	22,450
Vermont	260	5	235	65	565
Virginia	30,085	57,770	4,385	11,530	103,770
Washington	6,220	20,045	2,675	400	29,340
West Virginia	1,100	45	345	25	1,515
Wisconsin	2,030	65	820	165	3,080
Wyoming	185	—	675	80	940

Source: Department of Defense. Figures rounded to nearest "5".

Nonmilitary Agencies

Other agencies besides the Department of Defense utilize former military members with unique training and skills. The Central Intelligence Agency, the Federal Bureau of Investigation, and the Department of State, for example, all utilize military-trained intelligence and security personnel, specialized secure communications experts, cryptanalysts, and counterintelligence agents. And there are other specialized functions and jobs in many government agencies:

- Anyone interested in security and law enforcement as a career should not overlook the fact that the federal government operates more than two dozen law enforcement agencies. In addition to the Secret Service, the Federal Bureau of Investigation, the Immigration and Naturalization Service, the Drug Enforcement Administration, and the quasi-military U.S. Border Patrol, there are the U.S. Marshals, the Executive Protective Agency, the U.S. Forest Service, Treasury Department agents, and Postal Service investigators—and more. These organizations require a wide variety of administrative and support people of all kinds, not only law enforcement officers.

- The Federal Emergency Management Administration (FEMA) carries out or coordinates contingency planning and training for disasters that range from floods to nuclear, biological, and chemical warfare. The agency utilizes many former military members who have had training and experience as emergency management specialists, firefighters, damage control specialists, and law enforcement specialists, among others. FEMA's activities are frequently carried out in conjunction with state and local authorities.

- Nuclear engineers may find employment with the Department of Energy, the Nuclear Regulatory Commission, or the Tennessee Valley Authority.

- The National Aeronautics and Space Administration (NASA) has been an important source of jobs for former military aeronautical and space technicians and engineers, electronic technicians and engineers, and others in similar specialties. But NASA's programs reach into a variety of other support fields, such as space medicine, life-support systems, dietetics, meteorology, computer programming and systems analysis, communications, security, public relations, and so on.

- The National Oceanographic and Atmospheric Administration (NOAA) employs mapping technicians, space technicians, boat operators (including deep submergence vehicle operators), computer operators, pilots, oceanographers, various engineers and research scientists, and many others in military-related specialties.

Almost every agency of the federal government (excluding Congress and some special commissions) is under the jurisdiction of the Civil Service or Office of Personnel Management. The scope of federal Civil Service employment is almost without limit. The *U.S. Government Manual*, available at most libraries, describes every federal department, agency, and quasi-governmental agency and commission. The manual includes the names of key officials and the address of each agency. Do not hesitate to write for career and employment information.

State, County, and Local Government

State, county, and local governments maintain civil service establishments that in many cases parallel that of the federal government. In other respects, they are more comprehensive because they operate public works (water, sewer, and power plants), staff state and county educational institutions and hospitals, maintain police and firefighting forces, construct and repair roads and highways, and perform many direct-contact public, social, legal, and welfare services not commonly found in the federal Civil Service. Currently, state, county, and local government employment opportunities are increasing more rapidly than federal job opportunities.

Many jobs at this level are found in quasi-governmental "authorities," such as port authorities, housing and planning authorities, and transportation authorities. They usually have separate personnel systems. Local school boards may also operate their own employment systems; they can be valuable sources of employment for administrative and support workers as well as teachers.

Former and retired military men and women usually have job preference as veterans when applying for state and local government positions. A special category of employment counselors has been created, under a federal program, to help veterans find jobs. Furthermore, the "dual compensation" laws that plague retired career military officers do not apply at these levels.

State employment offices are usually scattered around each state, under the supervision of the Department of Labor in the capital. Opportunities for county and municipal jobs are often posted in county courthouses or administrative offices and at town halls and city halls; they may also be advertised in local newspapers. Jobs in state educational institutions and county or municipal community colleges are usually posted or on file in the institution's personnel office. (Some, by the way, have two personnel offices, one for professional staff (teachers and educational administrators) and one for administrative and support staff. Be sure you are in the right place!)

Even if you are not ready to make your transition, you can write for job circulars and bulletins. Or go to one of these places and examine the listings, check out the prerequisites for employment, find out application procedures, and note the pay rate or salary. Get past the "gatekeepers"—the secretaries in personnel offices are notoriously protective of their bosses—and talk to the personnel director about employment opportunities in your field. Everything helps.

International Opportunities for Lateral Entrants

Many military men and women develop an enduring interest in international affairs. In the growing "global village" of our time, thousands of American civilians are living and working abroad; other thousands live in the United States but pursue careers that provide opportunities for travel to foreign countries. The employers are the same as those already discussed: private businesses, nonprofit organizations, and governments.

Your own experiences living overseas (or as a foreign area expert, with foreign language skills) do not automatically qualify you for an international career, though they may be a valuable asset. Employers, rather, seek applicants who already have the professional or technical qualifications that they need to get a job done.

International opportunities with private companies that operate abroad are usually limited by the policies of foreign governments. In general, American companies are required to hire nationals of the country in which they operate, with exceptions for jobs for which no nationals are qualified. Those exceptions are relatively rare, especially in the multinational manufacturing companies that operate in the more developed countries. As a general rule, such companies train and develop their own international staff in-house. Most of them will never live abroad, though they may do a lot of traveling. Company employees who are transferred to overseas locations are likely to be managers, economic experts, engineers, and production specialists who have had long careers with the company. Breaking the established barriers is difficult.

The best opportunities for former and retired military lateral-entry personnel interested in working abroad for private American companies are likely to be with American airlines that operate over international routes; international construction and petroleum companies and travel agencies (e.g., American Express); defense contractors and other offshore contractors and consultants; and financial institutions (banks, securities, insurance). Many employees of these kinds of companies function as trainers or supervisors of foreign national employees, though there are opportunities for specialists in such fields as accounting, automotive maintenance, aviation and flight operations, communications, computer operations and repair, construction trades, demolitions, electronic weapons repair, engineering, food service, geodesists, health services, legal affairs, logistics, mechanics of all kinds, personnel and payroll specialists, photographers, public relations, radio and TV broadcasting, security transportation and travel, and many others that have military equivalents.

Directories of American companies that operate abroad are available from several sources (see Reading List). International Chambers of Commerce, located in many major cities, publish lists of members and usually newsletters highlighting member activities. They also hold luncheon meetings, which you may be able to attend as a guest and at which you can meet principals.

Many nonprofit organizations operate international programs, though not too many are likely to be sources of lateral-entry employment. Like private businesses, they are restricted to employment of nationals of the country where they operate. Nevertheless, disaster relief agencies like the Red Cross and CARE, service agencies such as the International YMCA and the USO, religious organizations like Church World Service, and a number of international medical service organizations are well worth investigating. *U.S. Nonprofit Organizations in Development Assistance Abroad* (see the Reading List) will assist you.

Government employment probably offers the best and most accessible opportunities for employment abroad, especially in the Department of Defense. Some military members are able to transfer directly into Civil Service jobs from their last overseas assignment. But many other federal departments and agencies operate overseas. A pamphlet, *Federal Jobs Overseas*, prepared by the Office of Personnel Management, is sold by the U.S. Government Printing Office, Washington, D.C. 20402. The *Federal Jobs Digest*, a commercial publication, contains notices of many federal jobs abroad. Or write for information to:

Agency for International Development. Opportunities in accounting and auditing, agriculture, community development, economics, engineering, housing, public health, public safety (police/security), transportation, and some staff jobs: secretaries, computer operators, administrative officers, etc.

    Recruitment Division, Room 1430, SA-1
    Agency for International Development
    Washington, DC 20523

Bureau of Public Roads. Overseas technical assistance program; construction of the Inter-American Highway. Employment opportunities in highway planning, design, construction, and maintenance; construction equipment operators and repairers.

    Bureau of Public Roads
    Washington, DC 20235

Central Intelligence Agency. Field agents, communicators, intelligence analysts, administrative support personnel.

    Director of Personnel
    Central Intelligence Agency
    Washington, DC 20505

Defense Intelligence Agency. Foreign intelligence jobs.

    Civilian Personnel Branch
    Defense Intelligence Agency
    Washington, DC 20301

Department of Agriculture. Foreign Agricultural Service (not limited to agricultural scientists); administrative support personnel.

Foreign Agricultural Service
Department of Agriculture
Washington, DC 20250

Department of the Army. Opportunities for cartographers, engineers, equipment specialists, recreation specialists, and many others.

U.S. Army Civilian Personnel Center
Attn: PECC-FSS, Hoffman II Building
200 Stovall Street
Alexandria, VA 22332

Department of the Air Force. A wide range of jobs.

Central Overseas Rotation and Recruiting Office
1947 HSG/MPKS, Room SE 871
Department of the Air Force
Washington, DC 20330

Department of Commerce. International trade, product and commodity analysis, trade fairs, etc.

Personnel Office, Room 5001
Department of Commerce
Washington, DC 20230

Department of the Interior. Employment opportunities in Alaska and elsewhere.

Office of Personnel, Room 2640
Department of Interior
18th and C Streets NW
Washington, DC 20240

Department of the Navy. Accounting, auditing, administrative support workers, engineering, medical research (Naval Medical Units), sciences, including social sciences (Office of Naval Research maintains offices abroad), and others.

Overseas and Return Placement
800 North Quincy Street, Room 1107
Arlington, VA 22203

Department of State. Foreign Service Officers (formal examination required) in Administrative Affairs fields: Budget and Fiscal, General Services (property management and maintenance, motor pools, supply management, procurement and contracting, transportation, shipping, and travel), Personnel, Security, Communications, and Information Systems; other fields are Consular Affairs, Economic Affairs, and Political Affairs. Foreign Affairs Specialists (no examination) who work as Foreign Service Secretaries, Support Communications Officers, Budget and Fiscal Officers, Communications Electronics Officers, General Services Officers, Personnel Officers, Security Engineering Officers, Security Officers, Building and Maintenance Specialists, Construction

(Civil) Engineers, Systems Managers, Physicians, Nurses, and Medical Technicians, Diplomatic Couriers, and Electronic Engineers.

    Recruitment Division
    U.S. Department of State
    P.O. Box 9317, Rosslyn Station
    Arlington, VA 22209

National Oceanographic and Atmospheric Administration. Meteorologists and electronic technicians for weather stations in Alaska, Puerto Rico, Hawaii, Guam, and Antarctica; engineers and electronic repairers in Antarctica.

    Chief, Personnel Division
    National Oceanographic and Atmospheric Administration
    6010 Executive Boulevard
    Rockville, MD 20852

National Security Agency. Radio intelligence specialists, cryptanalysts, computer systems analysts, etc.

    National Security Agency
    9800 Savage Road
    Ft. George G. Meade, MD 20755

Panama Canal Commission. Medical officers, medical technicians, machinists, cable splicers, heating and cooling mechanics, power plant operators, etc.

    Office of Personnel Administration
    Panama Canal Commission
    APO Miami 34011

Peace Corps. Peace Corps volunteers are needed in specialty fields: agriculture (farm mechanics, etc.), civil engineering, nutrition/hygiene, skilled trades (carpenters, electricians, masons, mechanics, sheet metal workers, plumbers, welders), vocational education, and forestry and fisheries (mechanics). Two years as a Peace Corps volunteer doesn't make you rich (living allowance and $175 a month), but you receive language and other foreign area training and work at a challenging job. It is a good apprenticeship for an international career: former PC volunteers have preference in the Foreign Service; many convert to PC staff positions, others have achieved high-level government positions, and some have made careers in international business. Note: there is no upper age limit, but PC will not accept anyone with a military intelligence background or a current "military obligation"—which may include a Reserve obligation.

    Office of Administrative Services
    Peace Corps
    806 Connecticut Avenue NW
    Washington, DC 20526

United States Customs Service. Customs inspectors and security officers, administrative support personnel.
U.S. Customs Service
1301 Constitution Avenue NW
Washington, DC 20229
United States Information Agency. Foreign Service Information Officers (same examination as for Department of State Foreign Service Officers): career fields emphasize public relations, newswriting, magazine journalism, radio/TV broad casting and other aspects of "public diplomacy" in an international environment; Foreign Service Specialists (no exam) work in the field as secretaries, administrative officers, librarians, radio engineers/technicians, printing plant technicians, security officers, radio correspondents (Voice of America), and English teachers (TESOL).
Office of Personnel Services, Room 518
U.S. Information Agency
301 Fourth Street SW
Washington, DC 20547

Finally, do not overlook possibilities for international careers with state government. The Constitution gives the federal government sole responsibility for developing and executing foreign policy, but many of the states operate aggressive programs in the field of international commerce, including the development of "free trade zones." California has a state commission on world trade. Port authorities compete for shipping and other business all over the world. According to recent reports, thirty-eight states maintain representatives in Japan alone. Others are located in key cities around the world.

State programs in the international field vary widely and are oriented toward economic development. I have visited half a dozen state offices, and each has its own focus: Nebraska concentrates on exports of corn and agricultural equipment and chemicals; South Carolina is concerned with the Port of Charleston and its declining role in the textile industry; Arizona deals with high-tech industries and export promotion. The former governor of Colorado, in a discussion of changes in the state during his twelve years in office, summed up the importance of international programs in all the states. When he took office, he said, his economic horizon was limited by the neighboring states. Twelve years later he was heavily involved with the Far East, Southeast Asia, Western Europe, and the United Kingdom.

Most state employees in international programs work in the state capital, though they may travel abroad. The program emphasis is on matters related to economics, but the scope of employment is much broader. Various states employ experts in public relations, vocational and technical training, foreign areas and languages, law, port management and security, statistics, accounting, and computer operations, among other military-related occupational fields. The coordination of state programs involves working with such diverse organizations as colleges and universities, technical institutes, federal agencies (Customs, the Commerce Department, Treasury, etc.), federal, state, and local law enforcement agencies, industry and trade associations and other nonprofit organizations, labor unions, and, of course, banks and other financial institutions and private industry.

International programs are usually included in the overall responsibilities of state development agencies or state departments of commerce. A list of the directors of these larger state agencies can be obtained from the National Association of State Development Agencies, Suite 526, Hall of States, 444 North Capitol Street NW, Washington, DC 20001. You will have to take it from there.

Chapter 10

Surveying the Job Market: Retreading

Many of those who leave the military services will not want to continue working in the occupational fields in which they were involved while in uniform. Others, especially those in combat arms specialties and other military-unique specializations, will not be able to pursue civilian careers in those fields. The two principal strategies available to people in these groups are: (1) *retreading*, or carving out a civilian career in a new field, and (2) working for themselves. In general, both strategies require additional education or training or retraining. This chapter discusses retreading; working for yourself is discussed in Chapter 11.

A career transition that involves retreading means that you move into a civilian career that does not parallel your military experience, though it may make use of some of it.

The assumption here is that you have done some serious transition planning as you look ahead to the time when you will leave military service. Too often both first-term and long-term (but noncareer) enlisted military members who have not established career objectives leave service with only the vague idea that they will find "something." Some have heard about veterans programs that offer opportunities for vocational training or retraining, and that is about as far as they get. No one who has reached this point in this book should be under such a delusion.

If anything, retreading requires more careful transition planning than lateral entry. First of all, almost any training, retraining, or advanced education undertaken after service has the effect of keeping the trainee or student out of the job market, usually at an economic disadvantage despite the availability of the various GI Bill provisions and veterans programs. Thus, the importance of an organized, "heads up" approach to transition planning. Everything that can be done in advance should be done to prepare for whatever after-service training or education is anticipated.

Second, many of the vocational training programs available to veterans are short-term and intended only to prepare trainees for entry-

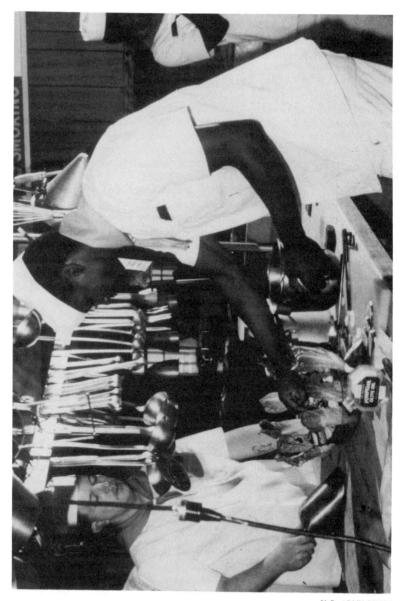

The food service industry is growing more rapidly than some other civilian sectors.

level jobs in traditional occupations that are growing slowly, if at all. Others virtually promise employment but at such a low skill level that the career potential is negligible. These "Band-aid" approaches are not what this book is about. They may keep veterans off the streets, but that is about all.

Third, some training programs that seem attractive do not or cannot fully qualify trainees for jobs. One such program that I am familiar with trains veterans to be tractor-trailer drivers. It is popular in my hometown among young first-termers who leave military service after a minimal enlistment in an Army combat arms specialty. The program does indeed train students to drive the huge trucks, but it does not necessarily lead to jobs as truck drivers. Why not, since trucking is big business?

A few minutes of discussion with a veterans' job counselor suggested some reasons. Most heavy trucking companies in my area hire only drivers who have logged five years or more of over-the-road experience. Insurance considerations favor hiring drivers over the age of twenty-five. Drivers in interstate commerce must pass written tests required by the Interstate Commerce Commission. The job of driver-helper that used to provide entry-level employment has all but disappeared.

Thus the student driver-trainee graduates with a certificate but has nowhere to go. He has paid hundreds of dollars (over the amount of the support grant available through the program), he has had living expenses to pay, and now there is no job in sight.

Moral: jumping into a training program just because it is available is dumb. Even a few hours spent looking into job prospects can prevent such a situation. The *Occupational Outlook Handbook* has all the necessary information and more, based on national trends. The state veterans' job counselors know the local labor market. In fact, the job situation is so dismal in my area that the counselors who speak at pretransition briefings discourage young soldiers from staying in the area after they are discharged. But every day I see the same big semis with the sign on the back: CAUTION! DRIVER TRAINEE. Take the advice.

Another form of retreading involves preparation for a professional career. Some examples are: teaching, sales (real estate, insurance, and securities), the clergy, law, medicine and health care professions, engineering, banking, and business management. All these career fields require advanced education, retraining, or experience beyond that available to most men and women who are serving in uniform. We will examine only a few of these potential careers in this chapter, however.

The premise here is that men and women whose career objectives include law, engineering, or health professions will have done more than the usual amount of pretransition planning. That is not always the case, of course. Several clergymen I know have felt the call under combat conditions and have, figuratively speaking, proceeded from foxhole to theological seminary. I have met physicians whose experience as enlisted medical technician spurred them on to qualify for and complete medical school. In general, however, the men and women who pursue these careers after military service are usually highly motivated, self-directed, and well aware of the rigid academic prerequisites and often strenuous professional training that lies ahead. Job and career placement services are usually available to these people at or through the colleges, universities, and professional schools they attend.

Suffice it to say, then, that all retreads should take advantage of the many educational and counseling opportunities available to them while they are in uniform. Career planning should focus on researching career objectives, improving or confirming educational qualifications even if that means nothing more than qualifying for the GED and improving basic communication skills, taking aptitude and vocational interest inventory tests, sitting for required college or professional school entrance exams, and, finally perhaps, working with an Educational Services Officer on the evaluation and selection of appropriate training or academic institutions. Failure to utilize these opportunities may turn a transition into a pilgrimage.

Those who plan to enter health care professions should, of course, be aware of the post-service career education opportunities available through the Armed Forces Health Professions Scholarship Program, the Uniformed Services University of Health Sciences, and the internships described in Appendix C. Various ROTC programs (especially the scholarship and the Army simultaneous membership programs) offer opportunities to utilize prior military service to reduce expenses while completing college.

The potential retread careers that we will look at more carefully are in the fields of real estate, finance and banking, insurance, and secondary school teaching. These occupational fields have several characteristics in common:

- They offer transitioning military men and women relatively easy access to important professional careers without much reliance on prior military technical training.
- They require training that cannot usually be acquired in military service or involves on-the-job training.
- Earnings are often based on the production of sales and paid as commission, not salaries (education excepted).
- Success depends on individual initiative, perseverance, enthusiasm, on-the-job training, and experience as much as on prior military or academic credentials.

Almost everyone these days deals with practitioners in one or more of the sales fields—real estate, insurance, and securities (stocks and bonds). All of us have met secondary school teachers in the course of our own education. Few of us, in or out of uniform, have more than vague ideas about how these people qualify for their profession or, possibly, what they do when they do qualify. Let us look a little more closely at them.

Real Estate Careers

Career changers are often attracted to residential real estate sales because of the potentially high income, but a real estate career can also involve commercial property sales, property management, sales management, appraising residential and commercial real estate, and service as a broker—who runs the show. Real estate professionals may become involved with investing and investment ventures and sometimes with the development of residential or commercial real estate projects.

Employment in the real estate sales field is growing at an average rate, though economic conditions and regional patterns of growth have more than the usual impact on the industry. A concise overview of the field can be found in the *Occupational Outlook Handbook*. The detailed discussion in the book *Your Successful Real Estate Career* is highly recommended. The author, Kenneth W. Edwards, is a retired military officer who writes from experience. The discussion here will deal largely with considerations that may influence your own career transition planning.

Preparation for a career in real estate requires independent study that leads first to a state license as a sales agent and subsequently to a broker's license or to certification in such specialties as real estate appraising. The introductory course in "Principles of Real Estate" has been more or less standardized and is offered by many community colleges, state colleges and universities, independent real estate schools, and some operating realtors. Courses are often scheduled in evening hours or on weekends. You should consider completing this basic requirement while you are still in uniform. In fact, many military members work as part-time sales agents while in service.

You are not likely to find this course offered on a military installation, however, and you probably will not qualify for tuition assistance. Moreover, because of variations in state laws, a course taken in one state may not prepare you for a real estate license examination in another. In your transition planning, therefore, you should probably already have decided where you will live and work before you take a real estate sales course. Some states do recognize real estate licenses issued by other states, on the other hand. A visit or a telephone call to the nearest Board of Realtors can clear up these points as they may apply to you.

The introductory course in real estate is only an entry-level licensing requirement. It does not substitute for other education. Although many successful real estate sales agents have never gone beyond high school, brokers are increasingly seeking agents who have college degrees. Subsequent career education—and there is plenty of it ahead—involves heavy doses of property and contract law, tax law, economics, government regulations, and finance.

Even though you have your sales license, you cannot sell real estate on your own. You must apply for a job with a broker or Realtor—a registered title for a broker who is a member in good standing of the local Board of Realtors and the National Association of Realtors. If you are accepted, however, you do not have a job in the ordinary sense of the word. Rather, you are an independent contractor and your income will come from the *commissions that you earn for the broker*. That is to say, the commission on the real estate that you sell is paid to the broker, not to you.

Varying arrangements govern the amount of the commission "split" between the broker and the sales agent. Generally, the agent receives 50 percent of the total commission, which now ranges from 5 to 7 percent of selling price for residential property and is 10 percent on commercial and farm property. Many considerations are involved in the amount of the split, but the sales agent's maximum income from annual sales of a million dollars worth of real estate—now becoming the minimum sales target—could be about $30,000. The median income in 1984 for real estate sales agents was, however, only about $19,000. This means that half the agents earned less than that amount. It also means that half of them earned *more*.

Beginning real estate agents seldom reach one million dollars in sales during their first year. In fact, the average sales agent does not sell anything at all for the first six months and may not earn even the median income for several years. Meanwhile, the hours are long; much of the sales work is done in the evenings and on weekends.

This evening and weekend pattern seems to have led to the idea that real estate sales can be a profitable part-time activity. Nothing could be further from the truth. The governing rule is: "Full-time sales is one of the highest paid occupations; part-time sales is one of the lowest paid occupations."

This kind of employment relationship imposes considerable burdens on beginning real estate agents, especially those accustomed to a structured work environment, regular hours, and a predictable income. Successful sales agents are self-starters who are highly motivated. The failure rate is very high.

Sales agents do more than show houses, write contracts, and collect commissions. They must *create* sales. Above all else, they hustle for "listings," the basis for a successful career in real estate. Postcard campaigns, door-knocking treks through whole neighborhoods, friendly calls on hopeful "For Sale by Owner" families (to convince them that they need an agent), passing out business cards at cocktail parties, weddings, bar mitzvahs, and wakes (the bereaved widow/widower may have to leave the family home), involvement in community service organizations (networking, again), telephone campaigns, and similar activities go on nonstop. Good real estate sales agents are seldom at their desks.

Beginning sales agents who do not meet the broker's standards for production are released after a trial period. Replacements are readily available. Anyone who plans to enter real estate sales must have the financial assets and other resources necessary to allow a comfortable survival without any additional income for at least the first six months or, better, the first year.

As independent contractors, furthermore, real estate sales agents are responsible for paying some or all the expenses associated with everything from advertising to washing their automobiles—which they provide and maintain. The broker or Realtor provides desk space, telephone, computer facilities, in-house training, and other services.

Sales agents are responsible for keeping their own tax records and paying federal and state income taxes and federal social security taxes. Courses on tax law, record-keeping, and tax filing are essential —and, usually, conducted in the evening hours. Try to take them while you are in uniform.

Real estate sales agents who succeed frequently become brokers by means of advanced professional courses that qualify them for the state examination. Courses developed by the National Association of Realtors are usually given under the supervision of the local Board of Realtors, often in the evening or on weekends. States require brokers to have several years of experience as sales agents before they can be licensed, but the courses may be taken while working as a sales agent.

Sales is not the only real estate career. Others in the field are sales managers, property managers, and appraisers—who may work on salary, salary-plus, or a fee basis. In most cases the people who work in these areas have had an "apprenticeship" of several years as a sales agent. The National Association of Realtors has also developed standards, training programs, and procedures for people who choose these allied occupations. Free information about real estate careers and available training programs is usually available from the nearest Board of Realtors; or write to the National Association of Realtors, 430 North Michigan Avenue, Chicago, IL 60611. Many state Real Estate Commissions, the governmental supervising agencies, publish handbooks, manuals, and newsletters. Contact the Real Estate Commission in the state capital.

Securities Sales Agents

The people who buy and sell stocks and bonds, mutual funds, and other financial investments are known variously as registered representative, account executive, or stockbroker. Their activities are on the *retail* side of finance and banking. Securities sales is a fast-track field; employment is available all across the country, but competition is stiff.

Account executives enter the field as trainees, but college degrees are usually required. Courses in business, finance, and economics are useful. An MBA may help you along the road to management, but most account executives do not seek management responsibilities. Seasoned producers may have such titles as senior account executive or vice president, but these titles do not imply that they have management roles.

Securities salesmen generally are hired and trained by the branch offices of large companies (Merrill Lynch, Shearson Lehman Hutton) or by locally owned independent brokerage firms. Training may last as long as a year and includes preparation for the Series-7 or Registered Representative exam. Some trainees are hired on salary but phase out into commission-only income by the end of the first year. Other firms take on only people who have passed the licensing examination and pay them nothing but commissions.

Trainees who become full-fledged account executives are paid on a commission-only basis; their status is that of independent contractor, much like that of real estate sales agents. (A trend toward salaried account executives may be emerging.)

Securities sales agents are more likely than real estate salespeople to be desk-bound. A computer terminal and a telephone are the account executive's tools. But the objective is the same: to create transactions that earn commissions for the company. An effective new account executive may earn $30,000 in his or her first year. Incomes of $50,000 to $100,000 are not unusual.

Beginners may be provided referrals generated by advertising campaigns or given walk-ins and telephone inquiries. Eventually they must conduct their own campaigns to develop client lists, often using the telephone to make cold calls or to follow up a mail campaign. They attend business and community events. Meetings with clients or prospects occupy evening and weekend hours. They conduct seminars on investing techniques or special-purpose financial instruments. Some become financial or estate planners with an eye to marketing their own products—which now often include insurance.

The work pace is relentless, sparked by the excitement generated by the volatile securities and commodities markets and fueled by the pressure to create more transactions today than yesterday. About two out of three who enter the field succumb to stress or the rejection syndrome after three to five years. Those who can handle such a situation and make it work for them can earn high incomes in a short time. Interestingly, many top sales producers are athletes who appear to have innate competitive instincts, know how to handle stress, and are good decision-makers. The same qualities are common to many former military members.

A useful overview of the field of Securities Sales Workers is given in the *Occupational Outlook Handbook*. Further career information is available from the Securities Industry Association, 120 Broadway, New York, NY 10271.

Two corporate sketches in *Inside Track* give thumbnail "inside" views of Merrill Lynch and Bear Stearns. For an informed, tell-it-like-it-is summary of the work and qualifications needed to become a successful account executive, I suggest Chapter 8 of *How to Get the Hot Jobs in Business and Finance*, a book by Mary E. Calhoun, a one-time sales trainee with Merrill Lynch. For information about how to become a Certified Financial Planner, write to the College for Financial Planning, 9725 East Hampden Avenue, Denver, CO 80231.

Insurance Sales

Retail insurance sales agents share many of the characteristics of real estate sales agents and account executives. They are usually trained in-house; they must be licensed by states; and they are independent contractors who are paid from the policy premiums they earn for their companies.

Entry-level sales agents in the insurance industry tend to be somewhat older than those in the real estate and securities industries, largely because the insurance industry cultivates a public image of sedate maturity. A college degree is not as important in this field, though an industry trend is increasing emphasis on financial and estate planning—which means that sales agents need a good background in finance, tax law, government, economics, sociology, and psychology. Employment opportunities are expected to be good through the mid-1990's, although they are growing more slowly than the average because of increasing productivity of existing sales agents and changing business practices, including the use of mail-order campaigns.

The *Occupational Outlook Handbook* has a useful summary of the training and other qualifications necesary for entry-level employment in insurance sales as well as the potential for advancement. Additional career information can be obtained from the American Council on Life Insurance, 1850 K Steet NW, Washington, DC 20006, and the National Association of Life Underwriters, 1922 F Street NW, Washington, DC 20006.

Entry-level sales agents are usually hired and trained by branch offices of large insurance companies, usually in the traditional field of life insurance. In some cases new agents are given some of their training at the home office. Product diversification in recent years has added health insurance, accident insurance, retirement annuities, and new forms of coverage such as the single-premium life insurance policy to the traditional sales program.

Insurance sales agents develop their own client lists. They participate in community affairs, and they are constantly studying professional courses in their field. Agents are paid a substantial portion of the first year's policy premium and fixed amounts of annual and renewal premiums over the lives of the policies they sell or "write." Earnings can grow quickly after a lean first couple of years.

Major insurance companies are now focusing on lucrative institutional sales of life, health, and other group policies to businesses and other organizations. Some successful sales agents establish themselves as independent insurance brokers and act as agents for several insurance companies, marketing multiple lines of casualty and life insurance and investments.

Professional development in the insurance field includes study for and certification as a Chartered Life Underwriter (CLU), a Certified Financial Planner (CFP), and a variety of other industry-supervised standards of achievement. Many states require continuing education for insurance sales workers.

Management opportunities are available for those who show sales ability and leadership, though many "high producers" prefer to remain in the sales field.

Banking and Finance

This is one industry where the "entry-level" jobs available to aspiring managers are at a professional level: entry into the fast-paced field of finance and banking is largely by means of internships and management training programs.

The commercial banks with which you are probably most familiar are no longer simply places where you store excess funds for the proverbial rainy day. Get beyond the lobby and you will find that they are somewhat sedate beehives of activity. Programs range across the financial spectrum from consumer and commercial loans to managed investment programs to high-tech credit card operations.

But financial insitutions also include *investment banks* that work primarily with corporations, other banks, and a few "high rollers" (Salomon Brothers, First Boston, and Morgan, Stanley), the *national brokerage houses* (Merrill Lynch, Shearson Lehman Hutton), big *insurance companies* (Aetna, Equitable), *diversified financial institutions* that are sometimes known as "hybrids" (Sears Roebuck, American Express), and national *accounting firms* (Arthur Andersen and Touche Ross, for example).

Trainees are usually recruited from among college graduates but not necessarily from those who majored in business, finance, or accounting. Many banks, in fact, prefer liberal arts majors (some courses in accounting, economics, computer science, statistics, and political science may be helpful). The combination of a liberal arts degree and an MBA is super! Some engineers, physical and biological scientists, and other technically trained professionals are needed in certain areas of the industry.

In addition to the management training programs, many technical staff jobs exist in the fields of accounting, computer operations, security, marketing, public relations, real estate, and other fields.

The career prospects are so attractive and so diverse, in fact, that no one in the retread category can afford to overlook them. In addition to the summary for bank officers and managers in the *Occupational Outlook Handbook*, you would do well to get your hands on two very readable books that cover the field of banking and finance. *Money Jobs* describes specific internships and management training programs and tells how to get into them. *How to Get the Hot Jobs in Business and Finance* is a bit more general but outstanding. Both books were written for college and graduate students, but each offers a great deal of valuable information for anyone seeking a career in the field. Eleven "insider" sketches of key corporations are in *Inside Track* (see Reading List for Part II), along with brief, readable, cogent industry surveys of the fields of accounting, banking, and financial services.

A job with Goldman, Sachs may not be in your career plans, but these books can also be valuable tools for senior officers and enlisted men and women and other more junior former service members who may not meet the entry standards for internships but may fit into technical staff functions in local banking and financial institutions or branches of the national ones.

Do not overlook local or state banks and bank holding companies, savings and loan institutions, credit unions, mortgage banks, and branch offices of national insurance, securities, and finance companies. Networking techniques often produce results.

Careers in Education

A joint announcement by the Secretary of Defense and the Secretary of Education, in September 1986, pledged the two departments of the federal government to work together to encourage retiring and retired military men and women to seek second careers in education and educational administration. In the formal ceremony, the Secretary of Education said, "Many men and women who served in uniform have excellent leadership and teaching skills" in, he later suggested, such needed subjects as science, mathematics, and foreign languages. He might have added others in the vocational training fields, including computers.

The field of education can offer a rewarding second career, but not to everyone. A number of former military officers that I know have carved out satisfying niches for themselves as secondary school teachers; a number of others that I have heard about have become highly effective educational administrators. But it is an unfortunate fact that experience as a military trainer or instructor does not qualify you to teach in a public school and may not qualify you to teach in a private preparatory school.

If you have had any thoughts about making a transition into a career as a civilian educator, you might as well know now that you need to do a lot of retraining and considerable rethinking on the subject of education itself no matter how much "platform" time you have logged.

The discussions of teaching fields in the *Occupational Outlook Handbook* are good places to begin an investigation. They include write-ups on elementary school teachers, secondary school teachers, and adult and vocational education teachers.

All fifty states and the District of Columbia require that prospective elementary and secondary public school teachers have at least a bachelor's degree, including certain Education courses (requirements vary), before they can be certified. Educational requirements for vocational education teachers vary from state to state and between occupational fields. State certification is not generally required for teachers in private preparatory schools, military academies, and technical schools.

Employment opportunities in elementary schools are expected to grow rapidly through the 1990's and then taper off, though many men who had been teaching at the secondary school level are moving into elementary school teaching. Conversely, employment for secondary school teachers is expected to decline until the mid-1990's, when the trend will be reversed as students complete elementary school. Meanwhile secondary school job opportunities will be best in the fields of science, math, and computer science. Some increase in teaching opportunities may result from the growing student enrollments in preparatory schools and secondary-level military academies—said to reflect widespread dissatisfaction with public education.

Vocational and adult education opportunities are expected to grow at about the average rate through the 1990's, with good opportunities for those qualified to teach automotive mechanics, computer technology, medical technology, and office skills.

Teacher certification is the principal problem facing the military men and women who accept the challenge laid down by the Secretaries of Defense and Education. The announcement sparked efforts by the Department of Education to encourage the states to revise or ease certification requirements in favor of military retirees and other former members. To date (February 1988), little seems to have been done. Rather, the issue has become something of a hot potato: Some states have protested that the Department of Education is attempting to move in where it is not wanted. On the whole, however, the prevailing situation is not hopeless.

Certification requirements normally include completion of a prescribed (or acceptable) undergraduate curriculum that includes a major and a minor teaching field and varying numbers of courses or credits in professional education, including practice teaching. In some states, a master's degree is required for certification at the secondary school level.

Educational programs that prepare military personnel for state certification as secondary school teachers are not usually available to active duty military personnel through the standard service-supported on-base, off-duty educational programs. (One exception may be the cooperative degree program in Vocational Education developed by Southern Illinois University. The Community College of the Air Force has offered an associate degree in vocational education.) Some serving members may be able to take qualifying courses in Education at state or community colleges and state universities located near military bases. Such courses are often given during evening hours and on weekends to accommodate employed teachers who are meeting continuing education requirements.

A number of universities have already structured special one-year graduate degree programs in Education designed to qualify former military personnel for teacher certification in the states or areas where they are located. Among them are Arizona State University (Tempe), George Washington University in Washington, D.C. (evening program), the University of West Florida, Memphis State University, the University of Southern Maine, George Mason University (Virginia), the University of North Carolina (Chapel Hill), and Wright State University (Ohio). Details of the degree programs must be obtained directly from the School of Education at the institution. (*Caution:* Certification standards vary widely from state to state; a degree program to satisfy Arizona state teacher certification requirements, for example, may not be acceptable in other states.)

It is not always necessary, however, to be fully qualified in advance.

Most state certification regulations provide for temporary or "emergency" employment of otherwise-qualified teacher applicants. The procedures vary but usually require that certification standards be met within a year or two of employment. "Otherwise-qualified" usually means that the candidate is prepared in a subject. About one third of the states require such teacher applicants to take a proficiency examination in their subject field. Some of these states also require teacher applicants to meet certain health requirements.

Alternative licensing procedures have also been developed in some states. In general, an applicant without adequate credentials (that is, professional education courses and practice teaching) but with superior subject-area preparation may be permitted to take a proficiency test, serve as a teaching intern under the supervision of experienced teachers, and complete specified professional education courses to become eligible for certification.

In January 1987 the Massachusetts State Board of Education announced such an alternate certification program as a means of meeting a projected demand for 10,000 to 20,000 new teachers over the ensuing five years. The Board also had reportedly developed another plan to certify teacher candidates on the basis of "life experience."

Since certification requirements vary widely from state to state, anyone interested in entering the field should write to the National Center for Education Information, 1901 Pennsylvania Avenue, Suite 707, Washington, DC 20006, or to the American Association of Colleges for Teacher Education, One Dupont Circle, Suite 610, Washington, DC 20036. For information on reciprocity between states (concerning other states' teaching licenses) write to the State Board of Education where you plan to teach.

The whole problem of state certification may sometimes be bypassed by targeting a job at a private preparatory school or a secondary-level military academy. Directories of these schools are available in public libraries. Or you can write directly to St. John's Military Academy, 1101 North Genesee Street, Delafield, WI 53018–1498, for a list of the thirty-six topflight military academies that belong to the Association of Military Colleges and Schools of the United States.

Before you jump in with both feet, however, a few other observations related to teaching at the secondary school level may be of interest.

First, military training is a form of what some professional educators call, with some disdain, "distributive education." Military instructors typically facilitate the transfer of facts from their memories (or manuals) to the notebooks and, they hope, the minds of their students. A great deal of military instruction involves rote learning and memorization of techniques for *doing* something.

There is nothing wrong with this kind of instruction. Indeed, it serves an important and necessary function. But it is not *education* in the sense that the Secretary of Education meant. I write as a former Army specialist in operations and training, and a sometime service school instructor in methods of military instruction, who recycled into a public school classroom thinking his eyes were wide open.

The generally agreed objective of public education is to help children (and others) learn how to reason, or to "think." The purpose of cramming "facts" into kids' heads is not so that they can pass tests or perform some action. Rather, it is to provide them with a "data bank" of information and ideas that they can use in their own independent thought processes. The product of thinking is *ideas*, not actions. The purpose of all this, in the United States at least, is to develop children into men and women who can function intelligently in the complex society in which they live, the point made in the book on *Cultural Literacy* discussed in Chapter 7.

These may seem to be lofty ideas that have little or nothing to do with teaching science, mathematics, foreign languages, computer operations, and vocational arts like automobile mechanics—all of which have in common the fact that they are often treated as if they were prime examples of distributive education and presented within the carefully drawn limits of their *disciplines*.

The problem is exactly that these subjects have been treated as though they were neatly wrapped packages of knowledge. But it is impossible to teach science without touching on English, math, or social studies—or even Greek and Latin. In life there are no disciplinary boundaries such as those that exist in most schools and no "building block" curricula.

Years ago, when I took over the Science Department at a preparatory school, I discovered that I (among others) was spending a great deal of time in my chemistry classes reteaching elements of algebra. The attitude of the students was that they had "done" Algebra (with a capital "A") the year before and that was that. Life is not that way at all.

What this all boils down to, when you consider the objective of education, is that every teacher is or should be teaching the same thing: how to study, how to think, and how to communicate ideas effectively orally and in writing. Children, even high school teenagers, do not arrive at these objectives by instinct or intuition. They cannot yet, by themselves, effectively integrate the vast amounts of information presented in the little boxes labeled English-I, Algebra-II, Biology, World History, or French-I. They need help. And that is the challenge of secondary school education.

The reward of teaching is not in knowing more about your subject or discipline than anyone else and being able to transfer it all to student notebooks in an orderly way. The reward of teaching comes as you watch students grow intellectually, emotionally, and ethically to become independent, reasoning adults. Military instructional techniques cannot be transferred unaltered into the secondary school classroom.

This is no place for a major essay on education or educational philosophy, but it is important that anyone who plans to enter the profession of education after military service realize that he or she is entering a whole new world. An excellent and thoughtful essay on what secondary school education can be like is available in *Horace's Compromise*, by a former preparatory school headmaster and state educational official. I heartily recommend it to anyone considering teaching.

Second, secondary school students are not military trainees. Children, especially teenagers, do not sit primly in classrooms like little baskets waiting to be filled with the fruits of their teachers' knowledge and experience. One of the most heart-rending experiences that confront many former military personnel—and especially experienced military instructors—who have turned to teaching is the almost utter lack of discipline that prevails in the classrooms of public schools and, to a lesser extent perhaps, in those of private schools.

In a word, teenagers reject authority even though, paradoxically, they welcome discipline under the right circumstances. Teenagers are obsessed with their own growing-up and how they look, even when they look pretty scroungy. They lack self-confidence and, worse, self-discipline. They are confused by the world around them. They are easily hurt by ridicule. Most accept the fact that their role in life for the time being is to go to school (which is a kind of "club"), but they have only a limited attention span and easily become "bored" or profess not to be "interested." Students typically test new teachers to see how much they can get away with. Some cheat and lie with easy facility because they are under great pressure to pass—which means to get it all over with. Coping with this situation in high school classrooms day after day destroys many would-be teachers, including many former members of the services.

The results of a national public opinion poll conducted in 1986 showed that military officers as a group represent the last practitioners of the patriarchal tradition in the United States. I would be inclined to add senior non-commissioned officers to that group.

Good officers and senior non-commissioned officers are the "fathers" (now, also "mothers") of their subordinates in rank. They have to be leaders: stern and positive, informed, self-confident, humble at times, and inspiring or cajoling—as necessary. They also have to be counselors: patient, empathetic, and concerned about the welfare of their subordinates. NCO's and officers are literally clothed with institutional authority, symbolized by the uniforms and insignia of rank they wear and the titles or assignments they hold: "Commander," "NCO-in-Charge," "First Sergeant." Good officers and NCO's do not invoke authority lightly and need not invoke it at all if they are leaders. Yet many former officers and NCO's literally flee from the classroom because they cannot control their students.

There are no easy answers to the problem. Approaches involve enhancing student self-confidence, inculcating self-discipline rather than relying on threats or punishment, and coaching as a means of helping students learn. Many former military members who are stripped of visible symbols of authority when they shed the uniform try to become *friends* with their teenage students. That doesn't work. But the same leadership traits that work in military service can work in the classroom.

Moving along to become an educational adminstrator may require even more ability to exercise leadership qualities acquired through military service. Educational administrators are almost always recruited from successful classroom teachers. The pathway to that kind of a career, of course, requires advanced study up to the doctoral level and is beyond the scope of this book.

International Opportunities in Finance, Banking, and Teaching

International finance and banking are rapidly growing fields in what is becoming a global community. As in manufacturing and other American industries that operate abroad, American banks and other financial institutions that have international branches often must limit the employment of American citizens in accordance with the regulations of their host countries. Similarly, those Americans who do work abroad for banks like Citibank, brokerage houses like Merrill Lynch, and insurance companies are generally established, trained employees.

A number of American institutions of higher education, nevertheless, do train students at the graduate level for careers in international banking and finance. Perhaps the foremost of these is the American Graduate School of International Management, in Glendale, Arizona, usually known simply as "Thunderbird." The school has an excellent record of job placement. Well-established graduate programs in international business are also located at Denver University, Georgetown University, Tufts University, the University of South Carolina, and more than fifty other major universities around the country. Consult *Peterson's Graduate and Professional Programs* or the *The Academic Journal* (P.O. Box 397, Newton, CT 06470).

Several American insurance companies service only members of U.S. armed forces abroad and therefore are less encumbered by foreign hiring regulations. The United Services Automobile Association and the Academy Insurance Company are two of these companies. American representatives of some U.S. casualty insurance companies sometimes live and work abroad, working largely with American companies and members of the resident American communities.

The World Bank, officially the International Bank for Reconstruction and Development, and its affiliated organizations, the International Monetary Fund and the International Development Association, operate under the United Nations. Americans who seek employment at these and other U.N. organizations and agencies should write to the Office of United Nations Affairs, U.S. Department of State, Washington, DC 20520.

Many international opportunities for experienced secondary school teachers are available in private schools, dependents' schools, and even foreign schools. The key word, of course, is "experienced." As a general rule, teachers who apply for these positions must have had at least two years of successful classroom experience in an accredited American secondary school. Information on international opportunities for teachers can be obtained from:

Institute of International Education
Attn: "Teaching Abroad"
809 United Nations Plaza
New York, NY 10017

Office of Dependent Schools (Attn: Personnel Division)
Department of Defense
2461 Eisenhower Avenue
Alexandria, VA 22331–1100

Office of Overseas Schools
U.S. Department of State
Washington, DC 20520

Teacher Exchange Section
U.S. Department of Education
400 Maryland Avenue SW
Washington, DC 20202

International Schools Services
Attn: The Directory
P.O. Box 5910
Princeton, NJ 08540

Overseas recruiting fairs for teachers provide important opportunities for experienced teachers to locate teaching positions abroad. Information on the locations and dates of such fairs can be obtained from:

Overseas Placement Service for Educators
152 Gilcrest Hall
University of Northern Iowa
Cedar Falls, IA 50614

Teachers Overseas Recruiting Center
P.O. Box 09027
Cleveland, OH 44109–0027

Chapter 11

Working for Yourself

A persistent urge of Americans, it seems, is to own and operate a business and work for themselves, and many people in the military services share that dream. More than four million small businesses are currently operating in the United States, and another estimated eight to ten million Americans are counted as self-employed. Altogether, small businesses employ an estimated one half of the entire civilian workforce.

The possibilities of working for yourself are almost endless. In the category of owning your own business, they include starting a small business, investing in (or buying outright) an established business, or investing in a franchise. The business structure may run from a sole proprietorship (e.g., a radio/TV repairman who works by himself) to a corporation. Opportunities for self-employment include freelancing (journalist/writer/editor, translator, photographer, graphic artist, etc.), consulting, and becoming a home worker.

The possibilities are almost endless, but the risks are often greater. The greatest risk, of course, is that of losing your shirt. I do not recommend that anyone leave military service to set up a business, or even retire to set up a business, without careful preparation and a clear knowledge of all that is involved. I hung up my uniform and started my own business thinking that I was ready, but I soon discovered that I didn't know much at all about how business really operates. Two long lean years passed before I felt that I was really on top of the situation. I have set up and operated several businesses since that time, building on the earlier experience. So what follows in this chapter is not just something I have read about.

An estimated half of all new businesses established each year, and there are thousands of them, fail within eighteen months. If you add to the licensed business establishments the numbers of would-be freelancers, home workers, and consultants who fail or barely eke out a living, the failure rate is probably much greater. The reasons for failure are many and varied, but a pattern exists. The principal factors in business failures are:

Highly trained military emergency management specialists may find jobs with federal, state, and local governments. Some have established businesses dealing with toxic and radioactive industrial wastes.

1. Undercapitalization (not enough money!).
2. Lack of understanding of market conditions.
3. Poor or inexperienced business management.
4. Unexpected changes in economic or political conditions.
5. The health of the proprietor or his or her family.
6. Legal and tax problems.

Some or all of these factors adversely influence the ability of almost anyone to establish and run a successful business. They can have an even greater impact on anyone who has recently been discharged or retired from military service. The prudent course of action generally recommended for those in the latter category who contemplate owning and operating a business enterprise is to work for someone else in the same or an allied field long enough to understand fully everything that is involved in such a venture. Some who have the means actually work without pay for this purpose. In some cases such a self-designed business "internship" or "apprenticeship" is an absolute prerequisite because of state or federal licensing requirements that cannot be met in the military services.

Obviously, hopeful entrepreneurs should take advantage of every opportunity during transition planning to prepare for a business career. In general, that means working for a degree in business administration or, if that is not possible, completing courses in accounting, marketing, business management, finance, business law, business information systems, computer operations, taxation, and whatever else you can fit in while you are in uniform. Do not overlook opportunities to expand your knowledge by attending the short courses the military services operate in business-related fields or to serve an assignment with industry.

Tuition-free practical courses on how to start and manage a small business are provided by many colleges and universities under the sponsorship of the Small Business Administration (SBA). The Internal Revenue Service offers free classes in tax-related matters to small business operators. Depending on where you are stationed, there is no reason why you cannot take advantage of these opportunities while you are still in service. Check with a Small Business Administration counselor or the local development authority to find out what is available. Check out, also, the local Chamber of Commerce, business associations, and business magazines. One thing will lead to another and your grasp of at least the local situation will rapidly expand in scope. If you are in a position to do so—on a recruiting assignment, detailed to a Reserve or National Guard unit, or serving in some other assignment that brings you into close contact with civilian business—join the local chapter of the JC's (Junior Chamber of Commerce), Rotary, Lions, Kiwanis, or one of the other service organizations. If you are in a professional field that has a civilian counterpart, join the local business association that serves members of that profession. But don't just join and attend occasional lunches. These organizations provide opportunities to meet men and women who are already in business. You can take it from there by networking.

These preparations provide only the minimal background, at best. The big questions remain: "What business?" and "Where do I get the money?" Assuming that you have that persistent urge to get into business for yourself, let's look at those questions.

What Business?

This question involves too many factors to permit detailed discussion here. But it should be obvious that you must know as much as you can about some kind of business before you move to enter it. And this goes far beyond being an expert in your field or proposed field, as you can see from the list of reasons for business failures. Knowing how to cook and manage a messhall or a military club, for example, is no guarantee that you will be able to run a successful restaurant. You have to know both the current *market* and future *trends*, as we have been insisting for anyone who seeks a civilian career following military service. And even then no one can be sure. Forecasts suggest a long-term growth in demand for food and beverage services, but they do not and cannot say what kinds of services the public will patronize.

Only a few years ago a business association published a list of the ten small businesses with the greatest future potential during the ensuing decade. They were, presumably in order of their potential:

1. Computer programming and software services.
2. Accounting services.
3. Medical laboratories.
4. Home computer stores.
5. Nursing homes.
6. Medical and dental instrument companies.
7. Restaurants (especially franchises).
8. Building materials stores.
9. Electronics supply stores.
10. Management consulting services.

How well have those predictions stood up?

Computer programming and software services. About 40 percent of the computer programmers employed in private industry were fired in 1986. While some of their functions may have been taken over by outside contractors, the programming and software business has been going through a difficult and entirely unpredicted period for more than two years of the three or four years since the optimistic prediction was published.

Part of the problem has been market saturation: The titles of software to meet almost every need already fill enormous catalogs. Part of the problem has been industry consolidation: A relatively few software companies have cornered a large share of the market. Part of the problem has been caused by standardization in the computer industry: IBM "clones," for example, that can run existing IBM programs. Part of the problem has been caused by the failure of the predicted mass market for home computers. The programming and software industry has become very competitive. Many small companies have collapsed.

Home computer stores. The boom in sales of home computers has faded. Merchandising methods have changed. Volume sales in what market remains are being handled by department stores, discounters, and franchised chains of computer stores. The corner computer store may be going the way of the corner grocery store.

Franchised Restaurants. Expansion continues, but in 1987 the industry leaders in the fast-food field were planning on about 5 percent per year growth in new stores instead of the 15 to 20 percent of previous years. Competition in the industry has produced the phenomenon of hamburger vendors who sell fried chicken and fish, fried chicken chains that sell fish and hamburgers, and fried fish outlets that have added chicken and hamburgers. They all feature salad bars. The major issue now may not be the menu but how the food is cooked: fried in high-cholesterol fat or broiled?

Not only is the market approaching saturation, but people seem to be turning away from fast-food outlets in favor of the "family restaurants" and somewhat classier places to eat out where the mature, more affluent population can enjoy a quiet meal preceded by cocktails and graced with a glass of wine.

Building materials outlets. The do-it-yourself craze may have peaked, but even if it hasn't, merchandising methods and consolidations now appear to be limiting business opportunities for building supply supermarkets—which in any case hardly fit the popular image of "small business." In the past two years, in Colorado alone, two large multistate operators of building materials supermarkets have closed their stores. A third chain is barely surviving. Meanwhile, giants in the forest-products industry like Cascade are opening their own retail building supply outlets; and the traditional "lumberyards" are diversifying their operations in an effort to reach the do-it-yourself and home craftsman market.

Time has taken its toll even of "sure bets" that follow well-established trends. The *nursing home* industry is plagued with the high cost of liability insurance, ever more demanding state and federal regulations, and shortages of qualified personnel, all of which drive up operating costs. *Medical laboratories* are closing in hospitals, their functions taken over by private laboratories operated off-site. The smaller laboratories that had already existed are facing increased competition from the large centralized or regional laboratory services better able to afford the expensive equipment now being introduced. Small retailers in the *electronics supply* business are closing their doors in the face of heavy competition from mass-market chains and discount houses.

Only two of the ten "most likely to succeed" businesses listed in 1984—all of them in the growing services sector, by the way—still look good from the point of view of the small businessman: accounting services and management consulting.

The point here is not to suggest that opportunities in small business are fading away. Rather, the direction of effort is changing, rapidly and even dramatically. No one who has the dream of owning his or her own business can afford to be overtaken by events before even getting started. On the other hand, new business ventures in previously undreamed of fields (almost all in the services area) are being reported every day—many of them responsive to public issues that are also reported in the press, on radio and TV, and in the business press. A wide-awake, heads-up approach is essential.

In line with earlier recommendations that everyone should watch the business press closely. I suggest that you subscribe to one of the magazines devoted to small business: *Entrepreneur, Inc., Venture*, or *Small Business Report*. Their coverage is more likely to report changing trends in the world of small business than the national magazines.

In addition to the national business press, almost every trade, business, or profession has an association and one or more trade journals. These are sources of information that cannot be overlooked when searching for an outlet to your talents. A little imagination will help, but imagination is not fantasy. Successful enterpreneurs may take risks, but they are not gamblers.

Where Do I Find the Money?

Sources of funding for new business ventures are limited. The majority of new businesses are established with personal funds. Some people mortgage their home or sell their stocks and bonds. The next most important source of money is friends and relatives. If you do not have enough money to start your own business, you cannot expect anyone to leap forward to hand you any. The consequence is that beginning entrepreneurs tend to be undercapitalized. Undercapitalized ventures usually fail.

An important exception to these observations are the loan programs for veterans and for minority and female entrepreneurs—Veterans Affairs Officers are available at every SBA district and branch office. Some state and local development authorities may have seed money (but not loans) available for new ventures. Some private nonprofit agencies—mostly those working in the minority populations—provide start-up loans and management counseling. Banks may make loans against stocks and bonds (or your home)—which merely means that (1) you do not have to sell them, and (2) the bank assumes very little risk. Small Business Corporations exist to provide "equity capital" (that is, they buy a share of your operation), but they seldom finance start-ups. Venture capitalists may jump into the breach to invest in promising new enterprises, but they are only in business for big returns and your business plan had better be a very compelling stunner.

As usual, however, success breeds success. If you actually get off to a running start and keep moving ahead, bank "customer representatives" will soon be knocking on your door offering you money. Clearing that initial hurdle is the real problem.

Getting a Running Start

The discussion to this point has already mentioned a number of things that anyone can and should do before jumping into a business venture. Other things you can do while you are still in uniform include the following:

1. Buy the study *Starting and Managing a Small Business on Your Own*, the first volume of a Small Business Administration (SBA) "Starting and Managing" series. You can find it at a Government Book Store or order it from the U.S. Government Printing Office, Washington, DC 20402. While you are at it, request the SBA publications catalog. It offers everything from a self-study business management course to manuals for specific businesses.

2. Buy and study the *Franchise Opportunities Handbook*, another SBA publication sold by the Government Printing Office. The publication includes summaries of more than twelve hundred franchise opportunities, under forty-odd classifications, in the retail and wholesale services sector. It also includes an extensive list of references on franchising and other aspects of small business operation and management.

It is worth noting that franchise operations generated nearly $600 billion in sales in 1986 and accounted for about one third of all retail sales in the country. The field is expected to continue to grow rapidly.

Franchise operators offer opportunities to start a business that has a recognized status with a relatively small investment. Most provide national advertising. Many provide management training and management consulting services for new franchisers. Some provide financial assistance, either directly or through third parties. Write for details to one or more that interest you. Seek out a franchiser in your field of interest and discuss his or her experiences. (Don't go in as a potential *competitor*, however.)

3. Locate a "business broker" (Yellow Pages or local newspaper) and make an appointment to discuss opportunities for buying a business. You do not have to be in the market yourself, but you should find out for yourself how such people operate and what kinds of businesses are available—and for how much.

Many successful businesses are offered for sale by owners who are retiring. In many cases, up-front capital requirements may be minimal, but annual payments (paid from the gross receipts) stretch out for years: The retired owner is usually more interested in income than anything else, for tax reasons. The broker should have on hand (or have access to) business records of the companies he is marketing. Watch out for "distress" sales, long-term downward business trends, unpaid loans and other liabilities, and other indications of a business in trouble or failing.

Check with the Chamber of Commerce and the Better Business Bureau to see what they know about a business that may interest you. Talk to an SBA Veterans Affairs Officer to see what financial and other assistance may be available.

4. Contact the Entrepreneur Group, Inc., 2311 Pontius Avenue, Los Angeles, CA 90064, for information on its small business programs. Call toll-free at 1-800-421-2300 from anywhere in the continental United States except California. In California, call 1-800-352-7449.

The Entrepreneur Group is not one of the nonprofit industry associations that have been mentioned elsewhere but, rather, a going business of its own. You will have to pay for publications and other assistance, but not very much.

The Group offers a comprehensive self-study business start-up and management course, based on practical experience. It also researches, publishes, and sells—at modest prices—start-up manuals on a wide variety of businesses. Many of the undertakings covered are at the leading edge of private business enterprise. In 1982 the Group's catalog included manuals on how to start a temporary-help agency and how to become a consultant. In 1986 other business consultants were just beginning to recommend these two as the hottest business opportunities to emerge in the past few years.

The manuals and other publications are available by mail, but you may be able to inspect the Group's wares at one of its many Start-a-Business stores around the country. A list of these stores is available from the Los Angeles office.

Membership in the Entrepreneur Group includes a subscription to the monthly *Entrepreneur* magazine, discounts on publications, and free counseling and advice by telephone.

Whatever your aspirations in the business world, of course, it is up to you to make them happen. Owning and operating a business requires knowledge, hard work, and a great desire to succeed. In a countrywide study of small business operations in 1985, I found that many businessmen who were then successful had earlier started one or more businesses that had failed. They had learned something from each failure and had gone on to succeed in their latest ventures.

Oddly enough, failure in business is neither a social nor a professional liability in the United States. Bank loan officers have told me that they generally prefer to talk to someone who has been in business before, even if the earlier business failed, than to someone who is trying to launch his or her first business venture. A bumper sticker that I saw recently seemed to sum it all up: "You are not a failure until you stop trying."

Remember, however, that business is business. Once you have set yourself up as a business owner, you have assumed certain moral, ethical, and legal obligations. Government authorities do not care whether you are the only one involved in "John Doe and Associates" or whether you are the sole stockholder, officer, and employee of "RST Corporation." Government authorities are out there to enforce the laws. You had better know what they are. A lawyer and a good bookkeeping or accounting service are essential for even the smallest business. The fees you pay them should be included in your operating or overhead costs and hence be a factor in the fees or prices you charge your own clients.

Other Ways to Work for Yourself

Operating a small business need not involve anything more than selling your knowledge or skills. Opportunities exist for free-lancers, consultants, and home workers, who are contractors to established businesses. For these activities, you do not need a store or an office; you can operate out of your own home without a lot of expensive equipment.

You do need, on the other hand, to have a marketable skill or a body of accumulated knowledge along with some idea of the market and how to penetrate it. You also need a good understanding of business structure and management principles, basic accounting, business and contract law, and federal, state, and local licensing and tax regulations.

Don't forget that you will be in business, after all. Self-employed people in the categories mentioned do not usually set up corporations (though there are good reasons for them to do so), but they are responsible for paying taxes on their business income and the full amount of federal social security tax based on that income. Federal income tax procedures provide that the income of sole proprietors be reported on a separate Schedule C and included in your individual tax return (Form 1040). Some states have similar requirements. What this means, then, is that you have to keep accurate records of your business income and expenses.

1. *Free-lancing* is the general term applied to experts and professionals who work for themselves in an occupational field that can also be the subject of full-time (or part-time) employment in a business activity or nonprofit organization. Free-lancers include many of the people who work in media fields: writers, editors, reporters ("stringers"), photographers, translators, and commercial artists are examples. Musicians and other performing artists and those in the fine arts often work independently, but they are not usually thought of as free-lancers.

Breaking into a field as a free-lancer can be difficult and very time-consuming. The rejection of a piece of writing, a photo, or some work of graphic art that you thought was your best is very disheartening. For that very reason a number of support organizations have been established. Most of them publish newsletters that discuss professional techniques, markets and marketing, and projects and opportunities. Some operate on a national scale, such as those for independent travel writers and photographers. You can find them listed in the *Encyclopedia of Associations*. Membership may be limited to established professionals, but there is no reason why anyone who is merely interested should not contact any of these associations for information. Among other things, such organizations typically offer such services as job banks, professional workshops and conferences, "how-to" guides, directories, legal services, and group insurance plans.

Many local organizations, such as the Washington Independent Writers (WIW), located in the National Press Building in Washington, D.C., also meet the needs of free-lancers, including newcomers. The WIW has in the past offered a minicourse called "Getting Started in the Freelance Life." It also operates a job bank and offers other membership benefits. Beginners may have difficulty finding these local organizations, and the best way may be to develop a contact in a newspaper office since many newspaper writers, editors, and photographers get their start as free-lancers—and some never give up the vocation. Check out the local "press clubs," as well.

There is nothing to lose and everything to gain if you begin free-lancing while you are in uniform—so long as you keep away from classified or sensitive subjects and refrain from critical essays on strategic issues. Stick to human-interest stories and photos. Start with the magazines published by the military services themselves: *Soldiers, Airman, Marines,* and others. They all welcome articles, photographs, and artwork from readers. They also specifically authorize direct communication with the editors for this purpose. At a higher level are the publications of the staff colleges, the war colleges, and DOD joint schools that seek well-written articles on professional topics.

Do not overlook the magazines published by the military-related associations and veterans organizations listed in Appendix D. Some of these magazines are oriented to members no longer in uniform, but even the "old soldiers" like to keep up with what is going on in the services. Be sure that what you submit fits the mood and tone of the publication. In most cases, that means you have to obtain copies of back issues and read them to get the feel of the editorial policy.

You may not make any money doing this kind of free-lancing while you are in uniform, but having a "portfolio" of articles, photographs, or artwork that has actually been published will confirm the ability that you think you have and help provide the credentials to ease your transition to professional free-lancing.

Valuable information on free-lancing is contained in the *Writers Digest*, a publication oriented toward independent writers and available only by subscription. Write to the *Writers Digest* at 205 West Center Street, Marion, OH 43305.

Associated Photographers International publishes a newsletter called *apidea* and claims to serve a network of 30,000 independent photographers around the world "sharing both money-making and creative photo ideas." Write to: Publication Office, Associated Photographers International, 22231 Mulholland Highway, P.O. Box 4055, Woodland Hills, CA 91365.

Marketing tips for free-lancers are available from a series of annual publications such as *Writers Market* and *Photographers Market* (see Reading List).

Translators with expertise in a technical field are frequently employed on contract by the U.S. government (Joint Publications Research Service in the Department of Commerce), by the Department of State, by publishers, by some manufacturers, and by local "language services" centers. A company that works by mail with contract translators of technical literature is Ad-Ex Translations International (see *The Work at Home Sourcebook* in the Reading List).

A field allied to free-lance writing is that of writing, publishing, and selling your own books by direct mall-order means. This popular and sometimes lucrative way to make money became attractive to many retirees (including military retirees) a few years ago and has recently acquired a certain aura of legitimacy because of the explosion of "desk-top publishing." Computers, peripherals such as printers, and software are available that enable anyone who can operate a computer to design and print professional-looking publications. The subjects are virtually endless; personal memoirs, "how-to-do-it" pamphlets and books, and newsletters are some of the products. Many articles on the subject are appearing in such magazines as *Writers Digest* and *Personal Computing*. The *Towers Club Newsletter*, dedicated to book self-publishers, is published ten times a year by the Towers Club, Box 2038, Vancouver, WA 98668.

2. *Consultants* have been described variously as "Beltway Bandits" in the Washington, D.C. area and elsewhere as "someone with a briefcase who is more than one hundred miles from home." But the consulting field is an established and rapidly growing one that reaches into every aspect of business and even into private lives. As usual, newletters, books, organizations, and central referral agencies have developed to serve those who are or aspire to be self-employed consultants. The *Encyclopedia of Associations* can give you leads on professional associations. Several pertinent books are included in the Reading List. Other places to investigate are:

Association of Part-Time Professionals
7655 Old Springhouse Road
McLean, VA 22102

The Consultants Clearing House
1301 Forestwood Drive
McLean, VA 22101

Consultants National Resource Center
Box RO
Gapland, MD 21736
(Publishes the bimonthly *Consulting Opportunities Journal*)

Being a consultant assumes that you know more about a particular subject than most people or that you look at things a little differently than those people who can't look around because they have their shoulder to the wheel. While you may be well informed in your professional field, there is no easy way to obtain experience as a consultant while in uniform.

3. *Home workers* or "worksteaders" are another rapidly growing breed of entrepreneurs who serve as independent contractors to established businesses. We are not talking here about the "get rich" schemes advertised everywhere these days with such slogans as "How to Become a Millionaire in Thirty Days without Working," or

pyramid schemes, or the usually bogus classified ads offering big money for addressing envelopes at home.

Self-employed home workers are in the vanguard of a projected future work ethic that makes good business sense. That is to say, employers can cut their overhead expenses by having routine jobs done by qualified independent contractors who work at home. Estimates are that as many as 1.8 million people already are working exclusively at home, and the number is expected to increase. Sarah Edwards, author of *Working from Home*, quotes futurists who predict that "twenty-five to thirty-five percent of all paid work will be done from people's homes by the turn of the century."

Unlike those who work as consultants, however, home workers or worksteaders are usually paid something close to the minimum wage or on a piecework basis. Many who work at home are physically handicapped. On the other hand, expert projections are that this kind of work will become closer to the norm within the next decade, with home workers hooked up to employing companies by computers and other electronic devices such as telecopiers. As that trend becomes confirmed, the likelihood is that wages will increase.

A recent guide to this field work, *The Work at Home Sourcebook*, provides the names and addresses of about five hundred companies that offer work-at-home opportunities in nearly sixty occupational fields. The author, Lynie Arden, has worked out of her home for two decades and knows what she is writing about. She also publishes *The Worksteader News*, a monthly newsletter that provides new sources of work, articles on special topics, and views and comments from readers. Both publications are available from *The Worksteader News*, 2396 Coolidge Way, Rancho Cordova, CA 95670.

Working for yourself can be both personally satisfying and financially rewarding. The several possibilities discussed in this chapter offer legitimate alternate careers or can develop into careers, but only if you are a self-starter dedicated to hard work and able to endure financially, psychologically, and socially the ups and downs that are almost inevitable. Some career military people who have been used to a highly structured work environment have great difficulty in adjusting to working for themselves. Others, of course, face the challenge with much enthusiasm. Whichever category you fit, you owe it to yourself and to your family, if that is appropriate, to explore with great care any career choice that involves working for yourself.

Chapter 12

Moving Toward Your Civilian Career: Help Is Not Far Away

To this point in our discussion of career transition, we have been emphasizing what service members can and should do to prepare themselves for the day when they will leave military service and resume their civilian role. My dictionary defines *transition* as "passage from one condition, state, stage, etc., to another." The time has come to move on.

A great deal of emphasis has been given to the idea that the transition does not begin on the day you pick up your discharge papers and pass, perhaps for the last time, out the gate of some military installation. Nor does transition planning end when you hang up your uniform. The average time required for transitioning military men and women to find their niche in a civilian career is reported to be six months. Good planning, before and after you leave military service, can significantly shorten that time.

One important consideration in planning that has only been mentioned in passing is that outside that symbolic gate, in civilian clothes, you are on your own. Whatever your military service may offer in the way of technical training and on-the-job experience, opportunities for advanced education, counseling, testing, and all the rest *while you are in uniform*, it drops you like a hot potato as soon as you take off that uniform. You can't go back again. And if you have not done some down-to-earth planning you may very well feel naked, alone, and confused.

Of course, if you are retiring you have all those benefits, and you can go back through the gate and enjoy them. If you signed up for an active Reserve assignment, you will be able to retain some of your former military status.

But when push comes to shove you are alone. Does anyone care?

The answer is a resounding "Yes!" In this chapter we are going to try to assure you that you may be alone but you do not have to be lonely. The help you need to work through the post-service portion of your transition will come from the civilian community that you have entered—and I include government agencies in that community.

Air Force meteorological technicians use sophisticated computers to interpret data received from dropsonde sensors and weather satellites.

Knowing where to turn for help (and where *not* to) and what to expect is an important part of your transition planning.

This chapter will introduce you to some of the programs, organizations, and agencies that not only can but want to help you make a smooth transition.

First, however, we will try to put into final perspective what civilian careers are all about and the ways in which your military experience can give you an advantage as you contemplate your future career plans.

Gaining a Perspective on a Civilian Career

A civilian career, as we have tried to describe it, often involves moving around from one employer or industry sector to another—as much to take advantage of opportunities to grow in your career as to improve income and other employment benefits. In the course of these moves, a person may perform different functions at different times. Administering, writing, teaching or training, counseling, planning, executing, selling, advising, and managing are among the many functions that may be performed during any particular civilian career.

The varied experience gained over a period of years enhances the person's value to a prospective employer and at the same time develops his or her potential to assume a senior management role or even to move out of the job market altogether to become a business owner and operator or a self-employed consultant. Civilian career patterns of this kind are already common in many professional fields and are beginning to become more prominent in technical career fields. One of the consequences of this changing career scene is that it influences the job market and hence the way people go about finding employment.

A moment's reflection will also tell you that this kind of civilian career pattern is not much different in content from that of a fully developed military career. And, in fact, military service accelerates the development of the *career-immaterial skills* that are developed only over long periods of time in civilian careers.

Beginning with enlisted basic training and officer procurement programs, the military services pound into their members the importance of accepting responsibility and instruct them in ways to plan, to execute plans "smartly," to teach and train, to advise and counsel, to lead, and to administer or manage everything from an infantry squad to a multibillion-dollar equipment development and procurement program. Many noncareerists will already have acquired transferable experience in at least some of these functional skill areas by the time they leave service.

A compelling Marine Corps recruiting pamphlet recognizes that.

"At 19, he has more responsibility than most people get in a life-time," says the blurb next to the cover photo of a young Marine in a spit-and-polish dress uniform. Turn the page and we find the same young Marine in battle dress performing as a ground controller for a helicopter assault landing. "When he's on the job," the text continues, "hundreds of men's lives and millions of dollars of equipment are in his hands."

You don't have to wear the stars and gold braid of a general or an admiral to have experienced responsibility or demonstrated leadership. But you do have to be able to transfer that experience and those personal skills—and others fostered by military service—to your civilian career. Employers, even those who may scoff at the idea of hiring people just out of uniform, quickly single out for promotion the men and women who can do just that. Take a minute to turn back to the lists of desirable personal characteristics in Tables 1 and 2 (Chapter 3) to refresh your memory on the subject.

The importance of some of these factors is confirmed, if you still have any doubts, by the results of an informal survey that I conducted among a group of military-related and veterans organizations closely associated with the transition process.

- Self-esteem, a positive attitude toward work, self-discipline, and adaptability were the personal attributes most often rated as *essential* to a successful transition.
- Military technical training and on-the-job experience tended to be rated "very important" or "somewhat important," but not essential, a finding that more or less agrees with the low ratings employers give to "entry-level job skills" (Table 1).
- College and university degrees were rated *essential* by three of the larger associations of former enlisted men and women that responded to the survey. The other respondents rated advanced education as "very important" or "somewhat important." The higher rating given by the enlisted organizations seems to support the strong recommendation in this book that enlisted members must strive to improve their educational status *while they are in uniform*. The slightly lower ratings, incidentally, were given mainly by associations of former officers and may reflect the fact that most officers enter military service with college degrees and that many leave with advanced university degrees.

A singular fact is that the responses to this survey were based on the experience of former military men and women who have already gone through the transition process—and experience can teach some hard lessons. When all the data has been sifted, the conclusions about the traits and qualifications needed for a successful transition are remarkably close to the sense of the three-word "secret-of-success" formula originated by the Non-Commissioned Officers Association: *Attitude, Adaptability, and Ability.*

Approaches to the Job Search

With all this said, however, there is still a catch: Many employers are wary of "career-changers" in any garb, civilian or military. They cannot easily tell where these people are "coming from" and thus cannot guess how they will perform in the new careers they seek. Job applications and résumés do not easily convey a sense of the self-confidence that is fostered by the intangible and "career-immaterial" military experiences just discussed.

Former military men and women who reach the interview stage often sense this hesitancy in interviewers and prospective employers, and they do not know how to react appropriately.

Once out of uniform, separating and retiring military men and women are no longer restrained by the remorseless emphasis that military service gives to identifying with the group and voluntarily accepting the concept of "service above self." Crossing the line from military service to the intensely competitive, highly individualistic civilian scene comes as a shock to many whose status, self-esteem, and self-confidence depended upon that military environment. But in the final analysis even those personal traits learned in military service can work for you. Employers value employees who can identify with group objectives.

The problem is, of course, that it may not be an easy matter to transfer the sense of group loyalty to an unknown employer. The solution of many former military people is therefore to seek employment where their experience and personal qualities seem more likely to be understood and appreciated. In many cases that means focusing job searches on the federal Civil Service and defense contractors—and many are disappointed.

It is seldom a good idea, however, to pick one employment field or even one source of jobs within an employment field and discard the others. You must consider all possibilities that will advance your career objective. You look for a job wherever you can see opportunities to demonstrate the personal qualities and the "career-immaterial" experience you have acquired during military service that are so greatly prized by employers. Certainly, not all the three hundred thousand or so separating military men and women who are looking for jobs can be absorbed by the Civil Service and defense contractors. By and large, the career planning approach of this book has been to help you gain confidence in your own ability to make a go of it on the "outside."

When you are looking ahead to a search for that first job, keep in mind that most employers try to fill job vacancies from within. Only when they cannot do so do they recruit, advertise, or engage employment agencies or outside recruiters—the latter of which are called "headhunters." This situation has led employment experts to describe the large number of jobs that are not advertised or referred to employment agencies as "the hidden job market." Estimates vary, but that market may account for more than 80 percent of all job vacancies.

With those facts in view, it is easy to see why the job search is seldom easy for transitioning military members. The essential task may be to penetrate the barriers that protect that hidden job market, and traditional job-search techniques seldom accomplish that objective. The most widely advocated solution to the dilemma is to employ networking, a technique discussed in Chapter 6 as part of the transition planning process. Now is the time to turn that technique to another use: finding a job. Let's see what lies ahead if you do not.

The Traditional Job Search

The traditional approach to a job search has involved answering "help wanted" or employment ads, scattering résumés among potential employers, registering with employment agencies and headhunters, and canvassing employers—that is, walking in cold and asking for a job. Millions of people rely on these techniques to find jobs that launch them into careers. But it is important to know how to assign your time and energy to make the techniques work for you.

What could be better than knowing how employers themselves go about finding new employees? About ten years ago a survey of employers in Oregon attempted to discover just that. Some of the results are shown in Table 6, based on information in the brief, provocative, and highly recommended book *How to Find Those Hidden Jobs*, by Violet Moreton Cooper, a career counselor herself.

Table 6 shows the techniques and resources that representative companies in Oregon used when they had jobs to fill, arranged in order of frequency of use. The resources rated: "direct hire" procedures (where a job-seeker goes directly to an office or shop to ask for a job), advertising, private employment agencies, state employment agencies or job centers, school and college placement services, and other organizations including trade and professional associations and labor union hiring halls.

The companies that participated in the survey were clustered in seven industries: construction, finance and insurance, government, manufacturing, services, transportation, and wholesale and retail trade.

Table 6. How Employers Recruit New Employees

Industry/Job Category	Direct Hire	Adver-tising	Private Agency	State Job Office	Schools/Colleges	Other
Construction						
Professional, etc.	6	3	1	4	2	5
Clerical	4	2	1	3	5	6
Sales	5	2	1	3	4	6
Skilled trades	5	2	4	3	6	1
Semiskilled	2	3	5	4	6	1
Finance and insurance						
Professional, etc.	2	1	3	4	5	6
Clerical	1	3	4	2	5	6
Sales	5	2	1	3	4	6
Skilled trades	3	1	4	2	6	5
Semiskilled	3	1	4	2	5	6
Government						
Professional, etc.	1	4	—	2	3	5
Clerical	2	4	—	1	3	—
Skilled trades	2	5	3	—	4	1
Semiskilled	1	4	3	2	—	5
Manufacturing						
Professional, etc.	3	1	2	4	5	6
Clerical	2	3	4	1	5	6
Sales	3	1	4	2	5	6
Skilled trades	1	2	5	3	6	4
Semiskilled	1	3	5	2	6	4
Service industries						
Professional, etc.	1	2	3	4	6	5
Clerical	1	3	4	2	5	6
Sales	1	3	5	2	6	4
Skilled trades	1	3	5	2	6	4
Semiskilled	1	3	5	2	4	6
Transportation						
Professional, etc.	1	2	6	5	3	4
Clerical	1	5	3	2	4	6
Sales	1	5	3	4	2	6
Skilled trades	1	3	5	2	6	4
Semiskilled	1	5	6	2	4	3
Wholesale/Retail Trade						
Professional, etc.	3	1	4	5	2	6
Clerical	1	4	2	3	5	6
Sales	1	3	2	5	4	6
Skilled trades	1	3	5	2	6	4
Semiskilled	1	3	6	2	5	4

Source: State of Oregon industry survey, 1977 (based on information published in V. M. Cooper, *How to Find Those Hidden Jobs*, 1986).

Five employment categories were used in the survey: professional, managerial, and technical; clerical; sales; skilled trades; and semi-skilled workers.

The results of this study of employers' recruiting practices showed that:

1. Direct hire was the most important employment technique used to recruit employees in the services, transportation, wholesale and retail trade, and government sectors. Direct hire was also the most important means for employing clerical or office workers in the finance and insurance sector and for workers in the skilled trades and semiskilled categories in the manufacturing sector.
2. Advertising, including ads in newspapers and trade journals and signs posted by employers at their own establishments, was next most frequently utilized by employers in every sector except government and transportation.
3. State employment offices (job centers) were used more often than private employment agencies in most categories. The principal exception was the use of private agencies (presumably headhunters) to recruit employees in the professional, managerial, and technical category by employers in construction, finance and insurance, manufacturing, and services.
4. College placement offices were likely to be preferred to the professional and technical associations (under "Other") for recruiting employees in the professional, managerial, and technical category.
5. Union hiring halls (included in "Other") were primary sources of skilled and semiskilled construction workers.

Knowing how employers recruit people for jobs can help you focus your job search. Even though the data in Table 6 is limited to one state and is more than a decade old, it is fairly well supported by other studies and my own observations of the labor market on the East Coast and in the Mountain States region.

Do not become so fascinated by the results, on the other hand, that you overlook the fact that employers may use more than one recruiting technique or resource at one time—or that they may shift their emphasis from one resource to another. Keep in mind also that local and national trends since the survey results were published have changed recruiting patterns. Two trends of immediate interest are the following.

The spread of "right to work" laws across the country has diminished the role of union hiring halls, especially in the construction trades, and increased the roles of direct hire, advertising, and private or state employment offices in recruiting skilled and semiskilled employees in other sectors of industry.

State employment offices or job centers are becoming even more important to the recruiting scene as employers develop more confidence in their methods of testing and screening job-seekers. The level of recruitment has also been raised to include placement of professional, managerial, and technical job-seekers. Furthermore, the 2,500 state employment offices are linked to each other and to a national job bank, a situation that can produce jobs for applicants who are willing to relocate to other states. These offices now operate free employment services for military veterans, under Department of Labor programs.

The study of recruiting practices in Oregon supports the importance of developing such job-search skills as résumé-writing, job application procedures (essential for direct-hire situations), and interview techniques. These skills are not discussed in detail in this book, though you will find some important observations and further references in Appendix F. You need to work on these skills before you leave military service. A good place to start is with your Educational Center or Educational Services Officer.

The following sections discuss some of the pros and cons of three of the job resources often used by job-seekers: direct contact with employers, responding to newspaper advertising, and using employment agencies. They also happen to coincide with the recruiting techniques most frequently used by employers.

Contacting Employers

Job-seekers of all kinds have resorted to "knocking on doors" for centuries, I suppose, asking shopkeepers, tradesmen, and artisans for work. The question in this day and age is not whether to do that, but rather: "What doors should I knock on?"

The Oregon study shows, somewhat surprisingly, that many employers still *prefer* to have job-seekers contact them directly. The information available in Table 6 provides some guidance. That is: check all the categories where the number "1" appears under the heading "Direct Hire." Recall also that the heading "Advertising" includes the use of such methods as posting signs on the employer's premises that invite job applications.

If you decide to use this technique in your own job search, it is essential to develop a plan of attack and mount a realistic campaign. You can waste a lot of valuable time and energy just stomping around town knocking on doors. A list of employers in your career field can easily be developed from a study of the Yellow Pages in any telephone book, or you can use a local business directory.

Before you establish any contact, however, it is essential that you find out everything you can about the company or nonprofit organization: check the Chamber of Commerce, the Better Business Bureau, the local business development council, and the *local* newspaper and business or professional newspapers and magazines (get to know your local librarian). Do not overlook nonprofit organizations.

In the process you will probably turn up the names of key people in the businesses or organizations you are researching; make notes about them—their positions *and* their backgrounds. Some consultants recommend that you call businesses and ask for the names of the supervisors in the departments where you plan to seek a job— they are usually the ones who actually select new employees. But, DO NOT ask to talk to them yet. You may want to try some networking at a later date, just calling on managers and talking to them about what it takes to get a job in your occupational field.

If your list of potential contacts includes local franchise operators or branches of national companies (or nonprofit organizations), consult business, industry, and association directories to find out what they do and how they do it.

Armed with this kind of information, you can probably narrow your list and call on the most promising businesses with considerable confidence. But remember that you are exposing yourself. A sound knowledge of job application procedures, a good résumé, and well-developed interview techniques are essential (see Appendix F). It hardly seems necessary to add that your personal appearance must be suited to the situation—figuratively and literally.

If you are networking, make sure the employer knows that you are not looking for a job. But do try to show that you have a good knowledge of his or her business and its problems and prospects. If you feel that you have made a good impression during your exploratory discussion, send your contact a thank-you note. Enclose a copy of your résumé and ask your contact to keep you in mind in case he or she hears of a job opportunity that meets your objectives.

Contacting employers directly may not result in immediate job offers, of course, even if there is a sign on the premises that "applications are being accepted." You may not get past a personnel screener, though you should try by using networking techniques. In many cases when employers are asking for applications, even the most promising applicants are told that they will be informed later when interviews will be scheduled. Do not be discouraged if the first few contacts do not produce results. Call-backs, preferably in person, are appropriate.

Reading "Help Wanted" Ads

Even though most job opportunities are not advertised, you cannot afford to overlook the classified and display ads placed by employers in local and national newspapers. Do not count on getting a job through any of them, however. Large numbers of job-seekers, sometimes numbering in the hundreds, answer these ads.

Newspaper classified ads tend to seek entry-level employees, and a majority of the advertised jobs are in unskilled or low-skill fields. On the other hand, random reviews of a local newspaper reveal a consistent pattern of jobs above the basic entry level (mostly placed by *identified employers*) in the construction trades, accounting, automotive maintenance, food services (including management training programs offered by franchisers), insurance, the engineering and technical fields, health care (including management opportunities), law (paralegals and legal secretaries), investments, banking, real estate, transportation, and protective services.

When dealing with local newspaper ads, look for those that have been placed by identified employers and that provide a date, time, and place for interviews. Those that request résumés by mail are often worth the effort, but you have little or no influence over the employment process unless you are called for an interview. The cover letter to your résumé is very important when answering this kind of ad.

You must be familiar with job application techniques, résumé-writing, and interview techniques in these situations where you directly expose yourself. Investigate employers in advance, to the extent possible, before you show up for an interview. If the ad does not give the name of the employer, be sure to find out when you call for an interview. Interviewers often ask such questions as "Why do you want to work for this company?" or "What do you feel you can contribute if you are hired?"

Employment ads in national newspapers (the *New York Times*, the *Wall Street Journal*, and *USA Today*) tend to be directed to "experienced only" job-seekers or job-changers. Most of these ads are in the professional, managerial, and technical category, but not all of them. So you can't afford to overlook these sources, especially if you are free to relocate.

Several national "employment opportunity" publications such as the *National Job Market* (biweekly, 10406 Muir Place, Kensington, MD 20895) and the *National Ad Search* (weekly, P.O. Box 2083, Milwaukee, WI 53201) extract display ads from newspapers all over the country. The ads cover federal, business, nonprofit, and international employment opportunities. Skip the agency ads and those for "Employment Services" and concentrate on ads run by identified companies that provide job descriptions and specify the credentials and experience required.

Both papers are sold at newsstands, but they may publish different editions for subscribers. Both also offer to send your résumé to hundreds of employment agencies and executive recruiters if you are a subscriber. The service is free and not a bad idea, providing you do not hold your breath waiting for hundreds of job offers. *National Ad Search* offers its subscribers free résumé kits.

The *Wall Street Journal* publishes display ads from its New York and regional editions in its *National Business Employment Weekly*, widely sold on newsstands. The Monday edition of *USA Today* features a weekly employment section. Follow the suggested guidelines if you decide to use these publications in your job search.

Most of the ads in these publications are legitimate, but all should be read with care and understanding. Newspapers and magazines do not screen advertisers. It also goes without saying that any employment ad that runs nationally is bound to pull in hundreds of responses. In a sense, it is like entering a sweepstakes. But as the promotional materials for sweepstakes say: If you don't enter, you can't win.

Reading Between the Lines

Unfortunately, some of the most attractive ads in newspapers are misleading—some intentionally so. It pays to be cautious. The rule of thumb is, "Forewarned is forearmed." Or, as the great entrepreneur of circus sideshows, P.T. Barnum, is supposed to have said, "There's a sucker born every minute."

- Blind ads that do not specify an employer, describe only "opportunities," and give only a telephone contact or a post office box number should be ignored. My favorite in that category read very simply: "Smallest Ad. Biggest Opportunity. Sm. inv. Call 567-8901." Smile, and forget it. "Sm. inv." means a *small investment*, by the way.
- Ads that state "Airlines are hiring" and specify "investment required," for example, or that "Key City Post Office Is Preparing to Hire," or that "20,000 Jobs Are Available from the Nation's Largest Employer" are promoting services, not jobs. Airlines, by and large, do their own recruiting. The Postal Service is a federal government agency—and is swamped with applications for jobs. The "nation's largest employer" is, of course, the federal Civil Service. One such ad in my local newspaper that seemed to offer job opportunities for air traffic con-

trollers specified "inv. req." (investment required). The same issue also carried a legitimate ad by the Federal Aviation Administration directly recruiting air traffic controllers. No agency can help you secure a federal Civil Service job.

- International jobs are often described as "available"—some ads even list specific jobs—by agencies that advertise in reputable publications. And they are telling the truth: Many international jobs are available every day—but not from these "agencies."

Some of these advertisers operate by mail, charge outrageous fees, promise much, and do nothing except bank your money. Several disreputable "agencies" of this kind operate out of Miami. While they may claim to be "registered in Florida," that state does not require employment agencies to register, nor does it otherwise regulate or supervise their activities. One recent ad in a national newspaper proclaimed that such an agency in Miami was a "member of the Chamber of Commerce." This is a variation on the phony "registered" claim. Even if the claim is true and the agency is a member of the Miami Chamber of Commerce, chambers of commerce do not necessarily investigate or vouch for member companies.

Others that advertise international jobs try to sell you a list of American companies that operate outside the country. A few sell monthly bulletins that actually list specific jobs for which you can apply—along with hundreds of other job-seekers. Most of the job ads are extracted from other publications and are stale. Stay away. (But see Eric Kocher's book in the Reading List.)

What About Employment Agencies?

Use them with caution, except for state job centers and reliable temporary employment agencies. As Table 6 shows, private employment agencies are a minor recruiting resource for most employers. Before you visit any private employment agency, check with the local Better Business Bureau office.

Several kinds of employment agencies exist. One is actually called *employment agency*. This kind usually specializes in entry-level jobs in low-skill areas, but some do offer more comprehensive job fields. Another is the *temporary* employment agency; these provide workers in all skill areas (depending on their specialty) to employers for a fee. Temporary agencies, by the way, often provide a route to a permanent job for people with outstanding qualifications; they get you "inside" where you can be observed and evaluated as a potential full-time employee. You also have a chance to size up the company. If you like what you see, and you did a good job as a "temporary," leave a résumé with your supervisor when you leave. A third kind of agency is the *executive recruiter* or headhunter. These firms usually work for employers, not for job-seekers.

Employment agencies routinely place ads in local papers to attract new clients and build up their files of candidates, even when the ads specify that jobs are available. Before you answer such an ad, check to see that it includes the statement: "Fee Paid." This means that the agency's fee is paid by an employer, not by the job-seeker. Other employment agencies may charge job-seekers a fee to "register" but do not say so in their ads, or they specify "fee" in tiny type. If you find a job through such an agency, you will also be charged a "placement fee," which is usually a substantial portion of the first month's pay.

Even the most reputable employment agencies often merely send your résumé or other credentials to their clients or other prospective employers. Some send "panels" of people from their pool of registrants to be interviewed for jobs. Getting the job is therefore up to you. The employment agency has done its job when it furnishes you the "lead," and it doesn't casre who is finally employed—especially if the employer pays the agency a fee for its role in recruiting, screening, and referring job candidates. The agencies that charge job-seekers do not care either, so long as one of the members of their "panel" is hired.

Some disreputable agencies, and unfortunately there are many, work the ranks of the unemployed. They promise much but deliver little. The name of their game is to get the initial registration fee, not to get you a job. If you wander into one of these agencies, remember that the "application" form you fill out is really a *contract*.

Some such contracts specify that the agency is your *exclusive* representative. Even if you find a job on your own or go to another agency, you may owe the first agency a sizeable fee for "placement." Don't sign anything until you have read the fine print and considered the consequences.

Other agencies work scams that are barely within the law. Some seek jobs in adjacent states, for example, and then make an "offer" to you. If you refuse because you want to stay where you are, you may be liable to a fee.

A few disreputable agencies have reportedly schemed with equally disreputable employers to make sure that you are hired—and that you are fired within two or three months. This game has obvious benefits for both the agency and the employer.

Executive recruiters, or headhunters, do not often advertise jobs (but may advertise their fields of expertise). Headhunters work the professional and middle- to upper-management fields. Good headhunters do not deal with individual job-seekers, though they may advertise to solicit résumés from highly qualified candidates. Generally, they recruit for their clients, the employers, who pay a fee to the agency. The *Directory of Executive Recruiters* lists such "fee paid" firms. Write for it to: *Executive Recruiter News*, Templeton Road, Fitzwillian, NH 03447. You may be able to get into the fold, possibly by cultivating one of the recruiters.

Executive search firms that advertise jobs and specify that the job-seeker pays a "fee" are in another category. Experiences vary with this kind of firm. Many have prestigious names and well-appointed offices. But, usually, before they will agree to do anything but a "screening interview," such agencies require the job-seeker to sign a contract that commits him or her to a fee amounting to thousands of dollars—some or all of which is payable in advance. The "employment counselors" you meet in such agencies are often very convincing commission-sales professionals who look and talk like MBA's and reek of success. They have to be good: The commissions they earn on your fees pay for their Brooks Brothers or "designer" clothes.

Some of these organizations do make reasonable efforts to secure a job for you, though they never promise anything. Many merely circulate copies of your résumé—which they prepare as part of their service —to confidential "house lists" of firms where they allegedly have "inside" contacts. Chances are that you will never know to which companies your résumé is sent. If you ask, you are liable to be told a category of employer: "A prestigious national insurance company near the top of the *Fortune* 500 list," for example. Then is the time for you to make a strategic withdrawal and lick your wounds.

Employment Services ads may also lead you to a *career counselor* or *career consultant*. Such firms, which sometimes run ads that sound as though they will find you a job, merely sell expensive pre-employment services like résumé-writing, interview techniques, aptitude testing, and training in job-search techniques. They do not provide jobs, and the best of them do not pretend to. In the end, you have to find your own. All the services listed are available free of charge from other sources, beginning right on your own installation.

There is no easy way to find a job when you are changing careers, and the traditional routes to employment are probably the most arduous. In the long run, they are the least productive, simply because most jobs are neither advertised publicly nor available from private employment agencies. What to do?

Help Is Not Far, But You Have to Go Get It

At the beginning of this chapter, I said that you have to know where to turn for help—and what kind of help to expect. Now that you understand the need better, where can you go for help?

A loose safety network of support organizations does exist that can assist you through your transition from military service to a civilian career. How you use it depends to a great extent on how much pre-transition planning you have done. In any event, any transition planning should consider all possible post-service sources of support, even if you do not have time to utilize them before you leave the service.

Those who have shrugged off the need for comprehensive career planning while in uniform can still have access to these support agencies and services after they are retired or discharged. But the time in service not used for advanced planning must be made up after they become civilians, a circumstance that can put them in great personal and financial jeopardy.

What kinds of support and services are available? Everything from advice on personal matters to full-scale employment services. And where do you look? Some services are directly related to the fact of military service and provided by government agencies that operate programs for veterans—a word that until now I have preferred not to use. Some are provided by membership organizations that provide transition services and other benefits to active-duty, reserve, or retired or former military men and women. Some are provided by national veterans organizations. Some are provided by private agencies that promote employment opportunities for former military personnel (and sometimes other career-changers). Some are provided by local and national nonprofit agencies that seek to help women and members of minority groups to realize their career potentials.

Government Organizations and Programs

Federal government departments and agencies that administer programs for veterans include the Department of Labor, the Small Business Administration, the Office of Personnel Management (Civil Service), and the Department of Defense, in addition to the Veterans Administration. Their programs range from unemployment benefits to job training and placement. Some of these programs are well known to men and women in uniform, but most are not until it is too late. Because of the large number of such programs, I have summarized them in Appendix G. But do not feel that they are not important to you.

Military-Related Organizations

Appendix D lists about sixty military-related organizations that provide direct services to former military men and women, from helping them to file claims for Veterans Administration benefits to employment services. The organizations are shown in three groups: national associations of active, reserve, and former or retired military men and women; military professional associations; and national associations of veterans. They all, however, have some characteristics in common:

- They are nonprofit membership organizations, and dues are likely to be very modest. Membership eligibility varies: *e.g.*: the Retired Officers Association welcomes all officers.
- Most them have chapters around the country (some operated internationally) that enable transitioning military members to interface on a social or professional level with members who have already gone through the process, have established success-ful civilian careers, and are willing to help others. They are, in effect, places where you can begin networking. Networking does reveal hidden jobs.
- Military professional organizations often include as members defense contractors and other industrial corporations in their fields. Some are affiliated with national professional associations. All are sources of jobs.
- They publish newsletters or magazines to inform their members of association programs and activities; many publications in-clude ads for employment.
- They hold national conventions that focus on serious issues but leave plenty of time for socializing—and networking. Many of the conventions feature military-related industrial displays; ex-hibitors often actively recruit employees at cocktail parties and in the hallways. Some conventions feature employment desks and other job services for members.
- They lobby in national, state, and local government arenas for improved (or continued) benefits for both active-duty and former military members. They are largely responsible for the Govern-ment programs summarized in Appendix G.

Some of these organizations operate continuing employment ser-vices of varying degrees of sophistication. Others may offer informal career counseling and job referrals (see Appendix D). Those offering established employment programs are:

Air Force Sergeants Association (through the Airmen Memorial Foundation).
American Legion
Armed Forces Broadcasters Association
Armed Forces Communications and Electronics Association
Association of the United States Army
Disabled American Veterans (serves all veterans)
Italian American War Veterans

Marine Executive Association
Marine Corps Reserve Officers Association
Naval Enlisted Reserve Association
The Non-Commissioned Officers Association
The Retired Officers Association
Veterans of Foreign Wars

The Airmen Memorial Foundation has collaborated in the development of a supervised correspondence course called "Career Search," which it highly recommends to enlisted men and women (see below). Among other activities, the Non-Commissioned Officers Association produces Job Fairs around the country for all veterans, in cooperation with the U.S. Department of Labor; it claims more than 500 regular employer "clients" and a high placement rate. The Retired Officers Association operates a full-service program known as The Officer Placement System (TOPS) that also claims a high placement rate as a result of its extensive contacts among employers. TROA also publishes and sells *Marketing Yourself for a Second Career*, an excellent job-search guide (see Reading List).

Private Organizations That Work With Military Personnel

Several privately operated organizations and agencies work closely or entirely with transitioning military people.

1. Transition Planning and Training Programs. Two reputable, successful, and low-cost courses of instruction have been developed specifically to ease transition problems. They are particularly useful for those who have not had time for the comprehensive career transition planning suggested in this book.

- *Identity Research Institute* offers a unique 42-hour course (conducted in several sessions) in the Washington, D.C., area and occasionally elsewhere. The originator of the course, a retired Air Force officer, claims 14,000 successful graduates. At the current cost of $475, no one can afford to miss out on this opportunity. Write: Stan Hyman, Identity Research Institute, 7845 old Dominion Drive, McLean, VA 22101.
- *Learning Process Center* has developed a comprehensive transition planning course called "Career Search," in association with the Airmen Memorial Foundation. The course was designed for enlisted men and women (not limited to Air Force members) and has been developed with the assistance of a former Air Force NCO who is now a successful executive recruiter. The course runs the gamut from career identification to interviewing techniques. It is offered by correspondence, but students are closely monitored by members of the Center staff. Tuition

charge and all necessary materials are $450, payable in install-ments. Write: The Learning Process Center, 222 West 24th Street, National City, CA 92050.

2. Suggested Employment Resources:
Several reputable private, profit-making organizations provide employment services to former military personnel and have access to the hidden job market. As a rule of thumb: Investigate before you invest.

- *Career Market Consultants*, 1003 Norfolk Square, Norfolk, VA 23502. Jobs in USA and abroad.
- *Holmes and Narver Services, Inc.*, 999 Town and Country Road, Orange, CA 92668. Jobs in USA and Middle East.
- *International Employment Hotline*, P.O. Box 6170, McLean, VA 22106.
- *Mil-Vets Associates, Inc.*, 156 Q Street SW, Washington, DC 20024. Established and operated by a retired Marine NCO, Mil-Vets concentrates on "job fairs" in the areas of Washington, DC., Norfolk, Va., and Cherry Hill, N.J. High-tech and manage-ment. No fees to job-seekers.
- *National Defense Data Bank*, 265 South Main Street, Akron, OH 44308. A high-tech job bank.
- *Resource Consultants, Inc.*, 1960 Gallows Road, Vienna, VA 22180. Wide variety of defense-related jobs in Virginia.
- *Search and Recruit International*, 114 South Witchduck Road, Virginia Beach, VA 23462. Stages technical and engineering conferences in various locations around the country where job candidates can meet with employer representatives. Recent lo-cations have been Washington, Norfolk, Charleston, Memphis, Jacksonville, Pensacola, San Antonio, San Diego, Sacramento, and Bremerton, WA. No fees.
- *Vinnel Corporation*, 10530 Rosehaven, Fairfax, VA 22030. Contractor for supplying military-trained personnel to support U.S. military assistance programs in Saudi Arabia.
- *World Job Centers, Inc.*, 396 West Greens Road, Houston, TX 77067. Publishes a weekly bulletin of job opportunities, special-izing in petroleum exploration and drilling, construction, airlines and cruise lines. Subscribers are assisted with résumés and con-tract negotiations. Expensive ($325/yr), but appears to be a reli-able source of job leads.

Nonprofit Organizations Providing Job Services

A list of associations that offer employment services ranging from free, or inexpensive, career counseling to placement can be found in

Appendix E. None of these is military-related, but one might qualify provisionally. *Helicopter Association International*, runs an employ- ment hot line or "Electronic Job Fair" designed to put helicopter pilots, mechanics, and others in the "vertiflite" field in touch with employers.

Other highly recommended organizations in Appendix E include *Forty-Plus*, a cooperative employment agency for older workers, and *Catalyst*, an employment resource center for women. Both of these organizations operate on a national scale.

Most of the other organizations listed in Appendix E are of special interest to women and minority members and include some devoted to networking.

A number of nonprofit agencies that can provide employment assistance to transitioning military members are mentioned in Chapters 9 to 11.

PART III. SUGGESTED READING

Juvenal L. Angel. *Directory of American Firms Operating in Foreign Coun-tries*. New York: Simon and Schuster.

Lynie Arden. *The Work-at-Home Sourcebook*. (Available from *Worksteader News*, 2396 Coolidge Way, Rancho Cordova, CA 95670).

Artists Market: Where and How to Sell Your Graphic Art. Cincinnati: Writers Digest Books (Annual).

Richard H. Beatty. *The Résumé Kit*. New York: John Wiley, 1986.

Richard Nelson Bolles. *What Color Is Your Parachute?*. Berkeley, CA: Ten Speed Press (Revised annually). Note: Get a copy, scan it, and forget this best-selling job-search book. It has little of substance to offer most transi- tioning military men and women, though it is iconoclastic, jazzy, and thought-provoking.

Mary E. Calhoun. *How to Get the Hot Jobs in Business and Finance*. New York: Harper and Row, 1986.

Doug Carter. *Marketing Yourself for a Second Career*. Excellent 45-page "how-to-do-it" publication of The Retired Officers Association, written by the Director of TROA's Officer Placement Service. Oriented toward officers, but useful for senior NCO's. Available to nonmembers at a nominal charge.

Violet Moreton Cooper. *How to Find Those Hidden Jobs*. (Available from author at Career Management Associates, 39505 Luckiamute Road, Philomath, OR 97370.)

Kenneth W. Edwards. *Your Successful Real Estate Career*. New York: AMACOM-American Management Association, 1987.

Paul and Sandy Edwards. *Working from Home*. Los Angeles: Jeremy P. Tarcher, Inc., 1985.

Federal Benefits for Veterans and Dependents. (VA IS-1 Fact Sheet). Washington, DC: USGPO (Revised annually). *Note:* Essential source of information about veterans' entitlement programs administered by the Veterans Administration, including job training.

Franchise Opportunities Handbook (Small Business Administration). Washington, DC: USGPO.

William H. Gentz. *Religious Writers Market Place*. Philadelphia: Running Press, 1985.

Herman Holtz. *Advice, A High Profit Business: A Guide for Consultants and Other Entrepreneurs*. Englewood Cliffs, NJ: Prentice-Hall, Inc., 1986.

Joseph J. Kelly. *The Poet's Market Place*. Philadelphia: Running Press, 1984.

Eric Kocher. *International Jobs: Where They Are, How to Find Them*. Reading, MA: Addison-Wesley Publishers, 1979.

Beatrice Nivens. *The Black Woman's Career Guide*. Garden City, NY: Anchor Press, 1982.

Photographer's Market: Where to Sell Your Photographs. Cincinnati: Writers Digest Books (Annual).

Marti Prashke and S. Peter Valunis. *Money Jobs: Training Programs Run by Banking, Insurance, and Brokerage Firms and How to Get Them*. New York: Crown Publishers, 1984.

Diane S. Rothberg and Barbara Ensor Cook. *Part-Time Professional*. Washington, DC: Acropolis Books, 1985.

Theodore Schwarz. *How to Be a Freelance Photographer*. Chicago: Contemporary Books, 1980.

Starting and Managing a Small Business on Your Own (Small Business Administration). Washington, DC: USGPO.

Becky Hall Williams (ed.). *Writers Market*. Cincinnati: Writers Digest Books.

U.S. Non-Profit Organizations in Development Assistance Abroad. Technical Assistance Information Clearing House, 200 Park Avenue South, New York, NY 10003.

Appendices

Appendix A

DOT Titles For Enlisted Military Occupational Fields

Military Occupation	DOT Title and Code	Growth Rate	APP
ACCOUNTING SPECIALISTS			
210382010	Audit Clerk	S/HBK	
210382014	Bookkeeper	S/HBK	
216382010	Accounting Clerk, ADP	S/HBK	
216382022	Budget Clerk	S/HBK	
216382034	Cost Clerk	N/SUM	
216382062	Statistical Clerk	S/HBK	
216482010	Accounting Clerk	S/HBK	
ADMINISTRATIVE SUPPORT SPECIALISTS			
203362010	Clerk-Typist	S/SUM	
203582078	Notereader	S/HBK	
209562010	Clerk, General	S/SUM	
216482010	Administrative Clerk	S/SUM	
AIRCRAFT ELECTRICIANS			
825281018	Electrician, Airplane	N?	
AIRCRAFT MECHANICS			Army
621910010	Air-Conditioning Check Out	N/HBK	
621281014	Air-Frame and Power Plant	N/HBK	
63928010	Aviation Support Equipment Repair	N?	
80621054	Tester, Plumbing Systems	N?	
80631014	Heating and Ventilating	N?	
806381054	Skin Fitter	N?	
807261010	Aircraft Body Repairer	N/HBK	

Military Occupation	DOT Title and Code	Growth Rate	APP
AUDIOVISUAL PRODUCTION SPECIALISTS			Army, Navy
149061010	Audiovisual Production Specialist	S/SUM	
AUTOMOBILE MECHANICS			Army, Marines
620261010	Automobile Mechanic	F/HBK	
620281034	Carburetor Mechanic	F/HBK	
620281062	Transmission Mechanic	F/HBK	
620381010	Radiator Mechanic	F/HBK	
AUTOMOTIVE BODY REPAIRERS			Army
807381010	Automobile Body Repairer	N/HBK	
845381014	Painter, Transportation Equipment	N/HBK	
BARBERS			
330371010	Barber	S/HBK	
BLASTING SPECIALISTS			Army
859261010	Blaster	S/SUM	
931261010	Blaster	S/SUM	
BOAT OPERATORS			
197133030	Tugboat Captain	N/SUM	
911263010	Deep Submergence Vehicle Operator	N?	
911663010	Motorboat Operator	N/SUM	
BOILER TECHNICIANS			Navy
805361010	Boilerhouse Mechanic	S/HBK	
BRICKLAYERS AND CONCRETE MASONS			Army
844364010	Concrete Mason	N/HBK	
861381018	Bricklayer	N/HBK	
BROADCAST AND RECORDING TECHNICIANS			Army
194262010	Audio Operator	F/HBK	
194261018	Sound Mixer	F/HBK	
194282010	Video Operator	F/HBK	

Military Occupation	DOT Title and Code	Growth Rate	APP
194362010	Recording Engineer	F/HBK	
962382010	Recordist	F/HBK	
962382014	Sound Cutter	F/HBK	

BUILDING ELECTRICIANS
Army, Marines

824261010	Electrician	N/HBK	

CARDIOPULMONARY AND EEG SPECIALISTS

078362018	Electrocardiograph Technician	N/HBK	
078362022	Electroencephalographic Technician	F/HBK	
078362030	Cardiopulmonary Technologist	F/HBK	

CARGO SPECIALISTS

911663014	Stevedore 1	S?	
921683050	Industrial Truck Operator	S/HBK	
921683082	Winch Driver	S?	
922687090	Stevedore 2	S?	
929687030	Material Handler	S?	

CARPENTERS
Army

860381022	Carpenter	N/HBK	

CASEWORKERS AND COUNSELORS

045107010	Counselor	F/HBK	
195107010	Caseworker	F/HBK	
195164010	Group Worker	F/HBK	
195267014	Human Relations/Drug and Alcohol Counselor	F?	

CLOTHING AND FABRIC REPAIRERS

782684010	Canvas Repairer	S/SUM	
785261010	Alteration Tailor	S/SUM	
785361014	Garment Fitter	S/SUM	
787682030	Mender	S/SUM	

COMBAT ENGINEERS

869687026	Construction Worker 2	N?	

Military Occupation	DOT Title and Code	Growth Rate	APP
COMPRESSED GAS TECHNICIANS			
549364010	Tester, Compressed Gas	N?	
549587010	Compressed Gas Plant Worker	N?	
552362014	Oxygen Plant Operator	N?	
COMPUTER OPERATORS			
213362010	Computer Operator	F/HBK	
2133822010	Computer Peripheral Equipment Operator	F/HBK	
COMPUTER PROGRAMMERS			
020162014	Programmer, Business	F/HBK	
219367026	Programmer, Detail	F/HBK	
COMPUTER SYSTEMS ANALYSTS			
012167066	Systems Analyst, EDP	F/HBK	
CONSTRUCTION EQUIPMENT OPERATORS			Army
859683010	Operating Engineer	N/HBK	
CORRECTIONS SPECIALISTS			
372667018	Correction Officer	F/HBK	
COURT REPORTERS			
202362010	Shorthand Reporter	S/HBK	
202362022	Stenotype Operator	N/HBK	
243362010	Court Clerk	F/SUM	
DATA ENTRY SPECIALISTS			
203582026	Data-Coder Operator	N/HBK	
203582030	Keypunch Operator	N/HBK	
203582070	Verifier Operator	N/HBK	
DATA PROCESSING EQUIPMENT REPAIRES			Army, Marines
633261010	Assembly Technician	F/HBK	
823281010	Avionics Technician	F/HBK	
828281010	Electronics Mechanic	F/HBK	
DENTAL LABORATORY TECHNICIANS			
712381018	Dental Laboratory Technician	N/HBK	

Military Occupation	DOT Title and Code	Growth Rate	APP
DENTAL SPECIALISTS			
078361010	Dental Hygienist	F/HBK	
079371010	Dental Assistant	F/HBK	
DETECTIVES			
375267010	Detective	N/HBK	
376267018	Investigator, Private	N?	
378267010	Counterintelligence Agent	N?	
DISPATCHERS			
221367066	Scheduler, Maintenance	N?	
249167014	Dispatcher, Motor Vehicle	N/SUM	
DIVERS			
899261010	Diver	N?	
DRAFTERS			Army
005281010	Drafter, Civil	N/HBK	
005281014	Drafter, Structural	N/HBK	
ELECTRICAL PRODUCT REPAIRERS			Army, Navy, Marines
721281018	Electric Motor Repairer	N/SUM	
721484010	Electric Motor Winder	N/SUM	
729281022	Electric Tool Repairer	N/HBK	
729281030	Electromedical Equipment Repairer	N/SUM	
829281014	Electrical Repairer	N/HBK	
ELECTRONIC INSTRUMENT REPAIRERS			Army
019261010	Biomedical Equipment Technician	N/SUM	
719261010	Biomedical Equipment Technician	N/SUM	
719261014	Radiological Equipment Specialist	N/SUM	
720281018	TV and Radio Repairer	N/HBK	
729281010	Audio-Video Repairer	N/HBK	
823281010	Avionics Technician	F/HBK	
828281010	Electronics Mechanic	F/HBK	
829261014	Dental Equipment Installer and Servicer	N/SUM	
829281022	Sound Technician	F/HBK	

Military Occupation	DOT Title and Code	Growth Rate	APP
ELECTRONIC WEAPONS SYSTEMS REPAIRERS			Army, Navy, Marines
806281030	Inspector, Missile	?	
823281010	Avionics Technician	F/HBK	
828281010	Electronics Mechanic	F/HBK	
828281018	Missile Facilities Repairer	?	
EMERGENCY MANAGEMENT SPECIALISTS			
199384010	Decontaminator	?	
378267014	Disaster or Damage Control Specialist	?	
ENGINE MECHANICS			Army, Navy, Marines
620281050	Mechanic, Industrial Truck	F/HBK	
620281058	Tractor Mechanic	N/HBK	
623281026	Machinist, Marine Engine	N/HBK	
623281038	Motorboat Mechanic	N?	
625281010	Diesel Mechanic	F/HBK	
625281026	Gas Engine Repairer	N/SUM	
806261010	Internal Combustion Engine Inspector	N?	
ENVIRONMENTAL HEALTH SPECIALISTS			
168267042	Food and Drug Inspector	S/HBK	
168287010	Inspector, Agricultural Commodities	S/HBK	
FIREFIGHTERS			Army
373267010	Fire Inspector	N/HBK	
373364010	Firefighter	N/HBK	
373367010	Fire Inspector	N/HBK	
373663010	Firefighter, Crash, Fire, and Rescue	N/HBK	
FLIGHT ENGINEERS			
621261018	Flight Engineer	S/HBK	
FLIGHT OPERATIONS SPECIALISTS			
193162-series	Air Traffic Controllers	N	
248367010	Airplane Dispatch Clerk	N	
248387010	Flight Operations Specialist	N?	

Military Occupation	DOT Title and Code	Growth Rate	APP
912367010	Flight Information Expediter	N?	

FOOD SERVICE SPECIALISTS

Army, Navy, Marines

313131014	Chef	F/HBK	
313361014	Cook	F/HBK	
313381010	Baker	N/HBK	
313381030	Cook, School Cafeteria	N/HBK	
315361010	Cook	F/HBK	
316681010	Butcher, Meat	S/HBK	
316684018	Meat Cutter	S/HBK	

FUEL AND CHEMICAL LABORATORY TECHNICIANS

Army

011281014	Spectroscopist	N/HBK	
022261010	Chemical Laboratory Technician	N?	
029261010	Laboratory Tester	N?	

GRAPHIC DESIGNERS AND ILLUSTRATORS

141061018	Graphic Designer	F/HBK	
141061022	Illustrator	F/HBK	
141061026	Illustrator, Medical and Scientific	F/HBK	
979382018	Graphic Arts Technician	F?	

HEATING AND COOLING MECHANICS

Army, Marines

637261014	Environmental Control System Installer/Servicer	N/HBK	
637261026	Refrigeration Mechanic	N/HBK	

HEAVY EQUIPMENT MECHANICS

Army, Marines

620261022	Construction Equipment Mechanic	N/HBK	
620381014	Mechanic, Endless Track Vehicle	N/HBK	

INTELLIGENCE SPECIALISTS

029167010	Aerial Photograph Interpreter	?	

Military Occupation	*DOT Title and Code*	*Growth Rate*	*APP*
059267010	Intelligence Specialist	?	
059267014	Intelligence Specialist	?	
199267014	Cryptanalyst	?	
249387014	Intelligence Clerk	?	
378267010	Counterintelligence Agent	?	
378382010	Airborne Sensor Specialist	?	
378382018	Unattended Ground Sensor Specialist	?	

INTERPRETERS AND TRANSLATORS
137267010	Interpreter	N?	
137267018	Translator	N?	

IRONWORKERS — Army
801361014	Structural Steel Worker	N/HBK	
801684026	Reinforcing-Metal Worker	N/HBK	

LEGAL TECHNICIANS
119267026	Paralegal Assistant	F/HBK	

LINE INSTALLERS AND REPAIRERS — Army, Marines
821261014	Line Maintainer	N/HBK	
821361010	Cable Installer/Repairer	N/HBK	
821361018	Line Erector	N/HBK	
821361026	Line Repairer	N/HBK	
823281022	Rigger	N/HBK	
829361010	Cable Splicer	N/HBK	

LODGING SPECIALISTS
238362010	Hotel Clerk	N/SUM	

MACHINISTS — Army, Navy
600280022	Machinist	S/HBK	
600280042	Maintenance Machinist	F/HBK	
600380018	Machine Setup Operator	F/HBK	

MAINTENANCE DATA ANALYSTS
221362010	Aircraft Log Clerk	N?	
221367038	Maintenance Data Analyst	N?	

Military Occupation	DOT Title and Code	Growth Rate	⌐ APP

MAPPING TECHNICIANS

Army

018261010	Drafter, Cartographic	S?
018261014	Drafter, Topographical	S?
018261018	Editor, Map	N/HBK
018261022	Mosaicist	N/HBK
018261026	Photogrammetrist	N/HBK
018281010	Stereo Plotter Operator	N?

MARINE ENGINE MECHANICS

Army, Navy

623281034	Maintenance Mechanic, Engine	N?

MEDICAL LABORATORY TECHNICIANS

078221010	Immunohematologist	S/HBK
078281010	Cytotechnologist	S/HBK
078361014	Medical Technologist	S/HBK
078361030	Tissue Technologist	S/HBK
078381014	Medical Laboratory Technician	S/HBK

MEDICAL RECORD TECHNICIAN

079367014	Medical Record Technician	F/HBK
205362018	Hospital-Admitting Clerk	N/SUM
205362030	Outpatient-Admitting Clerk	N/SUM
245362010	Medical Record Clerk	F/HBK
245362014	Ward Clerk	S/SUM

MEDICAL SERVICE TECHNICIANS

079364018	Physician Assistant	F/HBK
079367010	Medical Assistant	F/HBK
079367018	Medical Service Technician	N/HBK
079374010	Emergency Medical Technician	S/HBK
355374014	Medication Aide	S?

MILITARY POLICE

372667034	Guard, Security	F/HBK
372667038	Merchant Patroller	F/HBK
375263014	Police Officer 1	N/HBK

Military Occupation	DOT Title and Code	Growth Rate	APP
375263018	State Highway Police Officer	N/HBK	
377263010	Sheriff, Deputy	N?	

MOTION PICTURE CAMERA OPERATORS

Army, Navy

143062014	Photographer, Aerial	F/HBK	
143062022	Photographer, Motion Picture	F/HBK	

MUSICIANS

152041010	Musician, Instrumental	N/HBK
152047010	Choral Director	N/HBK
152047014	Conductor, Orchestra	N/HBK
152047022	Singer	N/HBK
152067010	Arranger	N/HBK
152067014	Composer	N/HBK

NON-DESTRUCTIVE TESTERS

011261018	Non-Destructive Tester	F/HBK
199361010	Radiographer	F/HBK

NURSING TECHNICIANS

079374014	Nurse, Licensed Practical	N/HBK
079374026	Pyschiatric Technician	N/HBK
355377014	Psychiatric Aide	S/HBK
355674014	Nurse Aide	F/HBK
355674018	Orderly	S/HBK

OCCUPATIONAL THERAPY SPECIALISTS

076364010	Occupational Therapy Assistant	N/SUM
355377010	Occupational Therapy Aide	N/SUM

OFFICE MACHINE REPAIRERS

Army, Navy

633281018	Office Machine Servicer	F/HBK
633281030	Statistical Machine Servicer	F/HBK

OPERATING ROOM TECHNICIANS

079374022	Surgical Technician	N/HBK

Military Occupation	DOT Title and Code	Growth Rate	APP
OPTICIANS			
713361014	Optician, Dispensing 1	F?	
716280014	Optician	F?	
OPTOMETRIC TECHNICIANS			
079364014	Optometric Assistant	F/HBK	
ORDNANCE MECHANICS			Army
632261010	Aircraft/Armament Mechanic	?	
632261014	Fire Control Mechanic	?	
632261018	Ordnance Artificer	?	
632281010	Gunsmith	?	
ORTHOPEDIC TECHNICIANS			
712661010	Orthopedic Assistant	F/SUM	
ORTHOTIC SPECIALISTS			
078261018	Orthotist	N?	
078361022	Orthotics Assistant	N?	
712381034	Orthotics Technician	N?	
PAVING EQUIPMENT OPERATORS			Army
853663010	Asphalt Paving Machine Operator	N/SUM	
853663014	Concrete Paving Machine Operator	N/SUM	
PAYROLL SPECIALISTS			
215482010	Payroll Clerk	S/SUM	
PERSONNEL SPECIALISTS			
205362010	Civil Service Clerk	N/SUM	
205362014	Employment Clerk	N/SUM	
209362026	Personnel Clerk	N/SUM	
PETROLEUM SUPPLY SPECIALISTS			Army
549387010	Cargo Inspector	S?	
638381010	Fuel System Maintenance Worker	S?	
869564010	Line Walker	S?	
891687022	Tank Cleaner	S?	

Military Occupation	DOT Title and Code	Growth Rate	APP
910384010	Tank Car Inspector	S?	
914167014	Dispatcher, Oil	S?	
914362014	Construction and Maintenance Inspector	S?	
914362018	Station Engineer, Main Line	S?	
914382014	Pumper-Gager	S/SUM	
914384010	Gager	S/SUM	
914667010	Loader 1	S?	
914682010	Pumper	S/SUM	
914687010	Laborer, Pipe Lines	S/SUM	
921663062	Truck-Crane Operator	N/HBK	

PHARMACY TECHNICIANS

074381010	Pharmacy Assistant	N/SUM	
074387010	Pharmacy Helper	N/SUM	

PHOTOGRAPHERS   Army, Navy

143062014	Photographer, Aerial	F/HBK	
143062030	Photographer, Still	F/HBK	
143062034	Photojournalist	S/HBK	
143620010	Biological Photographer	F/HBK	

PHOTOGRAPHIC EQUIPMENT REPAIRERS   Army, Navy

714281014	Camera Repairer	N?	
714281018	Machinist, Motion Picture Equipment	N?	
714281022	Photographic Equipment Technician	N?	
714281026	Photographic Equipment Maintenance Technician	N?	

PHOTOPROCESSING SPECIALISTS   Army, Navy

976267010	Quality Control Technician	F?	
976360010	Print Controller	F?	
976382018	Film Developer	F/HBK	
976681010	Developer	F/HBK	
976685026	Print Developer, Automatic	F/HBK	

PHYSICAL THERAPY SPECIALISTS

076224010	Physical Therapy Assistant	F/SUM	

Military Occupation	DOT Title and Code	Growth Rate	APP
076264010	Physical Integration Practitioner	F/SUM	
355354010	Physical Therapy Aide	F/SUM	

PLUMBERS AND PIPEFITTERS — Army, Marines
862261010	Pipefitter	N/HBK	
862381010	Aircraft Mechanic, Plumbing and Hydraulic	N?	
862381018	Pipefitter	N/HBK	
862381030	Plumber	N/HBK	

POSTAL SPECIALISTS
243367014	Post Office Clerk	S/HBK	

POWER PLANT ELECTRICIANS — Army
820261014	Electrician, Powerhouse	N/HBK	

PRECISION INSTRUMENT REPAIRERS — Army, Navy
710281026	Instrument Mechanic	N/SUM	
710281030	Instrument Technician	N/SUM	
710381042	Instrument Mechanic	N/SUM	
710681014	Calibrator 1	N/SUM	
711281010	Inspector, Optical Instrument	N/SUM	
711281014	Instrument Mechanic, Weapons System	?	
715281010	Watch Repairer	S/SUM	

PRINTING SPECIALISTS — Army, Navy, Marines
651380010	Printer 2	N/HBK	
651482010	Offset Press Operator	N/HBK	
651682014	Offset Duplicating Machine Operator	N/HBK	
653685010	Bindery Worker	N/HBK	
972381010	Lithographic Plate Maker	N/HBK	
972381022	Stripper, Photolithographic	N/HBK	
972382014	Photographer, Lithographic	N/HBK	

QUARTERMASTERS
197133026	Pilot, Ship	N/SUM	
911363014	Quartermaster	N/SUM	

Military Occupation	DOT Title and Code	Growth Rate	APP

RADAR AND SONAR OPERATORS
No direct equivalent; equipment is used by Air Traffic Controllers, Pilots, Navigators, Marine Salvage Operators, Weather Forecasters, and other civilian technicians.

RADAR AND SONAR EQUIPMENT REPAIRERS

Army, Navy, Marines

823261018	Radio Mechanic	N/HBK	
823281010	Avionics Technician	F/HBK	
828281010	Electronics Mechanic	F/HBK	

RADIO AND TELEVISION ANNOUNCERS

159147010	Announcer	N/HBK	
159147014	Disk Jockey	N/HBK	

RADIO EQUIPMENT REPAIRERS

Army, Marines

720281010	Radio Repairer	N/HBK	
822281010	Automatic Equipment Technician	N/HBK	
823261018	Radio Mechanic	N/HBK	
823281010	Avionics Technician	F/HBK	
823281014	Electrician, Radio	N/HBK	
823281018	Meteorological Equipment Repairer	N/HBK	
828281010	Electronics Mechanic	F/HBK	

RADIO INTELLIGENCE OPERATORS

193362014	Radio Intelligence Operator	?	
193382010	Electronic Intelligence Operations Specialist	?	

RADIO OPERATORS

Army

193262010	Airline Radio Operator	N?	
193262022	Radio Officer	N?	
193262030	Radiotelegraph Operator	S?	
193262034	Radiotelephone Operator	S?	

RADIOLOGIC (X-RAY) TECHNICIANS

078361018	Nuclear Medical Technologist	F/HBK	

Military Occupation	DOT Title and Code	Growth Rate	APP
078361034	Radiation Therapy Technician	F/HBK	
078362026	Radiologic Technologist	F/HBK	

RECREATION SPECIALISTS

195227014	Recreation Leader	F/HBK	

RECRUITING SPECIALISTS

166267010	Employment Interviewer	F/SUM	
166267026	Recruiter	N/HBK	
166267038	Personnel Recruiter	N/HBK	

RELIGIOUS PROGRAM SPECIALISTS

129107018	Director of Religious Activities	S/SUM	

REPORTERS AND NEWSWRITERS

131067014	Copywriter	F/HBK	
131067022	Editorial Writer	F/HBK	
131087010	Continuity Writer	F/HBK	
131087018	Screenwriter	F/HBK	
131267010	Newscaster	N/HBK	
131267014	Newswriter	F/HBK	
131267018	Reporter	N/HBK	
132017010	Editor, Managing, Newspaper	F/HBK	
132017014	Editor, Newspaper	F/HBK	
132037014	Editor, City	F/HBK	
132037018	Editor, Department	F/HBK	
132037022	Editor, Publications	F/HBK	
132267014	Editorial Assistant	F/HBK	
962264010	Editor, Film	N?	

RESPIRATORY THERAPISTS

079361010	Respiratory Therapist	F/HBK	

RIGGERS

			Army
921260010	Rigger	N/SUM	

SALES AND STOCK SPECIALISTS

290477014	Sales Clerk	N/HBK	
299367014	Stock Clerk, Self-Service Store	F/SUM	

Military Occupation	DOT Title and Code	Growth Rate	APP
SEAMAN			
911131010	Boatswain	S/SUM	
911364010	Able Seaman	S/SUM	
911364014	Boatloader	S/SUM	
911687022	Deckhand	N/SUM	
911687030	Ordinary Seaman	N/SUM	
SECRETARIES AND STENOGRAPHERS			
201362010	Legal Secretary	S/HBK	
201362030	Secretary	S/HBK	
202362014	Stenographer	N/HBK	
SHEET METAL WORKERS			Army, Marines
804281010	Sheet Metal Worker	N/HBK	
SHIP ELECTRICIANS			Navy
825281014	Electrician	N/HBK	
SHIPFITTERS			
806261026	Marine Services Technician	S/SUM	
806381046	Shipfitter	S/SUM	
SHIPPING AND RECEIVING SPECIALISTS			
222387050	Shipping and Receiving Clerk	S/HBK	
248367018	Cargo Agent	S/SUM	
920484010	Crater	S/SUM	
920587018	Packager, Hand	S/SUM	
920685078	Packager, Machine	S/SUM	
921683050	Industrial Truck Operator	S/HBK	
SPACE SYSTEMS SPECIALISTS			
No DOT information available. Employment in NASA, NOAA, DOD, U.S. Weather Service, AT&T, COMSAT, INTELSAT, etc.			
STOCK AND INVENTORY SPECIALISTS			
219367034	Stock Control Clerk	S/SUM	
222367038	Magazine Keeper	S/SUM	
222367042	Parts Clerk	S/SUM	
222387026	Inventory Clerk	S/SUM	

Military Occupation	DOT Title and Code	Growth Rate	APP
222387034	Material Clerk	S/SUM	
222387058	Stock Clerk	S/SUM	
222387062	Storekeeper	S/SUM	
249367066	Procurement Clerk	S/SUM	
921683050	Industrial Truck Operator	S/HBK	

SURVEYING TECHNICIANS
Army, Marines

018167010	Chief of Party	N/HBK	
018167014	Geodetic Computer	N/HBK	
018167034	Surveyor Assistant, Instruments	N/HBK	
018167038	Surveyor, Geodetic	N/HBK	
018167046	Surveyor, Marine	N/HBK	

SURVIVAL EQUIPMENT SPECIALISTS

739381054	Survival Equipment Repairer	?	
912684010	Parachute Rigger	?	

TELEPHONE OPERATORS
Army

235462010	Central Office Operator	N/HBK	
235662010	Command and Control Specialist	?	
235662022	Telephone Operator	N/HBK	

TELEPHONE TECHNICIANS
Army, Marines

822261022	Station Installer/Repairer	S/HBK	
822281014	Central Office Repairer	S/HBK	
822281018	Maintenance Mechanic, Telephone	S/HBK	
822281022	Private Branch Exchange Repairer	S/HBK	
822361014	Central Office Installer	S/HBK	
822381018	Private Branch Exchange Installer	S/HBK	

TELETYPE OPERATORS
Army

203582018	Cryptographic Machine Operator	?	
203582050	Telegraphic Typewriter Operator	S/SUM	

Military Occupation	*DOT Title and Code*	*Growth Rate*	*APP*
TELETYPE REPAIRERS			Army, Marines
822281010	Automatic Equipment Technician	S/HBK	
822381010	Equipment Installer	S/HBK	
823261018	Radio Mechanic	S/HBK	
823281010	Avionics Technician	F/HBK	
828281010	Electronics Mechanic	F/HBK	
TRAINERS			
099167022	Educational Specialist	N?	
099227030	Teacher, Adult Education	N/HBK	
153227014	Instructor, Physical	F/HBK	
153227018	Instructor, Sports	F/HBK	
166227010	Training Representative	N/HBK	
378227010	Marksmanship Instructor	?	
378227014	Recruit Instructor	?	
378227018	Survival Specialist	?	
TRANSPORTATION SPECIALISTS			
214362014	Documentation/Billing Clerk	N/SUM	
238167010	Travel Clerk	S/HBK	
238362014	Reservation Clerk	S/HBK	
238367010	Gate Agent	S/HBK	
352367010	Airplane Flight Attendant	F/HBK	
352377010	Host/Hostess, Ground	S?	
912367014	Transportation Agent	S?	
TRUCK DRIVERS			
903683018	Tank Truck Driver	N/HBK	
904383010	Tractor-Trailer Driver	N/HBK	
905663014	Truck Driver, Heavy	N/HBK	
906683022	Truck Driver, Light	N/HBK	
913463010	Bus Driver	N/HBK	
WATER AND SEWAGE TREATMENT PLANT OPERATORS			Army, Marines
954382010	Pump Station Operator, Waterworks	N/HBK	
954382014	Water Treatment Plant Operator	N/HBK	

Military Occupation	DOT Title and Code	Growth Rate	APP
955362010	Wastewater Treatment Plant Operator	N/HBK	

WEATHER OBSERVERS — Navy
025267010	Oceanographer Assistant	?	
025267014	Weather Observer	?	
248362014	Weather Clerk	?	

WELDERS — Army, Marines
810384014	Welder, Arc	N/HBK	
819281018	Weld Inspector 1	N/SUM	
819361010	Welder-Fitter	N/HBK	
819384010	Welder, Combination	N/HBK	

WELL DRILLERS — Army
859362010	Well-Drill Operator	N?	

Notes:

1. Abbreviation *HBK* following a job title indicates that a detailed description of the occupational field is given in the *Occupational Outlook Handbook* (Department of Labor).

2. Abbreviation *SUM* following a job title indicates that the field is described briefly in Appendix A of the *Occupational Outlook Handbook*. Consult the *Dictionary of Occupational Titles* for job description and training requirements.

3. A question mark (?) following a job title means that no information on trends is available for that job. In some cases, however, an estimate has been made based on trends in the general occupational field. When only a question mark (?) appears, the presumption is that these jobs are in highly specialized fields that may be peculiar to the federal government or to defense contractors. For example:

Intelligence and radio intelligence specialists (CIA, DIA, NSA, FBI, DEA, etc.)

Emergency Management Specialists (Federal Emergency Management Administration and allied state and local programs, Nuclear Regulatory Commission, nuclear power plants, etc.)

Electronic Weapons Technicians and Ordnance Mechanics (DOD and service activities (Civil Service), defense contractors).

Marksmanship Instructors (FBI and other federal law-enforcement agencies; state and local police forces).

4. The existence of an Apprenticeship program in any military occupational field does not necessarily mean that an apprenticeship is available in each of the DOT job titles that appears under the occupation. Consult your Educational Services Officer or base Education Center.

Representative Officer Professional Fields

Military Career Field	Civilian Occupations	Growth
Administration	Administrator	Faster
	Office Manager	Average
	Public Administrator	Average
Aerospace Engineering	Aerospace Engineer	Faster
	Technical Writer/Editor	Faster
Atomic Energy/	Nuclear Engineer	Slower
Nuclear Energy	Nuclear Safety Inspector	Average
	Technical Writer/Editor	Faster
Aviation	Pilot	Faster
	Flight Engineer	Slower
	Air Traffic Controller	Average
	Air Safety Inspector	Slower
Biomedical Sciences	Biological Scientist	Average
	Biochemist	Average
	Physiologist	Average
	Ecologist	Average
Cartography and Geodesy	Surveyor	Average
	Geodesist	Average
	Drafter	Average
	Cartographer	Average
Chaplain	Catholic Priest	Faster
	Protestant Minister	Slower
	Jewish Rabbi	Average
	Director, Religious Programs	Slower
	Counselor	Faster
	Teacher	Average
Civil Engineering	Civil Engineer	Faster
	Surveyor	Average
	Urban Planner	Slower
	Technical Writer/Editor	Faster

Military Career Field	*Civilian Occupations*	*Growth*
Club Management	Food Services Manager	Faster
	Club Manager	Faster
	Hotel Manager	Faster
	Apartment Manager	Faster
	Retirement Home Manager	Faster
Communications-Electronics Engineering	Electronics Engineer	Much Faster
	Technical Writer/Editor	Faster
Comptroller	Accountant, CPA	Much Faster
	Auditor	Faster
	Comptroller	Faster
	Bank Officer/Manager	Much Faster
	Insurance Underwriter	Faster
Contracting and Procurement	Contract Manager	Average
	Purchasing Agent	Average
	Purchasing Manager	Average
Counterintelligence/ HUMINT	Investigator	Average ?
	Government Agent	Average ?
	Personal Security Manager	Faster
Criminal Investigation	Police and Detectives	Average
	Investigator	Average
	Security Manager	Faster
Education and Training	Elementary Teacher	Faster
	Secondary School Teacher	Slower
	University Professor	Slower
	School Administrator	Slower
	Counselor	Average
	Adult Education Instructor	Average
	Vocational Education Instructor	Average
Electronic Data Processing	Computer Programmer	Much Faster
	Computer Systems Analyst	Much Faster
	Statistician	Average
	EDP Manager	Faster ?
	Technical Writer/Editor	Faster
Electronic Warfare	Electronic Engineer	Much Faster
	Technical Writer/Editor	Faster
Emergency Management	Emergency Management Specialist	Average ?
	Nuclear Safety Inspector	Slower

Military Career Field	Civilian Occupations	Growth
	Environmental Health Inspector	Slower
Finance and Accounting	Accountant, CPA	Much Faster
	Bank Officer	Faster
Fixed Telecommuni- cations Systems	Electronic Engineer	Much Faster
	Technical Writer/Editor	Faster
Food Management	Food Management	Faster
Health Services	Dentist	Faster
	Dietitian	Faster
	Environmental Health Inspector	Slower
	Nurse	Much Faster
	Occupational Therapist	Faster
	Optician/Optometrist	Faster
	Pharmacist	Slower
	Physician	Faster
	Podiatrist	Much Faster
	Psychologist	Faster
	Social Worker	Faster
Health Services Management	Health Services Manager	Much Faster
	Hospital Manager	Faster
	Group Practice (HMO) Manager	Much Faster
	Retirement Home Administrator	Faster ?
	Nursing Home Administrator	Faster
Intelligence	Government Agent	Average
	Security Officer	Faster
	Civil Service (DIA, CIA, etc.)	Average
	Market Researcher	Average
Law Enforcement	Police and Detective	Average
	Security Officer	Faster
	Customs/Immigration Inspector	Slower
	Meat and Agricultural Inspector	Slower
Legal Affairs	Attorney	Much Faster
	Public Administrator	Average
	Legal Advisor (Corporate)	Faster
	Trust Officer (Bank)	Faster

Military Career Field	Civilian Occupations	Growth
	Arbitrator	Faster
	EEO Specialist	Average
	Legal Assistance Officer	Faster
	Labor Relations Specialist	Average
	Title Examiner	Average
	Lobbyist	Faster
Logistics Management	Material Manager	Faster
	Contract Manager	Average
	Purchasing Agent/ Manager	Average
Maintenance Management	Mechanical Engineer	Much Faster
	Electrical Engineer	Much Faster
	Civil Engineer	Much Faster
Marine and Terminal Operations	Port Manager	Average ?
	Terminal Manager	Average ?
	Security Officer/ Manager	Faster
	Safety Inspector/ Manager	Average
Meteorology	Meteorologist	Average
	Radio/TV Announcer	Average
Oceanography	Oceanographer	Average
Operations Research/ Systems Analysis	Systems Analyst	Much Faster
Personnel Administration and Management	Recruiter	Average
	Personnel Specialist	Average
	Personnel Manager	Average
	Labor Relations Specialist	Average
	EEO Specialist	Average
	Training Officer	Average
Petroleum Management	Petroleum Engineer	Average
	Chemical Engineer	Faster
	Mechanical Engineer	Much Faster
Political-Military Affairs	Foreign Service Officer	Average ?
	Civil Service (DOD, State Department, etc.)	Average ?
	International Business and Banking	Faster ?
Public Affairs	Public Relations	Much Faster
	Radio/TV Announcer	Average

Military Career Field	Civilian Occupations	Growth
	Writer/Editor	Faster
Security	Guard/Security Officer	Faster
	Police/Detective	Average
	Government Agent	Average ?
	Security Manager	Faster
Shipping Management	Transportation Agent	Slower
	Shipping and Receiving Manager	Average
Traffic Management	Traffic Manager	Slower ?
Veterinary Services	Veterinarian	Faster
	Epidemiologist	Faster
	Public Health Officer	Faster
	Environmental Health Inspector	Slower
	Meat and Food Inspector	Slower
	Toxicologist	Faster
	Pathologist	Average

Source: Career fields from DOD and military service publications. Job projections from *Occupational Outlook Handbook*, U.S. Department of Labor, 1986–87 Edition, except for those followed by (?).

Appendix C

Educational Opportunities Available to Military Personnel

A. Active Duty Programs

1. Non-traditional educational programs from DANTES.

The Defense Activity for Non-Traditional Education, or DANTES, has developed servicewide programs that are administered or supervised by base Education Centers and/or Educational Service Officers.

a. The Independent Study Support Program provides opportunities to complete education goals by means of correspondence course offered by regionally accredited colleges and universities. Courses are available at high school, undergraduate, and graduate levels.

b. Servicemembers Opportunity Colleges, a network of more than 400 colleges and universities that minimize residency requirements, offer credit for non-traditional educational achievement (correspondence courses, examinations, service training), and accept credits by transfer. Associate degree programs are administered by the Army (SOCAD) and the Navy (SOCNAV).

c. Subject Standardized Tests (DSST's) offer opportunities to earn college credits in 55 subject areas; successful completion of each test results in the award of three semester hours of college credit.

d. Military Evaluation Program, under a contract with the American Council on Education, provides for the award of college credits for service school courses and other military training, based on standards published in the ACE's *Guide to the Evaluation of Education Experience in the Armed Services*.

e. High School Equivalency Tests, for the General Education Diploma (GED), GED pretests, and interest inventory tests.

f. College Admissions Testing Program makes available the Scholastic Aptitude Test, the Test of Standard Written English, and the Student Search Service. Pretest "prep" courses are usually available from Education Centers.

g. Professional Certification Programs, through formal agree-

ments with nationally recognized certification agencies, offer opportunities to qualify for certification in more than twenty professional
fields, recognizing skills acquired as a result of military training and
experience as well as through formal or informal advanced education.

2. The College Level Examination Program (CLEP), a nationally
recognized testing program developed by the College Entrance
Examination Board (known also as the College Board), is available
through base education centers. The testing program includes a five-
part General Examination (in English Composition, Social Sciences
and History, Natural Sciences, Humanities, and Mathematics) and
forty-four Subject Examinations. Successful completion of all five
parts of the General Examination can result in credit for the entire
freshman college year. Subject Examinations are equivalent to the
"final" or end-of-course examinations given in resident undergraduate
college programs. Individual preparation for CLEP tests includes
personal reading, on-the-job experience, television or VCR courses,
and correspondence courses.

3. Service institutions and programs that administer DANTES and
other non-traditional educational programs and sponsor or coordinate
on-base, off-duty formal education courses include the Navy Campus,
the Program for Afloat College Education (PACE, which provides
academic and technical courses on Navy ships), the Community
College of the Air Force, and the Army Continuing Education
System. The Community College of the Air Force, for example,
offers associate degrees in more than seventy fields and provides
college credit for completion of Air Force basic training, technical
school courses, and non-commissioned officer academies.

4. Education Centers and Educational Service Officers (ESO's)
provide on-base services that vary from base to base or from service
to service. Common services include:

    a. Basic education courses (reading, writing, and arithmetic);
and preparation for the GED;

    b. Courses in English as a Foreign Language;

    c. Educational and career counseling;

    d. Educational and vocational interest tests;

    e. Foreign language courses;

    f. College entrance and graduate placement tests;

    g. National Apprenticeship Program (Army, Navy, Marines);

    h. Coordination of off-duty college programs;

    i. Tuition assistance and financial aid.

5. Appointment to service academies is available for qualified enlisted men and women, including attendance at service-operated
preparatory schools with full pay and allowances.

6. "Bootstrap" college programs offer opportunities for both
enlisted personnel and officers with some college credit to complete

degree requirements by attending college full time, with full pay and allowances; the student pays tuition and fees.

7. Enlisted commissioning programs of the various services send members to complete college degrees prior to entering officer training.

8. Full-fledged academic institutions are maintained by the Air Force (Air Force Institute of Technology) and the Navy (Naval Postgraduate School); officers may be assigned to these schools, or through them to civilian universities, for graduate study. Courses at these institutions are not necessarily limited to members of their own service.

9. Army, Marine, and Coast Guard career officers are usually eligible for graduate degree programs at civilian universities, under fully funded programs.

10. Uniformed Services University of Health Sciences: full-scale medical degree program for qualified enlisted personnel and officers of the Army, Navy, and Air Force. Applicants are commissioned in the appropriate reserve component in grade of O–1 upon acceptance and serve in uniform with full pay and allowances. Enlisted applicants must arrange for a discharge to accept appointment; officers may be transferred.

11. Legal Education programs for qualified Army and Air Force officers on active duty provide for graduate study in civilian law schools on a fully funded basis.

12. Professional Military Education: college credit awarded for attendance at some senior NCO schools, warrant officer advanced courses, and officer career development courses; cooperative graduate degree programs are available to officers attending the various war colleges.

B. Special Situations for Post-Service Educational Assistance.

1. *Reserve Officers Training Corps (ROTC) Programs.* Write to:
Army ROTC, Post Office Box 9000, Clifton, NJ 07015
Air Force ROTC/ROR, Maxwell AFB, AL 36112
Naval ROTC Information, P.O. Box 500, Clifton, NJ 07015

2. *Service Academies.* Write to Director of Admissions at:
United States Military Academy, West Point, NY 10996
United States Naval Academy, Annapolis, MD 21402
United States Air Force Academy, Colorado Springs, CO 80840
United States Coast Guard Academy, New London, CT 06320

3. Students in Medical and Allied Health Fields:

a. *Uniformed Services University of Health Sciences.* Applicants must be eligible for a Reserve commission, not more than more 32 years of age as of June 30 in the year of graduation, and meet the physical and security requirements for a Regular commission in the armed forces, in addition to academic qualifications. Members serve in uniform in grade of O–1 in the appropriate service Reserve, with full pay and allowances. Graduates are offered Regular commissions (O–3); they serve on active duty at the rate of 21 months for each year spent in medical training. Write: Admissions Office, Uniformed Services University of Health Sciences, 4301 Jones Bridge Road, Bethesda, MD 20814.

b. *Armed Forces Health Professions Scholarship Program.* Applicants must be enrolled in or accepted for admission at an accredited school of medicine or osteopathy in the United States or Puerto Rico and qualified for a Reserve commission (Army, Navy, or Air Force). Those accepted are commissioned in grade of O–1 in their service's Inactive Reserve and remain at that grade while students. Students receive stipends of $530 a month, except during a required 45 days of active duty training each year, when they receive pay and allowances as O–1's. Tuition, fees, and other expenses are paid by the military service. Active duty obligation up to three years, depending on prior service. Write:

ARMY: Commander, USAMEDD Personnel Support Agency
             Attn: SGPE-PD
             1900 Half Street, Washington, DC 20324

NAVY: Chief, Bureau of Medicine and Surgery Navy Department, Washington, DC 20372
             HQ AFMPC/SGEP

AIR FORCE: Randolph Air Force Base, TX 78150

c. *Air Force ROTC Pre-Health Professions Program.* AFROTC students are guaranteed Armed Forces Health Profession Scholarships under this program, provided they are accepted by an accredited school of medicine or osteopathy upon completion of ROTC and an undergraduate degree. Other terms are the same as above, except that active duty obligation may be up to six years.
Write: HQ AFMPC/SGEP, Randolph AFB, TX 78150.

d. *Air Force ROTC Nurse Program.* Scholarships and monthly subsistence allowances available for students who have completed two years of nursing training in a school accredited by the National League for Nursing and affiliated with an AFRCTC unit. Minimum academic record, age restrictions, and USAF physical standards apply. Up to four-year active duty obligation, depending on prior service. Write: HQ AFMPC/SGEP, Randolph AFB, TX 78150.

e. *Army and Navy Medical Internship/Residency.* Provides appointment as O–3 in appropriate service to graduates of approved schools of medicine or osteopathy, and active duty service with full pay and allowances for minimum of three years. Age restrictions: Army, under age 32; Navy, under age 41. Write:
ARMY: USAMEDD Personnel Support Agency, address as above;
NAVY: Chief, Bureau of Medicine and Surgery, address as above.

f. *Army, Navy, Early Commissioning Program* for medical, osteopathic, dental, and, for Army, veterinary students. Students (except final-year students) who are enrolled in or accepted for admission by an accredited school are appointed Reserve officers in grade of O–1 and placed on inactive status while in school. Summer training in military facilities is available, with full pay and allowances. Graduates serve on active duty for three years with entry grade as O–3 (veterinarians as O–2), which includes first-year graduate education. Age limits apply. Write: Addresses given under *b* above.

g. *General Practice Dental Residency.* Graduates of accredited dental schools are appointed to the grade of O–3 in their service Reserve component and perform their general practice residencies in uniform, with full pay and allowances. Minimum service obligation is three years; further residency training is possible. Write: Addresses as in *b*, above.

h. *Army Early Commissioning Program.* Students of sanitary engineering, social work, optometry, podiatry, and psychology who have completed bachelor degrees and are enrolled in, or accepted by, an accredited graduate school are appointed 2nd Lieutenants, Army Medical Service Corps, and placed on inactive status while in school. Graduates serve on active duty for three years in their specialty assignment. Write: Commander, USAMEDD Personnel Support Agency, address as in *b*, above.

i. *Army and Air Force Dietetic Internships.* Graduates of accredited colleges are appointed Reserve 2nd Lieutenants; they serve on active duty at a military hospital during the internship. Applicants must meet academic requirements for a Hospital Dietetic Internship established by the American Dietetic Association. Age limits: Army, age 29; USAF, age 27. Obligation: three years from date of entry. Write: Army and USAF commands at addresses under *b*, above.

j. *Army Occupational Therapy Clinical Affiliation.* Graduates with a bachelor's degree who have completed a curriculum in occupational therapy are offered a nine-month clinical affiliation. They serve on active duty for up to three years. Write: Commander, USAMEDD Personnel Support Agency, address as above.

k. *Army Clinical Psychology Internship.* Graduates with a doctorate in Clinical or Counseling Psychology are appointed in the Army Medical Service Corps; the one-year internship is conducted at

Army medical facilities in an active duty status. Active duty obligation is four years, including the internship. Write: Commander, USAMEDD Personnel Support Agency, address as above.

l. *Army Reserve Student Commissioning Program* for medical, osteopathic, dental, and veterinary students. Qualified students, age 28 or less, are appointed 2nd Lieutenant, Medical Service Corps, USAR, and placed in reserve status while in school. Students may participate in paid drills in selected reserve units or serve on short tours of active duty (up to 45 days) for summer training at military health care facilities. Upon graduation, participants are reappointed in the Army Medical, Dental, or Veterinary Corps. No active duty obligation; a Reserve obligation may be involved, depending on prior service.

4. *Chaplain Candidate Programs.* Students enrolled at, or accepted by, a recognized theological seminary may be appointed to the grade of O–1 in the Navy, Air Force Reserve, or Army Reserve (or Army National Guard); ecclesiastical approval required. They remain in an inactive status except for active duty for training during summer vacation periods (may include Chaplain School). Upon graduation, ordination, and with ecclesiastical endorsement, participants are commissioned in the appropriate Chaplain Corps. Age limits apply. No mandatory active duty, though extended active duty may be requested. Write:

ARMY: Office of the Chief of Chaplains
               Department of the Army
               Washington, DC 20314

NAVY: Office of the Chief of Chaplains (OPO1H4)
               Assistant for Recruitment
               Department of the Navy
               Washington, DC 20370

AIR FORCE: Command Chaplain
               ARPC/HC
               Denver, CO 80280

Note: Military-supported education programs listed in this appendix are subject to change or augmentation.

Appendix D

Military and Veterans Associations

1. *National Military Associations (General)*

Air Force Association
1501 Lee Highway
Arlington, VA 22209

None. Industry members, reps at annual conventions.

Air Force Sergeants Association
Contact: Airmen Memorial
           Foundation
           5211 Auth Road
           Suitland, MD 20746

Counseling, testing, résumé service. Sponsors *Career Search* course.

American Military Retirees
  Association
P.O. Box 973
Saranac Lake, NY 12983

Informal. VA counseling, claims.

Army and Navy Union (1886)
P.O. Box 537
1391 Main St.
Lakemore, OH 44250

None reported. VA counseling, claims.

Association of the United States Army
  (1950)
2425 Wilson Boulevard
Arlington, VA 22201

Career Assistance Service (Career planning kit, résumé service, counseling, job referrals).
Members only (small fee).

Fleet Reserve Association (1922)
1303 New Hampshire Avenue NW
Washington, DC 20036

Career counseling and assistance.

Marine Corps Association (1913)
Box 1775, Marine Corps Base
Quantico, VA 22134

Informal; participate in
   USMC retirement
   seminars.

Marine Corps League (1923)
956 North Monroe Street
Arlington, VA 22201

None reported. Veterans
   counseling.

Marine Corps Reserve Officers
   Association (1926)
201 North Washington Street
Alexandria, VA 22314

Retirement seminars;
   career counseling,
   résumé service, job
   bank.
Career desk, conventions.
Recruiters at conventions.

Marine Executive Association
1111 14th Street NW
Washington, DC 20005

Informal (networking).
Expansion planned.

National Association for Uniformed
   Services
5535 Hempstead Way
P.O. Box 1406
Springfield, VA 22151

None reported. VA
   counseling and claims.

National Guard Association of the
   United States
1 Massachusetts Avenue NW
Washington, DC 20001

None

National Naval Officers Association
   (1971)
P.O. Box 46214
Washington, DC 20050

None

National Officers Association (1981)
1304 Vincent Place
McLean, VA 22101

None

Naval Reserve Association (1954)
1619 King Street
Alexandria, VA 22314

None

Naval Enlisted Reserve Association
   (1957)

Career planning seminars;
   job referrals (informal);

6703 Farragut Avenue
Falls Church, VA 22042

VA counseling and claims.

Non-Commissioned Officers
 Association of the USA (1960)
P.O. Box 33610
San Antonio, TX 78233

Career counseling.
Job Fairs under DOL/
 VETS program.

Reserve Officers Association
1 Constitution Avenue NE
Washington, DC 20002

None reported.

Retired Armed Forces Association
135 Garfield Avenue
New London, CT 06320

Counseling (VA benefits).

The Retired Enlisted Association
 (1963)
P.O. Box 1218
Aurora, CO 80040-1218

Counseling (VA benefits).

The Retired Officers Association
201 North Washington Street
Alexandria, VA 22314

The Officer Placement
 Service (TOPS):
 counseling, résumé
 service, job leads, job
 referrals. Magazine
 carries employment
 opportunities
 announcements. No fees
 to members.

U.S. Army Warrant Officers
 Association (1973)
P.O. Box 2040
Reston, VA 22090

None. Refers members to
 TROA/TOPS (above).

United States Armor Association
Box 607
Ft. Knox, KY 40121

Unknown.

U.S. Coast Guard Chief Warrant
 Officer and Warrant Officer
 Association (1929)
482 L'Enfant Plaza East, SW
Washington, DC 20024

None reported.

Women Marines Association (1960)
1008 Scenic View Drive
College Park, WA 99324

None.

2. *Military Professional Associations*

American Association of Military
  Controllers (1949)
P.O. Box 91
Mt. Vernon, VA

None reported.

American Defense Preparedness
  Association (1919)
1700 North Moore Street
Arlington, VA 22209

Solicit employment
  opportunity ads in
  publication.

American Helicopter Association
217 North Washington Street
Alexandria, VA 22314

Informal (affiliated with:
  Army Aviation Assn.,
  Naval Helicopter Assn.,
  Airborne Law
  Enforcement Assn.,
  Aerospace Industries
  Assn., and Helicopter
  Assn. Int'l.

American Logistics Association (1920)
1133 15th Street NW
Washington, DC 20005

None reported.

American Society of Naval Engineers
1432 Duke Street
Alexandria, VA 22314

Unknown.

Armed Forces Broadcasters
  Association (1982)
P.O. Box 12013
Arlington, VA 22209

Retirement seminars;
  résumé service; job bank
  (members only).

Armed Forces Communications and
  Electronics Association (1946)
5641 Burke Center Parkway
Burke, VA 22015

Career Planning Center
  and job bank for member
  C3I professionals.

Army Aviation Association of
  America (1957)

Unknown.

1 Crestwood Drive
Westport, CT 06880

Association for Unmanned Space   Unknown.
   Vehicles
1133 15th Street NW
Washington, DC 20005

Association of Jewish Chaplains of the   Unknown.
   Armed Forces (1967)
28611 West 12 Mile Road
Farmington Hills, MI 48018

Association of Military Surgeons of   Solicit employment
   the United States   opportunity ads in
10605 Concord Street   publication.
Kensington, MD 20895

Association of Naval Aviation (1975)   None.
5205 Leesburg Pike
Falls Church, VA 22041

International Military Club Executive   Unknown.
   Association
1438 Durke Street
Alexandria, VA 22314

Judge Advocates Association (1943)   None reported.
P.O. Box 2731
Arlington, VA 22202

Military Chaplains Association of the   Unknown.
   United States
P.O. Box 645
Riverdale, MD 20737-0645

Military Educators and Counselors   Unknown. Affiliate of
   Association   American Association
5999 Stevenson Avenue   for Counseling and
Alexandria, VA 22304   Development.

Military Operations Research Society   Unknown.
101 South Whiting Street
Alexandria, VA 22304

National Counter-Intelligence Corps Association 3969 Applewood Lane Kettering, OH 45429	Unknown.
National Military Intelligence Association c/o GTE Government Systems Corp. Strategic Systems Division Springfield, VA 22151-4381	Unknown.
Retired Army Nurse Corps Association (1977) P.O. Box 39235, Serna Station San Antonio, TX 78218	None.
Society of Air Force Physicians USAF/SGPC HQ Bolling AFB Washington, DC 20332	Unknown.
Society of American Military Engineers 607 Prince Street P.O. Box 21289 Alexandria, VA 22320-2289	Unknown.
Uniformed Services Academy of Family Physicians P.O. Box 11083 2314 Westwood Ave. Richmond, VA 23230	Unknown.

3. *National Veterans Associations*

American Legion c/o National Economic Commission 1608 K Street NW Washington, DC 20006	Counseling, résumes, job referrals, seminars at posts; Job Fairs in some Departments; Employment Newsletter. Department Employment Officers work with DOL/VETS Posts work with State Job Service counselors.

American Veterans Committee (1944) 1735 DeSales Street NW Washington, DC 20036	VA counseling, claims.
AMVETS (1944) 4647 Forbes Boulevard Lanham, MD 20706	VA counseling, claims.
Catholic War Veterans of the USA 2 Massachusetts Avenue NW Washington, DC 20001	None reported.
Disabled American Veterans (1921) 3725 Alexandria Pike Cold Spring, KY 41076	VA counseling, claims for veterans, through Posts, Outreach Centers, and 260 National Service Officers in 67 cities. Employment programs in selected cities and joint projects with VA DOL/VETS in others.
Italian-American War Veterans of the United States 514 Sumner Street East Boston, MA 02128	VA counseling, claims. Résumé service. Informal referrals.
Jewish War Veterans of the USA 1811 R Street NW Washington, DC 20009	VA counseling and claims.
National Association of Black and Minority Veterans (1970) 4185 North Green Bay Road Milwaukee, WI 53209	VA counseling and claims. Job referrals.
Paralyzed Veterans of America (1946) 801 18th Street NW Washington, DC 20006	VA counseling and claims.
Polish Legion of American Veterans of the USA 2141 Vernon Drive Trenton, MI 48183	VA counseling, claims. Placement services.

Regular Veterans Association of the United States (1934) P.O. Box 1941 Austin, TX 78742	VA counseling and claims. Placement services.
Veterans of Foreign Wars of the United States Attn: Veterans Service Office 200 Maryland Avenue NE Washington, DC 20002	VA benefits, employment counseling, résumés, job referrals by Post Employment Officers. Work with State Job Service offices at local level.
Veterans of the Vietnam War 2090 Wilkes Barre Road Wilkes Barre, PA 18702	VA counseling and claims.
Vietnam Veterans, Inc. POB 1411 Pittsburgh, PA 15230	VA counseling and claims.

Note: Many organizations that have no formal career services offer informal guidance or networking opportunities.

Appendix E

Selected Nonmilitary Sources of Career Assistance

Many of the following organizations are actively engaged in networking or operate their own network. They tend to be advocacy organizations, aggressively promoting the interests of special groups within the population: women, minorities, and older workers. Contact with one or more of these organizations often leads to contacts with others less well known.

Affirmative Action Register, 8356 Olive Boulevard, St. Louis, MO 63132. Publishes a job information journal.
Business and Professional Women's Foundation, 2012 Massachusetts Avenue NW, Washington, DC 20036.
  Offers scholarships and fellowships to women in the fields of management and engineering education.
Catalyst, 250 Park Avenue South, New York, NY 10003.
  A voluntary agency that furthers career development for women, operating through a network of 150 local chapters. Résumé-writing, job referrals, career publications, job-search guide, list of Catalyst Network chapters.
Federation of Organizations for Professional Women, 2437 15th Street NW, Washington, DC 20009.
  Job development and placement programs. Publishes *A Woman's Yellow Book*, a directory of organizations involved in women's issues.
Forty-Plus Clubs are found in most cities. A nonprofit cooperative executive job support organization for older workers, manned by volunteers. Check classified employment ads or telephone book for local address; some chapters are located at State Job Service offices.
National Association for the Advancement of Colored People, 186 Remsen Street, Brooklyn, NY 11201.
  Counseling and employment services; 1,800 local offices.
National Association for Female Executives, 1041 Third Avenue, New York, NY 10021.

Coordinates a NAFE network of 1,200 resource-sharing groups nationwide. Career workshops and seminars, management aptitude testing, résumé guide, unsecured loans, credit guide for women.

National Association of Negro Business and Professional Womens Clubs, 1806 New Hampshire Avenue NW, Washington, DC 20009.
Educational and career services; placement service; 300 local affiliates.

National Career Development Association, 5999 Stevenson, Alexandria, VA 22304.
Association of career counselors; publications; placement service (for counselors).

National Career Development Project, P.O. Box 379, Walnut Creek, CA 94596.
Career information clearinghouse. Publications.

National Council of Negro Women, 701 North Fairfax Street, Alexandria, VA 22314.
Coordinates career services; list of 30 affiliated organizations. Sponsors Women's Center for Education and Career Advancement in New York, engaged in programs for minority women who wish to pursue non-traditional careers.

National Urban League, 500 East 62nd Street, New York, NY 10021.
Job training and employment program; veterans programs; 113 local chapters.

OPTIONS, 215 South, Broad Street, Philadelphia, PA 19107.
Career counseling, etc., for women and minority members (local).

SER—Jobs for Progress, 1355 River Bend Drive, Dallas TX 75247.
Job-training and placement programs for Spanish-speaking Americans; 82 locations across the country.

Wider Opportunities for Women, 1325 G Street NW, Washington, DC 20005.
Professional, managerial, and administrative jobs program for women; 350 locations nationally.

Women's Bureau, U.S. Department of Labor, Washington and Regional Offices.
A government agency, unlike the others, that provides advice and assistance of various kinds to women seeking careers.

Young Men's Christian Association, 101 North Wacker Drive, Chicago, IL 60606.
Educational counseling and employment services at 2,200 local YMCA's under a central career assistance program.

Young Women's Christian Association, 726 Broadway, New York, NY 10003.
Educational counseling and employment services at 4,600 local YWCA's under a central career assistance program.

Appendix F

Job-Search Tools: Applications, Résumés, Interviews

It is almost axiomatic that no matter how well prepared you are professionally, technically, and personally to embark on the course to your career objective, you are going to have to fight all the way to your first objective: a job.

The weapons in your arsenal when you are looking for a first job, or any job, are job applications, résumés and the cover letters that go with them, and effective interview techniques. All are likely to pose problems to former military personnel, especially to those who have been career NCO's and officers. You can and should develop your skills in these areas while you are still in uniform.

Many military installations can provide assistance through Education Centers, ESO's, and other service offices established to work with transitioning military personnel. Many of the military, military professional, and veterans organizations listed in Appendix D and several of the nonprofit organizations listed in Appendix E provide how-to materials. Some will review your draft résumé; others will prepare a résumé for you. Other information is available from several publications listed in the Reading List for Part III. This appendix is limited to general guidance with special reference to job applications and what they can mean to you. I have yet to run across a publication that gives this subject more than a few words.

Translating Military Terms and Experience into English

One big problem, of course, is that of translating military training and experience into civilian terms. As we have already pointed out, one approach to that problem is to become familiar with the job descriptions and discussions of civilian occupational fields found in the *Dictionary of Occupational Titles* and the *Occupational Outlook Handbook.*

Someone may tell you, by the way, that neither of these publications is used to any great extent by civilian employers. That is quite true. But the reason is that the publications summarize information acquired from employers themselves, who already know what they need to know because they *originate* the jobs, job descriptions, training requirements, work conditions, and wage and salary standards. You should use these publications precisely because you need to know what the employers know and what they expect of new employees. (I hasten to add that these publications are used regularly by career counselors—a fact that should tell you something about their value to transition planning.)

Translating your military experience into terms familiar to civilian employers is a must. Avoid military jargon and abbreviations. For example, if your job ended when you were reassigned to Headquarters, U.S. Army Europe, say so. Scrawling "PCS/HQ USAREUR" doesn't mean much to most civilians. Another example: the NCOIC, EDP Opns, 357 Finance Det. (EDP), HQ MDW, has to translate his or her title, functions, and command. You can translate *NCOIC* as Office Manager, Chief of Section, or Data Processing Center Manager. Doug Carter's *Marketing Yourself for a Second Career* (Reading List Part III) has a list of suggested job titles that you may want to consider if you are an officer.

A brief civilianized description of the NCOIC's job might read:

"Managed a central electronic data processing unit of 28 employees, including three shift managers, two programmers, and a computer repair technician in around-the-clock operations. Established work and maintenance schedules to provide payroll and other financial data for a workforce of 50,000. Developed standards and supervised training of new employees in the operation of XYZ computers systems. Qualified programmer (COBOL)."

Translate or explain the titles of technical and professional military courses. "EDP Operations 23-A, USAFAC" isn't very helpful. "Sergeant Majors Academy" is not much better. And "Transportation Officers Career Course" doesn't say anything.

Junk the Jargon

Another problem is to clean up your speech and written communications and toss out the military jargon, abbreviations and acronyms, made-up words (nouns turned into verbs, like *prioritize*), malapropisms, and generally tortured English that tend to permeate both. While all these expressions are useful and generally understood between military men and women, they are neither when it comes to most civilians. Military jargon is the butt of many jokes in Hollywood movies and TV serials. It is no joke when its use prevents communication.

Reading civilian publications in your career field can help, though it may substitute one jargon for another. Take note of the way trained radio and TV announcers speak on national network outlets; their speech is generally considered to be "standard American English." Imitate it.

Some seemingly minor corrections are needed in references to time and dates. The civilian community does not use the twenty-four-hour clock. Many civilians, in fact, consider its use to be affected or foreign. So don't confirm an appointment at "0-niner-hundred" or "0-niner-four-five." The usage telegraphs to the listener that you are a former military member, something you may not want to do.

For reasons not very clear, military usage inverts the date system commonly used in civilian life. Again, it may sound affected or foreign. The accepted way to date an application or a letter is to put the number of the day *after* the month, not before it: December 5, 1987, not 5 December 1987. Once again, the military usage telegraphs something to the reader.

Civilian correspondence uses standardized formats that are about as rigid as those used in the military services. The widely used military "subject-to" format is not acceptable in the civilian world of business, even though it has many advantages. Military correspondence is often further distinguished by listing references in the first paragraph. Military correspondence uses the word *inclosure* for things included with a letter; civilian practice is to use *enclosure*. A few minutes spent with a secretarial handbook can help you sort out these and other differences between military and civilian correspondence, including the accepted forms of address, salutations, and closings.

Job Applications

Job applications can present terrible problems to former military men and women simply because they are designed for civilians who generally show visible progress in their career field by successively more responsible jobs in the same general occupation. Abrupt changes in military assignments can cause confusion among civilian employers, who tend to equate job-changing with personal instability or lack of goals. In a period of ten years I had four different job titles, none related to the others in any apparent way. In one Army assignment, I supervised five civilian employees in the grade of GS-13. When I later applied for appointment to a special Civil Service register of "executives," I was turned down because the examiners rated my military experience as equivalent only to GS-11.

Formal job applications are used in many pre-employment situations. They include the applications required for government jobs, for "walk-ins" (when someone looking for a job arrives unannounced at a company office and is referred to the Personnel Office or

"Human Resources Office"), for those who respond in person to local employment ads, for those who respond by mail to employment ads (and are invited to complete an application), and—sometimes —after you have actually been offered a job but the company needs a formal application for its files.

Forms similar to job applications are also used by employment agencies, employment counselors, headhunters, and others. *Beware*: These are often not applications but *contracts*; be sure you read all the fine print and understand what is involved before you sign any such form.

A typical application requires you to write out—often on the spot —your employment objective and a reverse chronological record of all previous employment (that is, the last job is listed first). It may require some or all of the following information:

Job titles or position titles;
Brief job description of each job held;
Number of employees supervised;
Beginning and ending dates;
Beginning and ending salary/wage;
Reason for leaving the job;
Name, address, and telephone number of each employer;
Name, title, and telephone number of each supervisor.

Other information required may include both your current and previous home addresses, the name and address of the nearest living blood relative (and/or telephone number), the names of all the schools and colleges you have ever attended (including technical schools), foreign travel, foreign language abilities, information about other job skills (use of office machines, computers, photographic equipment, etc.), a brief statement about your goals if you are employed (e.g.: What do you expect to be doing in five years? Or ten years?), the names of three or more personal or business references (with titles, home addresses, and telephone numbers) other than relatives and former supervisors, the name of your bank and other credit references (with account numbers), and hobbies or personal interests.

Applications routinely ask for information about military service; if appropriate, they may ask for a copy of your DD-214.

If the job you seek involves handling money (bank teller) or requires a security clearance, you may be asked some personal questions that are not otherwise permitted: age, sex, marital status, divorces, arrests and/or convictions, names of foreign friends and contacts (with profession and address), and so on.

Before you get in a situation that requires this kind of information, you would do well to dig out the facts and write them down in an organized way on a sheet of paper that you can carry around with you. Have a supply of *copies* of your DD Form 214 with you, too—*never* give away your original.

Job Applications Screen Applicants

Just as it is important to know what you may have to write out on a job application, it is essential that you understand why the employer wants the form at all.

Job applications are used for screening purposes. Employers want to know "where you are coming from." Can you read and write intelligently (and legibly!)? How much formal education or technical training have you had? What kinds of jobs have you held and for how long? Are you a stable, reliable, responsible person who can grow in the company if hired? State the facts, simply and clearly, and do not exaggerate or falsify.

Always answer every question on the form. If a question does not apply to you, simply note "NA" (for not applicable). In cases where no gaps in your chronological employment record are allowed, you may have to explain where you were and what you were doing. A short note such as "attending military technical school," "on leave awaiting new assignment," "hospitalized for major surgery" will suffice in most cases. However, you may be asked to explain in detail on another part of the form or on a separate piece of paper.

If you are working on a federal Civil Service Standard Form 171 or other government application form or completing an application to be submitted by mail, consider using a typewriter. Neatness is always important, but submission of a carefully typed form suggests that you are serious about the application.

When you hand in an application that you have filled out in a personnel office, a secretary or employment screener may size you up for general appearance and deportment and your verbal abilities—making mental notes that may later be transferred to paper. Even if you are a "walk-in," dress and act properly.

Employment screeners are assigned to scan applications for disqualifying information. In some cases screeners may go over applications with the job applicant to clarify questions that may arise. This procedure also gives the screener an opportunity to evaluate the applicant's communication skills, attitude, and appearance. In some cases employers may use the direct-hire techniques to screen out minority members, workers who are too old (or too young), handicapped, or just "look funny" in contravention of the Equal Employment Opportunity laws. Be advised. You will never know for sure. You will get a firm handshake, a warm farewell, and a note in the mail after a couple of weeks saying that your *employment* qualifications were good but not good enough and that your application will be kept on file for future reference.

In small companies informal screening may be done by the manager or an assistant. Be sure you know to whom you are talking when you go in for a job. And watch what you say, not only how you look.

Some of the disqualifying factors employment screeners look for:

- Incomplete or sloppy application: It suggests lack of enthusiasm, lack of self-esteem, no goals; applicant may be hiding information.
- Vague employment objective: "I'll do anything" suggests lack of goals, lack of self-esteem, an ambivalent attitude toward working at all.
- Insufficient formal education and training: May suggest that applicant will be unable to learn and grow in the job.
- Excessive formal education and training: Applicant may be rejected as overqualified; may expect too much; may be source of discontent among other employees; may pose threat to existing management. (Also often used by employers who do not hire former military men and women as a matter of policy.)
- "Job-hopping": A series of short-term jobs in several companies or locations, each lasting a year or less with no advancement, suggests an unreliable, unstable person with no goals.
- No bank or credit references: Is applicant hiding something?
- Vague career expectations: Applicant is unmotivated.
- Excessive career expectations: Applicant is unrealistic; may be a disruptive influence.

When all the applications for a day or other period have been screened, those of qualified applicants are forwarded to the manager of the office where the vacancy exists for further review and evaluation. The best qualified or most likely candidates for the job will then be called in for interviews. Checks of claimed educational qualifications, personel and business references, banks and other credit references, and police records are seldom made. On the other hand, if a false claim or outright lie is discovered during an interview or after the applicant has been hired, the consequences can be severe.

The object of the job application is to bring out the best that you have to offer and gain the attention of the employer (or personnel screener). Neat, legible handwriting and good, plain English will go a long way to help. Complete every answer (or make the notation "NA"), but keep your comments brief and within the bounds of the prepared form if at all possible.

If you really need an extra sheet to explain yourself, fasten it securely to the official application form. Print or write your name, address, social security number, and the title of the job for which you are applying at the top of each such extra sheet. Indentify comments by referring to numbered sections of the official form. Whoever reviews your application will appreciate your professionalism.

Anyone who is intimidated by all this should probably obtain several copies of SF-171, the form used when applying for federal employment, from the nearest civilian personnel office and work on completing it. The SF-171 is probably the most complicated application form that you will ever see. Ask your ESO for a critique.

The Controversial Résumé

In my view the whole subject of résumés has been blown up way out of proportion to their usefulness. About the only thing everyone agrees on is that almost everyone needs one. That is something of a switch because the device originated with civilian professionals and executives who were moving up the career ladder, not just reaching for the first rung. Surveys of "Employment Opportunities" ads, however, have turned up requests for résumés from electricians, computer operators, cooks, and others.

Very little agreement exists on how transitioning military men and women should prepare a résumé or when they should use one. Most people simply adapt the tried and true examples in any number of books and manuals on writing résumés. Detailed guidance is available from several of the publications included in the Reading List for Part III and from organizations listed in Appendices D and E.

In any case, the term comes from the French word, *résumé* (pronounced *reh-zoo-may*), which means nothing more than *summary*. So prospective employees *summarize* in their résumé education, training, work experience, and something of their life experiences to support their claim that they are qualified for a particular kind of employment. Despite differing views, a few general rules seem to apply:

- Keep it brief. One page. Those who screen résumés spend an average of less than thirty seconds reading each one.
- Omit anything that does not point up your experience and future *potential*. Résumés are not histories.
- Write in the third person, as if you were someone else.
- Unlike job applications, when listing prior jobs do not give a job description. The emphasis is on *accomplishments*. Use action words: "Supervised computer maintenance" says it better than "I was the the supervisor of computer maintenance..."

  If you are a short-termer whose military training may be a very significant part of your military experience, emphasize that fact. Short-termers might also consider including experience and accomplishments gained before military service. Summer jobs related to career goals, service on a school or college project, achievement of Eagle Scout rank in the Boy Scouts, and academic honors like election to the National Honor Society or receipt of a college scholarship can all suggest desirable personal traits that employers look for. Don't overlook accomplishments.

The résumé of the NCO-in-Charge of the Finance unit, used above as an illustration, might include the following statement after the job title:

MANAGER, DATA PROCESSING CENTER:

"Directed financial data processing service for a workforce of 50,000. Designed work and maintenance schedules that permitted optimum utilization of installed EDP equipment with no increase in staff. Improved services resulted in net savings of $240,000. Awarded Army Commendation Medal."

- Do not include personal data. Equal Employment Opportunity laws prohibit employers from asking for photographs and such data as age, sex, religion, race, and health.

  In some cases, however, you may have to specify such information to clarify your status. If the job involves age limitations, you might give your age or state "Age qualified." In most cases names imply sex, but if yours doesn't you may want to state it. I once served with a lusty six-foot male Texan named Rose Beverly Conover.

- Stay away from professional résumé preparers. Screeners can spot them quicker than an eagle can spot a mouse. When they find them, the résumés are filed in the circular file. End of story.

- Consult friends or an Educational Services Officer if you need help or a critique.

- Have your résumé *typed* professionally and *printed* on good quality 20-pound white offset paper. Avoid fancy type styles and colored paper, though ivory and light buff papers are acceptable. If you can afford it, electronic typesetting techniques can squeeze more onto a page than a typist.

Chronological and Functional Résumés

Two kinds of résumés have been developed over the years. One is essentially a chronological listing of what you have done. The other is a functional résumé that organizes your experience and accomplishments to support your job search in a particular field. Both have their advantages and disadvantages.

RONALD   2341 VIRGINIA AVENUE   SOUTHPORT,
J. DEBUSSEY   (909) 555-3333   PA 99999

OBJECTIVE: Sales and Service Technician, Microcomputer Equipment

SUMMARY: Six years of progressively responsible experience in off-site systems analysis and design, installation, and maintenance of microcomputers and peripheral equipment. Academic degree in business communications systems.

EDUCATION AND TRAINING:
  Associate Degree in Business Management; Completed Air Force junior management training program; Computer Maintenance Management Course (8 weeks, U.S. Air Force); Field Installation and Repair Course (4 weeks, IBM Corporation); Basic Electronic Technician Course (21 weeks, U.S. Air Force.)

EMPLOYMENT RECORD:
  1985–87 Assistant Field Supervisor, EDP Facility serving a workforce of 10,000. Supervised installation and repair activity under the direction of Field Supervisor. Conducted systems analyses and designed microcomputer office automation systems. Developed operator training and preventive maintenance program that reduced downtime 80 percent. (Cash Performance Award.)
  1984–85 Maintenance Supervisor, Financial Records center. Scheduled and supervised work assignments for five microcomputer repairers in support of administrative staff of 500. Assisted commercial tech reps with systems design. Improved maintenance service by developing mobile repair team and initiating modular maintenance techniques that resulted in better use of staff and resources.
  1982–84 Computer Technician, Telecommunications Center, Belgium. Maintained microcomputer equipment in support of center as member of two-man crew. Assisted commercial field reps with design and installation of new system K-28. "Technician of the Year" 1983.
  1981–82 Computer Technician (Trainee). Personnel Records Center. On-the-job training in off-site installation and bench repair of microcomputers and peripheral equipment. "Trainee of the Quarter," October 1981.
PERSONAL:
  Completing Air Force service as Staff Sergeant (E-5), October 1987. Thirty-six credits toward bachelor's degree in Business Administration (Business Information Systems). Fluent French (native speaker). Single. Available for employment worldwide.

The chronological résumé recites everything you have done; you are more or less obliged to show dates (last job first). Thus, if the best and most useful experience was acquired in a job that you had ten years ago, it may be overlooked in the reading. Furthermore, you may have had such diverse experience during your military service that nothing much supports your employment objective. If you were in only a few years, on the other hand, this may be the best way to go about writing a résumé. In it you may give more prominence to education and training than to actual work experience.

The functional résumé overcomes both those problems but may create another: You may have to write separate résumés for specific employment opportunities. A problem that can arise with too specific an objective is that you may not get the job you want *and* you will not be considered for any other.

The essential task is to extract from your military service what you learned and did to form a pattern of experience that communicates your expertise and future potential in a civilian occupational field. Educational achievement plays a secondary role unless it directly supports your career objective. The structure of the functional résumé makes it more applicable to career and long-term noncareer service members than to those with minimal service.

A composite résumé that uses elements of both the above types is illustrated in the accompanying example. It clearly shows both accomplishment and potential. A question may arise about why an apparently up-and-coming Air Force Staff Sergeant is leaving the service. That can be taken care of in the cover letter that is an essential part of the résumé process.

The cover letter is used to identify the position you are applying for, along with information that will indicate whether you are responding to an employment ad or whatever. Then it discusses the reasons why the employer should interview you and eventually hire you. This is done by stating what you can *contribute to the employer's operations.* If, as in the sample, you have a record of improving your own job performance, thinking up better ways to get a job done, and reducing operating costs, say so. But do not repeat a lot of what is in the résumé. If, as in the sample, you had experience with the products of a number of different manufacturers, stick to your experience with IBM equipment when you write to IBM. On the other hand, if you write to a distributor you may want to mention your experience with a wide range of products of different manufacturers.

Note that much of this suggests that you know a lot about the company to which you are writing. Do your homework first!

Next, make a brief reference to the fact that your résumé is enclosed.

Finally, in the closing paragraph, ask for an interview. It is good form to close with a statement or question that invites a reply. Perhaps you will be in the city where the prospective employer is located; mention that fact and propose a date for an interview. Or suggest that you will call when you arrive to set up a time and place. Invite additional inquiries, if it seems useful.

Résumés are used for other purposes than first attempts to find a job. As already suggested, they can be provided to networking contacts for their information. They can be sent, along with a thank-you note, to networking contacts who are in hiring positions but whom you did not ask for a job. They can be attached to applications in direct-hire situations.

Interviewing Techniques

Short but sweet: Dress properly and behave yourself. Show that you are self-confident and can think on your feet. Prepare yourself by accumulating information about the company where you seek a job and, if possible, the interviewer. Be respectful.

With that said, it may be worth observing that the military chain of command tends to make junior members uncomfortable in the presence of senior members—and, possibly, subservient.

Respect is owing to an interviewer whom you have never met but who is more than likely to be an officer of the company where you are seeking a job. But subservience is as much out of place as a false bravado that you hope will put you across as a great guy or gal. Courtesy, enthusiasm, and confidence are important. And so is your *participation*. An interview is a two-way street.

Prepare yourself in advance by collecting all the information you can about the company and the way it operates. Ask intelligent questions about things that may puzzle you or about which you need more information. Show an interest in the company. Compliment the interviewer on the company's policies and products, if you can.

Interviews are predictably unpredictable. Interviewers like to pop questions just to see how you react and how well you think. You can prepare yourself to some extent. Some typical questions:

- Why do you want to work for this company?
- Tell me something about yourself.
- What are your best qualities?
- What are your weaknesses?
- What can I tell you about our company?
- What would you do if . . . . . . ?
- What are your long-term goals?

About the best way to go about acquiring good interview techniques is role-playing under the supervision of a qualified counselor.

If there is no such program at your installation, ask your ESO or Education Counselor to help you set up a group, complete with equipment and a counselor. Increasingly, counselors videotape such sessions and play them back to the participants. But do not discount the advice on interview procedures that you can obtain from a number of manuals on the subject. And remember that there are good interviewers and bad interviewers. You won't know which you get until you sit down across a desk from him or her.

A book that has become a classic in the field is:

Sweaty Palms: The Neglected Art of Being Interviewed, by H. Anthony Medley.

Many job-search guides contain sections on successful job interview techniques, including several books listed in the Reading List for Part III. Some local nonprofit organizations may run workshops on the subject, including the two Y's and the Forty-Plus Club. Adult education programs may also have such workshops among their course offerings.

Appendix G

Government Employment Benefits for Veterans

1. *U.S. Department of Labor*

- Unemployment benefits (Weekly benefits vary by state; since you only apply once and you will draw that state's benefit wherever you move, for as long as you are eligible, apply to a state with high weekly benefits if you can. Apply to state employment service offices.)
- Reemployment rights, up to five years of active duty; also applies to Reserve and National Guard members who left jobs for required active duty training. *Contact*: Assistant Regional Administrator for Veterans Reemployment Rights (ARA/VRR), Veterans Employment and Training Service, at the appropriate regional office of the Department of Labor (see Federal Government listings in telephone book).
- State Job Services, operated jointly with DOL, offer help with interviewing, counseling, aptitude testing, training opportunities, job referrals (24-hour advance preference to veterans), and job placement. Each of 2,500 local job service offices around the U.S. has at least one specially trained Local Veterans' Employment Representative (LVER) to work with you; most are retired or former military members.
- Job Training Partnership Act (JPTA) provides job training and related aid, usually for entry-level mid-skill level jobs. The program operates in a variety of ways, including local public/private partnerships. Inquire at Job Service for details.
- Vietnam-Era Veterans Rights. Outreach and community service programs under local veterans committees in cities with large populations of Vietnam veterans. Employers with federal contracts of $10,000 are required to assist Vietnam veterans and to list suitable job openings with the State Job Service office. Inquire at State Job Service.
- Apprenticeships and Training opportunities are available through State Job Service.

- Jobs for women: Information available from Women's Bureau, U.S. Department of Labor, Washington, DC.
- Disabled Veterans' Outreach Program (DVOP) helps to develop training and employment opportunities. DVOP representatives are stationed at most State Job Service offices and at many VA hospitals and Readjustment Counseling Centers.
- Jobs for older workers (military retirees) are a special concern. Contact State Job Service office.

2. *Office of Personnel Management (Federal employment)*

- Veterans Preference: provides "points" for service, disabilities, and award of Purple Heart. (Retired military members are no longer qualified unless below the rank of O–4 or disabled.) Also extends to preference in examinations and appointments, and to reopening examinations. Includes job retention rights and waivers of some physical requirements.
- Federal Job Centers maintain lists of available federal jobs; centers are listed in telephone directory "white pages" under Federal Government.
- Noncompetitive appointments may be made for disabled veterans (30 percent or more disabled). See DVOP representative.

3. *Small Business Administration Programs*

Veterans Affairs Officers in SBA district and branch offices administer or coordinate programs that provide:

- Financial assistance to small businesses operated by veterans (19 different loan programs);
- Management assistance;
- Procurement assistance: providing subcontracts to veteran-owned businesses.

4. *Veterans Administration Programs*

- On-the-Job Training Program
- Readjustment Counseling (Vietnam veterans)
- Veterans Job Training Act (Vietnam veterans)
- Vocational Rehabilitation (disabled veterans)
- Non-Contributory GI Bill (veterans who served at least 180 days before January 1, 1977; expires December 31, 1989.) (See for details: *Federal Benefits for Veterans and Dependents* or local VA office.)
- New GI Bill benefits are available through college financial aid offices.

5. *Department of Defense Programs*

- Education and training: See Appendix C.
- Employment in defense establishment Civil Service jobs.
- Reserve organizations: Membership can provide supplemental income; units become networking sources for job searches.

Index